THE PERFECT Wedding

Maria McBride-Mellinger

CollinsPublishers

A Division of HarperCollinsPublishers

TO BRETT, RYAN, AND EVAN, THE PRECIOUS REWARDS OF MY OWN VOWS

First published in the USA 1997 by Collins Publishers
HarperCollins website: http://www.harpercollins.com

Produced by Smallwood & Stewart, Inc., New York City

TEXT © MARIA McBRIDE-MELLINGER
PHOTOGRAPHS © ROSS WHITAKER/NEW YORK
ALAN RICHARDSON
MARILI FORASTIERI
TANYA MALOTT LAWSON

Copyright © 1997 Smallwood & Stewart, Inc.

Library of Congress Cataloging-in-Publication Data
McBride-Mellinger, Maria.
    The perfect wedding / Maria McBride-Mellinger. — 1st ed.
        p.   cm.
    ISBN 0–06–258663–7 (hardcover)
        1. Weddings—United States—Planning—Handbooks, manuals, etc.
I. Title.
HQ745.M326   1996
395' .22—dc20   96-19111

Printed in China

10 9 8 7 6 5 4 3 2

ART DIRECTOR: Susi Oberhelman
BOOK DESIGNER: Pat Tan

ents

Introduction

You are going to be married ~ my warmest congratulations to you! If you're like I was, you will want everything about your wedding to be perfect. But each bride's idea of perfection is as individual as she is, and no two couples, or weddings, are ever the same. Some brides may have only a vague feeling about what they want, while others are clearer about the details of their day, almost down to the length of the bride's veil and the flower in the groom's boutonniere. Yet, however vague or vivid the fantasies, most people ~ even those brides who have married before ~ simply don't know how to make their dreams happen.

That information is in your hands now: *The Perfect Wedding* tells you how to create the wedding of your dreams. Whatever your budget, whatever your ideal wedding, here you'll find answers to practical questions as well as tips for adding style to the mix. The text explains where to locate exactly what you want; how to deal with professionals, from photographers to florists, bakers to limousine services; and, most importantly, how to save money by spending wisely.

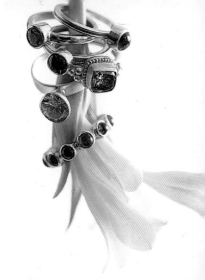

In *The Perfect Wedding*, you will discover the difference between a karat and a carat, the distinctions between a good dress and a great dress, and definitions of the terms bakers use to describe wedding cakes. Each chapter introduces you to all the questions and options that face every bride. Then turn to the second part of the book, where I've included my own "insider's Rolodex," a listing of hundreds of the best bridal resources across the country, distilled from my years as a bridal stylist and editor. Armed with these resources and enough time ~ I recommend at least a year for a large wedding, six months or less for smaller weddings of fewer than a hundred guests ~ you can organize the wedding you want.

A successful wedding is always the result of successful collaboration, first between bride and groom and other family members, and then between the couple and each of their vendors. Working with professionals to maximize their performance, and the return on your dollar, is a major aspect of this book. The photographs serve as a starting point for discussion with your vendors; show them the colors, textures, arrangements, and other details that you love. Being able to actually show suppliers what you want will save you time and potential headaches later. Use the Credits list on page 196 to identify your favorite objects (and their providers) in the photographs. Feel free to contact vendors who are not in

your town ~ many are willing to travel or may be able to ship products to you. Not surprisingly, a good number of these people are experienced at working long distance, and can "read" your style and goals in the course of a long telephone chat. Before they begin any custom work, they should provide you with preliminary sketches, outlines, estimates, and budgets for your approval.

YOUR WEDDING SIGNATURE

Today there is no one season for weddings, and the rules of nuptial etiquette have relaxed considerably; you can pretty much dictate the style of your wedding. If you prefer an intimate ceremony, consider charming country inns, romantic restaurants, and hotel suites, perfectly sized for smaller wedding parties. Grand ballrooms, art museums, and historic estates offer ultra-formal venues. If you want an outdoor wedding, municipal parks and botanic gardens are modest alternatives. Do you want to marry unlike anyone you know? Erect a tent at the city zoo or take your closest family and friends away for a wedding weekend to an island, a mountain resort, or a lakefront hideaway.

Celebrate your individuality as a couple by introducing personal touches into the ceremony and reception. For instance, marry where you first met or at the site of your most frequent dates. If you're a gardener seek out a wedding cake artist to craft your cake with your favorite flowers. Whatever you collect, whether it's folk art or antique linens, include them in the decorations at the reception. If you're dedicated to jazz, hire a classic combo. Have a monogram designed incorporating both names and use this as a repeating motif on all programs, menus, place cards for your wedding day ∼ your monogram can even be printed in gold on the dinner plates for the bridal table.

Instead of having your portrait shot in an anonymous studio, go outside to a scenic local backdrop: gardens, beaches, estate terraces, verandas, country roads, bridges, and carousels are just a few options. Take the time to drive about to find just the right spot, then shoot a "test" portrait with your own camera to determine if you like the view.

⊱ TEN STEPS TO YOUR PERFECT WEDDING ⊰

HAVE A FRANK CONVERSATION with your fiancé and your parents about the wedding you want: its size, style, and the budget. There will be a lot to organize, so begin to delegate: agree on family members' responsibilities, and reevaluate these regularly. But be thoughtful. In the face of the hundreds of details to attend to, be careful that you don't turn into a drill sergeant. Remember that your family and friends are not

hired help. And when there is some detail you really care about, handle it yourself.

SET THE DATE. If you're determined to be wed in the grand ballroom of your favorite hotel or in the lobby of an art deco skyscraper, or if you're set on a swing band or steel drums, or if you wouldn't think of celebrating without your favorite caterer or florist, book this resource first. Many of the best locations, wedding consultants, caterers, photographers, musicians, and florists get booked early and can accommodate only a single major event a day. Check your date against a calendar of local events so that parades, street fairs, or holidays won't play havoc with your timing.

BE REALISTIC about calculating expenses for rings, your bridal ensemble (including all accessories), formal wear, location, photography, invitations, flowers, catering and staff, bar, cake, linens, transportation, gifts, and fees (clergy, license, parking). More money is spent on the reception, especially for catering services, than any other element, so that will offer the greatest opportunity for saving.

SEEK OUT GOOD RESOURCES. Look everywhere ~ most vendors service a wide assortment of events. Did you see a beautiful arrangement of flowers in a magazine or the windows of a local department store? When you do find a good resource, request references and ask them if they would hire the vendor again. Shop smartly ~ what's most important is value, not bargains. Determine what you're actually receiving for the price quote; compare details and quality.

PUT IT IN WRITING. The most crucial component in your relationship with any and all vendors is a written agreement. It is your guarantee of services and it is important for your peace of mind. Insist on a purchase order or a contract for each product and service. A good agreement specifies what is being paid for, who is providing the service or product, the payment and timetable, and the method of payment (expect to pay the final installment immediately before the wedding). Your wedding date, the location, and the time of delivery should appear, as well as overtime fees and gratuities. Above all, understand the fine print before you sign and never sign a contract under pressure.

DEVISE MASTER TO-DO and contact lists for vendors, your gift registrations, the wedding party, and the guests. Choose a tracking format that works for you ~ a computer-generated list, file cards, or a notebook. Just be sure the lists are easy to update and portable. And carry fabric swatches, table measurements, photos of locations and of your gowns at all times. Clip them into a notebook small enough to tuck into your purse; you may come across a great calligrapher or the perfect ribbon when you least expect to.

TRUST YOUR OWN JUDGMENT. Once you've hired a resource, don't try to micromanage their efforts. If you have done your homework, you should be able to let them do what you are paying them to do. Usually you are free to renegotiate the details to suit your needs up to three weeks before your wedding.

APPLY FOR YOUR LICENSE at your local county clerk's office; call the marriage license bureau at least a month before your wedding to inquire about details ∼ necessary IDs, waiting periods, blood tests, fees, divorce records ∼ that you will need to have available. Very often couples must apply together in person, so be sure to allow time in your schedule for this critical detail.

RECONFIRM ALL DETAILS one to two weeks before your wedding and be sure the service providers ∼ from the caterer and the band to the limousine drivers ∼ as well as members of the family and wedding party all have copies of the master schedule, with important phone numbers in case of emergencies, and accurate directions.

REMEMBER OTHERS: The Second Harvest National Food Bank Network, 312-263-2303, will provide you with the number of the food bank nearest you, that can arrange to pick up leftovers for redistribution.

Whether it is two months or two years from now, remember this will be *your* wedding. The distance you travel, the dilemmas you face, the problems you solve should pale in comparison to your happiness and joy. But organizing even a simple wedding celebration can require the tact of a diplomat, the financial dexterity of an accountant, and the patience of a saint. To get through it all, you owe yourself and your fiancé an indomitable, unshakable sense of humor, as well as some time together to indulge and nurture the real reason for all the planning frenzy ∼ your love.

You will want to recall your wedding with fondness for all the years to come. On the day itself, enlist someone else to manage the details so that you and your new husband can enjoy yourselves. If there are subtle changes in the game plan, chances are you will be the only one who notices. And if something does go awry, the best ∼ and perhaps only ∼ antidote is a shrug and a smile. Be the epitome of grace under pressure. And allow yourself to have a good time. That, after all, is the essence of a perfect wedding.

Maria McBride-Mellinger

a Question
a Promise
a Kiss

You haven't even begun the real planning, and already there are so many details that require your attention: shopping for an engagement ring and wedding bands that are as beautiful as they are heartfelt; communicating your good news to your family and all your friends; and, perhaps, having an engagement party. Of course, you and your groom should soon select your wedding party. Now is also the perfect time to register for gifts (do this early for the benefit of those who send engagement presents). This chapter will take you through these preliminary steps as you start to plan for the big event. No one day is as full of emotion, as steeped in family dynamics as your wedding day, so make the most of this "quiet" time and sit down with your fiancé for a candid discussion about the type of wedding you both want ~ your dreams, your realities, and your finances. You should agree on definite "must haves" as well as absolute "no ways." If you plan realistically now, you'll save yourself headaches ~ and heartaches ~ later. But as important as such planning is, don't let the details overwhelm you. Your engagement should be, more than anything else, a time for joyous celebration with family and friends and, most importantly, with one another. You will want to look back on this time in your life fondly.

WEDDING RINGS

A lot of wistful daydreaming is devoted to the matter of the engagement ring. Most of us immediately think of the fabulous gemstones ~ diamonds, emeralds, amethysts, rubies, and sapphires. Diamonds, of course, are virtually synonymous with engagement rings, and we cannot help but be dazzled by them. Yet an engagement ring can just as easily have other stones. If you love garnets, by all means choose one for this special ring; a pearl, too, is appropriate, as is any semi-precious stone. In fact, you may decide that you want an engagement ring with no stone at all.

Begin with a trip to a reputable jeweler; look for a shop with an appealing selection of merchandise and a knowledgeable staff. Ask questions about each ring's value and quality. Consider a wide variety of stones and settings ~ the most important requirement is that you love the ring. Since so many factors contribute to a stone's quality, I recommend obtaining a certificate attesting to the gem's characteristics and value. Most jewelers are happy to provide this paper.

Choose a setting that fits your lifestyle ~ if you work with your hands you may prefer one of the two settings that are more protective: a bezel, where the band hugs the middle section (or girdle) of the stone, or a channel setting, which has the stones set between two strips of the band so that they are held at both top and bottom.

I have always adored antique jewelry for its charm, beauty, and craftsmanship. More and more jewelers are offering estate rings, and many fine auction houses have special sales for brides-to-be. (Whenever you are looking at estate jewelry, keep an eye out for antique necklaces, clips, and bracelets; these are one-of-a-kind, truly memorable gifts for your attendants. A handsome antique wristwatch or pocket watch for your fiancé is a gift that will mark your engagement for all time.) When you look at antique rings,

Invest in a handsome ring box that will protect and showcase your engagement ring. I found these sterling silver ring boxes *(opposite)* **at an estate jeweler. The rings, top to bottom, are a South Sea pearl ringed with round diamonds; an estate Edwardian period round-cut sapphire and a round-cut diamond set side by side in a filigree setting; an emerald-cut diamond flanked with baguettes and set in platinum.**

The Perfect **Wedding**

On a stack of sterling silver bands *(above left)*, **the top is a posy ring stamped with the virtues "truth" and "respect." The middle ring is a heritage ring, and the bottom rings are a matching pair of simple polished sterling silver bands. The stack of rings** *(above right)* **are all yellow gold bands of different styles. The top ring is etched and granulated and designed to resemble a crown. Below this is a basic polished gold band on a granulated band. Just under these is a four-knot band on top of a Celtic-styled band. And finally, the bottom ring is a hand-cast leaf-motif band.**

bear in mind that though the stone can always be reset, the real value is likely to be the setting itself; these older rings are prized for their superb period design.

⁓ WEDDING BANDS: LASTING SYMBOLS ⁓

Your wedding band and engagement ring need not match but should be compatible. They may be variations of each other: One couple I know both wanted slender gold bands, but the bride had a dozen tiny diamonds set randomly, like a glittering galaxy, in hers.

Custom-designing rings this way is a wonderfully personal idea. Seek out a silver- or goldsmith or gemologist rather than a jeweler who sells from inventory. A reputable jeweler may be able to recommend someone, or you can visit a local craft and jewelry fair to look for work you admire. When you visit the goldsmith, examine the stones and materials there. This is a good time to think about what you might like ⁓ designs such as a swag or bead and bow, for example, or a leaf or flower motif. Once you have agreed on the basics, the gold-smith will show you sketches before creating the rings.

Often a wedding band is yellow gold, but it's just as appropriate for it to be white gold, rose gold, silver, or even platinum. Platinum, however, is not to be confused with white gold; it is stronger, rarer, and more costly. The best gold, 24 karats, is 24 parts gold with no added alloy; it's pure, but very malleable and too soft to be practical. Most rings are 18 karats, with 6 parts alloy, although 14-karat rings also look great and wear well. Jewish couples wishing to remain loyal to tradition may want to consider the traditional plain gold band, which is free of any stones to avoid any misrepresentation of its value.

A wedding band is a symbol of the bond you share. A brief inscription engraved inside each band makes these rings truly special. The classic signature will include each of your initials and your wedding date. A romantic couple I know chose to engrave their rings with the date they met. I also recommend adding a poetic sentiment you'll treasure always.

Sterling silver wedding bands are an untraditional choice. If you are choosing silver, why not go one step further and really personalize your band. The top ring is an example of three-dimensional ridge detailing, and the bottom one is granulated with hearts, spades, diamonds, and clubs.

DIAMONDS

*P*ure, brilliant, and virtually indestructible, the diamond is an apt symbol for everything a marriage yearns to be. Although purchased as a token of love, this precious stone is also an investment and should be procured wisely. A good jeweler will show you examples of different shapes and colors, and styles of settings, while explaining the value of each stone. Jewelers have developed a system of classification to assist buyer and seller alike. The "four C's" ~ carat, clarity, cut, and color ~ distinguish every stone. But equally important in this aesthetic decision are the setting and shape of the stone, so do your research carefully.

THE FINE POINTS

CARAT • "Carat" refers to the weight of a diamond. A carat is one-fifth of a gram. Stones weighing more than one carat are rare.

CLARITY • This is a system of rating a stone on the basis of its naturally occurring blemishes and geological debris. The highest rating is flawless (FL), followed by internally flawless (IF), very, very small inclusions (VVS), very small inclusions (VS), small inclusions (SI), and, lastly, imperfect (I). A flawless stone is very rare.

CUT • Cut is generally regarded as the most important of the criteria. The way a diamond is cut determines its brilliance and beauty. A stone is faceted in a series of flat, angled surfaces that reflect light off one another, causing the stone to sparkle. A round stone cut with fifty-eight facets is classified as brilliant.

COLOR • Diamonds are also scaled according to their color. A rating of D is the highest, meaning that the stone is clear and virtually colorless. The lowest rating is Z, indicating a stone that generally contains traces of earthy color. Some diamonds naturally exhibit some blush of color and are a specialty category known as "fancies." Canaries, for example, are prized yellow diamonds.

CHOOSING A WEDDING PARTY

While it is perfectly fine to marry without any attendants, most couples do want to share their wedding with their closest friends and family. Smaller wedding parties, of two or four or six attendants, are fine for informal weddings and weddings with shorter guest lists. Formal and very formal weddings with hundreds of guests, however, are elaborate events where it is common for the bride to have as many as twelve bridesmaids.

Organizing your wedding party is just the first of many delicate political maneuvers you will execute as you plan your nuptials. Extending an invitation should be not a spontaneous gesture but a thoughtful consideration. Before you enlist new acquaintances, long-absent friends, business colleagues, and extended family members, think through the risk of personality conflicts and hurt feelings. Draw up your list, then put yourself in each friend's place to see if this could be an imposition or a cause of friction.

Decide before you enlist your attendants if you are

Dress your wedding party uniformly to match the style and formality of your wedding. Accessories ~ boutonnieres, ties, and pocket squares for the men, bouquets, jewelry, and shoes for the women ~ should also be equal in style. Groom, best man, and groomsmen all sport handsome navy suits for an outdoor semiformal wedding.

prepared to cover or contribute to the costs of their wedding attire or accessories (a thoughtful gesture, especially if you'll want an ensemble that is rather pricey for the group).

Bear in mind that agreeing to be an attendant is a little like joining an exclusive club: Attendants will be closer to the center of activity and excitement but, as with any club membership, there are dues to be paid. Most attendants are expected to cover the costs of their wedding attire and their transportation if they live out of town; the bride generally provides accommodations. They will present the bride with a wedding gift. And most likely there will be showers and engagement parties to attend.

Approach your friends about participating in the wedding party soon after you become engaged (if you'll have an extended engagement, solicit your bridesmaids, ushers, and other attendants about a year before the date). Once your party is definite, give everyone a list of participants, including home and business addresses and telephone numbers.

Bridesmaids and the maid of honor wear off-the-shoulder silk gowns and carry nosegays of roses ~ a perfect match to semiformally dressed men. The simple, spare use of jewelry plays up the understated elegance of the gowns.

ON THE SHOULDERS OF THE TRUSTED

A MAID OR MATRON OF HONOR has significant responsibilities, from helping to choose bridesmaids' attire to keeping the wedding party up-to-date on events and developments. Before the wedding, she'll help you dress, and throughout the day she will be alert to your attire, fluffing and arranging the train and veil as necessary. At the ceremony she will hold your bouquet during the ring exchange, and as a witness, she will co-sign the wedding certificate.

THE BEST MAN should also be a responsible sort, and he will be busy. He must make sure that the groom is dressed and at the wedding in plenty of time. He will carry your wedding rings, co-sign the wedding certificate, pay the officiant's fee, and make the first toast at the reception.

GROOMSMEN (or ushers) escort wedding guests to their seats, so their number should correspond to guests at a ratio of about one usher per forty guests.

Assorted small gilt frames
(above left) **are perfect to
wrap individually and give as
gifts to your bridesmaids.
Tie gold-leaf perfume bottles**
(above right) **with silk ribbon
and cut tags to resemble
little pennants.**

Cufflinks *(opposite)* **make
ideal gifts for the groomsmen:
vintage mother-of-pearl and
silver snap; blue crystal granulated with dark blue crystal
dots, edged with silver;
gold pinecone with toggle;
carnelian inset into square
sterling silver cufflink
cast in the Bauhaus style;
estate abalone shell
button knotted with vermeil,
gold over sterling, braid.**

You will probably not be able to include everyone who is important to you in the group, but fortunately there are many other significant roles for loved ones. Ask a good friend to give a reading, recite a poem or a prayer, or sing. Your friend the graphic designer might create the invitations or wedding programs, your teenage sister with the beautiful hand may pen the calligraphy for place cards, your artistic cousin can design baseball caps to wear at the rehearsal dinner.

TOKENS OF GRATITUDE

It is customary to give gifts to your attendants as tokens of your gratitude. Typically, the gifts for the groomsmen and those for the bridesmaids are identical or similar. Look for special, enduring treasures: Pearl earrings or gold lockets that can be worn to the wedding, fine leather gloves, and silk chiffon scarves are lovely for the women; sterling-handled razors and handsome fountain pens are smart choices for the men. Distribute the gifts at the rehearsal party or any party the week before your wedding. Always include a personal card expressing your appreciation, written in your own hand or composed by your calligrapher and signed by you.

ANNOUNCEMENTS

Laminate or make a copy of your newspaper announcement *(above)* on acid-free paper so that it lasts forever. Unlike invitations, announcements *(right)* can be more frivolous, and freely sent to those unable to attend. A fanciful decorative patterned card with a printed vellum overlay attached by a silk ribbon is a personal statement. There are many options to choose from. Why not incorporate a shared interest such as boating and devise a nautical announcement? Perhaps one of your fond memories is of apple picking in the early autumn ~ how about an apple tree card? And of course, there is always the simple heart.

*J*ust as soon as you kiss and promise to wed, it's time to spread the news. Giddy couples should contain their impulse to reveal the exciting announcement until they have notified their parents, as it is their honor to know first. Of course, you'll want to notify your closest friends and family with handwritten notes or phone calls. I heartily endorse the note over a telephone call: Even if your dearest ones live nearby and you see them regularly, it is a wonderful gesture to tell them the news in a written keepsake message.

A printed announcement is an efficient and beautiful way to share the news with all the other people you both know. You need not match the style of the wedding, since chances are you and your groom haven't yet decided on most of the specific details. The announcement is only a proclamation of your intentions, and even if you know the wedding date do not include it.

While you are designing your announcement, order a batch of cards printed with your maiden monogram to send as thank-you notes throughout your engagement. You may also wish to have your new monogram designed now: While traditional monograms bear the two initials of your first names with the initial of your shared last name, consider a monogram with four initials if you keep your own last name.

KEEPSAKES TO TREASURE

Carefully clip newspaper and journal notices and save copies of your printed announcement in a keepsake box. You will find archival boxes at fine stationers, or you can contact a bookbinder to create a custom box from handmade papers or hand-tooled leather. The size and shape are really up to you, but I have found that a box at least eight by eleven inches will be large enough to hold your invitation, menu, photographs, and most of the ephemera you will want to save.

Mrs. Anne Moffitt
the pleasure of your com
t the engage
Mill

Mary and Brian Garfield
cordially invite you
to celebrate the engagement of
Nicole Tagert
to
Michael Rand
Saturday, the nineteenth of July
seven o'clock
2764 Crested Bluff
Minneapolis
r.s.v.p. 994-5445

S.S. CREASY
HANK   SUSAN

asy
ng of
Toasting
rof
Susan
ary 6, 190
cast off
ntry Club
. Virginia

January 2, 1905
Henry Creasy

Michael
Christopher
Grisby
request the
in

ENGAGEMENT PARTIES

Use your own interests and loves as a starting point. Whatever the season, my party tables are inevitably decorated with family heirlooms ~ one grandmother's vintage quilt as a tabletopper, another grandmother's collection of milk glass plates and sponge ware pitchers for decor. Flea markets can be the perfect place to find just such treasures. I collect square and folksy handkerchiefs from flea markets and use them as place mats and napkins *(opposite and above)*. The handkerchiefs are presented pinned with a sterling pin designed by a jeweler and meant to be kept by the guests.

Backyard barbecues, bridesmaid teas, Champagne and cake toasts, country inn luncheons: Your engagement will give you the greatest reason yet to entertain. If you and your fiancé have entertained lavishly in the past, you might host a *grande fête*. If you prefer something more low-key, hold a series of informal, intimate dinners to tell all your friends of your plans throughout your engagement. Just before you marry, about two weeks before the wedding itself, host a ladies' luncheon for your bridesmaids or a party with your groom to which you invite all your attendants. And finally, the penultimate event, on the eve of the wedding, is the rehearsal dinner.

A PRELUDE TO YOUR RECEPTION

Any good party is a collaborative venture, between the hosts and guests and between the mood and environment. And because every party has a guest list, a location, invitations, table settings, music, and a menu ~ just as your wedding will ~ entertaining before you marry is a wonderful opportunity to fine-tune your wedding plans. In the course of all these parties, you may realize that a smaller, more intimate wedding will be most meaningful to you. Or you might discover that you really love the excitement of the crowd and are comfortable negotiating hundreds of details and hundreds of guests.

THE SEARCH FOR VENDORS

Despite the glowing recommendations you hear about any vendor, I recommend you have your prospective caterer or wedding consultant orchestrate one of your early engagement parties, as this is a great way to experiment before the big event. Don't be concerned that your party is too small for a professional: Caterers regularly handle intimate affairs, and hotels and clubs have smaller, private dining rooms. Chances are you will enjoy a well-priced party, and the

For a bridesmaids' lunch, create personalized tea bag tabs *(opposite)*: **little squares of paper are lettered with your monogram and the flavor of the tea on the back. Capture the quintessentially feminine spirit of the day with vintage vases** *(above)*, **swank mademoiselles filled with delicate blossoms and clusters of fruits. Some of the many luscious combinations are pansies and baby oranges, lilies of the valley, grapes and heather, and cherries and mini-roses.**

caterer or location might even offer improved rates with the hope of booking your wedding. Value ~ not cost ~ should be the bottom line. You will get a true sense of what to expect before you have to make binding decisions for the reception.

Your caterer and consultant are the most important wedding professionals to evaluate, but consider also a test run with your florist, baker, photographer, even makeup stylist. A good working relationship is based on the ability to communicate freely, and everyone expresses ideas in a different manner. Try to be as detailed as possible when describing what you want: Words like "beautiful" and "delicious" are vague and open to interpretation. You are more effective if you specify that you want centerpieces of "pale pink sweet peas and lady's mantle, no higher than fifteen inches from the table" and a dessert of "poppyseed genoise, raspberry filling, and real buttercream flavored with Cointreau." Only when you speak the same language and create a bond of trust can you feel confident your message is getting across.

GIFT REGISTRIES

Why not choose a registry with a theme? If you're a garden enthusiast, play up that love and register at a botanical shop. Cast-aluminum gardening pots and gardening tools as well as potting soil and seeds (above) **can make the perfect gift. If you would rather not stray too far from convention, choose a shop that will be able to provide all the entertaining and homemaking essentials. A box filled with china, crystal, and silver from the bridal registry** (opposite) **is exciting to receive.**

*H*appily, custom dictates that everyone invited to your wedding offer a gift celebrating your nuptials. And even more happily, many retailers have some version of a registry program, saving time and anxiety for your guests while guaranteeing that you get exactly what you want.

Register for gifts as soon as you are engaged. Call or visit the stores you both love, and browse during quiet off-hours, when bridal directors are less frenzied and they can help with selections. Register for items in a broad range of prices, as you want guests to be able to purchase a gift they will be comfortable giving. This will also allow guests to use the registry for shower gifts, typically less expensive presents.

National retailers will computerize your registry and provide current information about your selections to each of their outlets. Larger department stores will allow you to register with them a year in advance. Smaller, more specialized shops, with less inventory and more eclectic selections, tend to have somewhat stricter parameters. With a small store and a long engagement, you may have to update your list periodically to keep up with the changing or seasonal inventory.

BEYOND THE CONVENTIONAL

Do not feel limited to conventional registry shops. If you and your fiancé love music, register at your favorite record shop, or a bookstore if you are a couple of bookworms. Antiques shops, wine merchants, plant nurseries ~ even hardware stores ~ are all suitable. Put a little time into this decision, as you'll be using these gifts for a long while.

Tradition suggests that gifts be sent ahead rather than brought to the wedding. Begin a gift log, recording on index cards the giver, the gift received, and the store it came from. Write a thank-you note within two weeks of receiving any gift and record the date on the index card.

With love
Ross

The joy which the two of us,
_____ Arak and Nathan Kanofsky,
give to each other,
share with our family and friends.

Our parents
_____ and Michael Arak
Toby Kanofsky
and
Alan Kanofsky

The Pierre
Grand Ballroom

SCALE

Bringing the Dream to Life

Creating the wedding of your dreams begins with a series of evaluations. Often, the type of ceremony you choose sets the tone for the rest of the celebration. But it could just as easily be the date or the location you want for your reception. For these major elements, be logical: evening receptions are less practical in winter, when weather may be a factor; travel time between the ceremony and reception should be less than thirty minutes; the degree of formality you establish should be constant throughout. Once you have settled on the date and place, decide if you want to hire a consultant to implement your plans, and choose a caterer and musicians. Unless your location is perfectly accessorized, you will need a few showpiece props to enhance the decor. Ordering stationery early on will leave you free for other details. Finally, prepare for the memories of your day, with a photographer and a videographer. Most importantly, you must be comfortable with the financial scale of the wedding. Generally, couples underestimate expenses, or during the planning process they yield to temptation and choose an option beyond their budget. A good hard look at what you are really prepared to spend will help avoid needless misunderstanding and aggravation.

THE CEREMONY

*O*ften the decision to marry in a church or temple is based on practice and circumstance. If you are considering a religious ceremony, contact your clergy as soon as you're engaged. If you have no religious affiliation but desire to marry in a house of worship, you will probably be asked to join a congregation. And if you want a religious ceremony in an alternative location, check with your local clergy to see if your wishes are acceptable to their doctrine.

Make an appointment with the parish office to reserve your date and to discuss the options and requirements. If more than one ceremony will be performed on your day, allow plenty of time to set up and retreat, and for your guests to park and retrieve their cars. If there is another wedding besides yours, ask the church if you may contact the other couple to coordinate timing and perhaps to share floral decorations. Inquire about restrictions: music, bell ringing, decorative details; many churches now prohibit aisle runners, pew adornments, and tossing birdseed or petals. Some churches restrict photography or videography.

Inspect the space to be sure it will accommodate the comfortable seating of your guests and the acoustics of your music. Check to see if the foyer is large enough for a receiving line; if not, greet guests outside or at the reception.

❧ CIVIL RITES ❧

If you are having a civil ceremony, you can research the legally authorized officiants at the office of your town clerk, where marriage licenses are also obtained. Most civil servants perform weddings in their chambers or offices, and requests to marry at other locations may not always be honored. Interfaith and independent clergy can perform civil ceremonies, too. Do expect to pay a fee for the officiant's service, and do invite the officiant and spouse to join the reception.

A plush diamond jacquard silk pillow lends a wonderfully romantic touch when used as the ring bearer's pillow; the wedding bands are knotted to the pillow with vintage golden silk ribbon. (Do make certain that the rings are fastened securely.) One of the rings is a basic gold band; the other is detailed with a circle of X's symbolizing kisses.

CHOOSING A LOCATION

hoosing the perfect place for your wedding celebration may be tricky. For one thing, travel time between the ceremony and the reception should not exceed thirty minutes. This alone may narrow your options considerably. But before you even begin to look, talk frankly with your groom and make these preliminary decisions:

HOW FORMAL WILL YOUR WEDDING BE? Most of us equate formality with expense, and for good reason, so factor your budget into this decision. A sit-down dinner with multiple courses is the most formal reception; a wedding lunch is often casual. In between are lunches, teas, suppers, and buffets.

WHAT KIND OF ATMOSPHERE DO YOU REALLY LIKE? If deep down you find the country club stuffy, scratch it off your list. If your wedding will be in the height of hay fever season, cross off the botanical garden, too. You want to book a space feeling confident that everything will run smoothly; if the site manager is not responsive to you now, before you have made a commitment, choose another location.

HOW MANY GUESTS WILL YOU HAVE? Even two hundred people will disappear in a grand ballroom. By the same token, it's hard to squeeze fifty people, a band, and a wedding party into a living room. One good rule of thumb: The fewer guests you plan, the more eccentric your location can be. If you are inviting children, pass on the manor house or sailboat and book a space that is more kid-friendly. Once you decide, book your spot ~ good places fill early.

⟡ THE SETTING FOR YOU ⟡

List the places that excite you: a historic home or a museum, a garden, loft, photographer's studio, town house, yacht or ferry, even the marina. Be inspired by your surroundings: a mountain lodge, the beach, a winery; if you met at college, look at campus halls, the library, the dean's office.

Some of the best receptions take place in unconventional locations. For example, a girls' school, with its arched entryways, gothic columns, and stone courtyard, lends an element of stateliness. Contrast imposing stonework with luxurious flourishes: quirky gilt containers, quilted silk overlays with others of crushed silk, lush flowers on a stone chair are wonderful complements to the formal style of the space.

Call ahead to check availability, capacity, and cost, then see the space in person, during the hours you will want it. Some rules: Conventional sites offer peace of mind, as well as options from linens to menus, but they're less flexible about personalization. Unusual venues provide the bare necessity of space, and your customizing options are unlimited. A space full of beautiful details will stretch your reception budget, for it needs less adornment. A room that is spare may mean that you'll have to bring character into the space yourself, a costly ~ but potentially thrilling ~ undertaking.

Whatever your choice, look out for hidden costs. As utterly romantic as your wedding will be, booking the space should be entirely logical, so bear in mind:

FACILITIES Must you use the on-site caterer? Is there a kitchen that can handle your demands? Are there tables, chairs, table settings, linens? Amenities such as icemakers and ice buckets? How much will you really have to rent?

FEES What is the basic cost for the space? What are the extras and overtime charges? How is payment made?

HOURS How much time is included in the rental, including setup and cleanup? I allow four hours for crews to set up in a traditional site, but add more for an unusual location.

INSURANCE Is the facility ~ and are other vendors ~ fully insured? If not, increase your homeowners' coverage.

PRIVACY Will there be another event scheduled at the same time? Can it be kept apart from your wedding?

RESTRICTIONS Will your guests be restricted to certain rooms? What's not allowed? One sentimental bride wanted her dog to be part of the wedding celebration, and took care to choose a location that would welcome him.

STAFF What personnel are included in the rental fee? Will the manager be on-site? How will the space be maintained ~ restrooms tidied, flowers primped, ashtrays emptied?

You will also want to verify that there is access for delivery vehicles and wheelchairs and adequate electrical power, lighting, parking, and security.

The location you choose speaks volumes about the style of your wedding: The iron gates (top left) **of a historic inn heighten guests' anticipation; a dramatic spiraling staircase** (top right) **is the focal point of a grand town house and a magnificent entrance for the bride and her father. A hotel's majestic ballroom** (bottom left) **epitomizes nuptial elegance; and a grand pavilion** (bottom right) **at a landscape architect's nursery is a hidden treasure.**

HOTEL WEDDINGS

Choose a hotel with luxurious Old World decor or an ultramodern site but expect a seasoned staff, central location, elegant amenities, ancillary lodgings, a versatile kitchen and an appealing wine list, and an unflappable banquet manager. One-stop shopping and exquisite attention to detail are the primary benefits when you decide on a classic hotel wedding.

THE FINE POINTS

 MEET with the banquet manager or catering director as soon as you want to book a date. Review options, packages, fees.

 TOUR the accommodations. For a large wedding, consider ballrooms; suites are best for smaller guest lists. Most hotel spaces easily host the wedding and reception and happily provide a room in which the bride may dress.

 REQUEST a suite for the wedding night and a preferred rate for wedding party and guests.

 TASTE the menu and beverage options. Best choices should reflect time of day ~ brunch, luncheon, tea, dinner, late-night dessert.

 INQUIRE about staffing and gratuities: valet, coat-check, wait staff, busboys, general help, security.

 REVIEW and approve stylistic details ~ linens, table settings, floral decor, lighting ~ with banquet manager.

THE HOME WEDDING

Welcome guests with flowers that reflect the style of the home. Do not try to emulate the sleek style of a professional florist; you want these decorations to look natural and guileless. For instance, fill some pots ~ these are McCoy ~ with fresh-cut garden flowers and line them up along the porch rail. Use galvanized flower buckets or even watering cans to hold vibrant bouquets; then set them out randomly, at gateposts, on porch steps and garden tables.

*I*f you want to celebrate your marriage at home (it was my choice) or if a dear friend or favorite aunt has offered her exquisite house, stop to consider the realities. Many romantic couples tend to underestimate the demands this kind of wedding will make. The most common obstacles are insufficient space, inadequate catering facilities, and a far greater stress load for you and your family. But if you are determined to marry at home, my advice to you is simplify, simplify, simplify: Simplify the guest list, simplify the menu, simplify the decorations.

The first step: Look at your home with the clear eye of a party planner. (Incidentally, a consultant may be the key to having your cake and eating it, too: She will be able to handle the problems that inevitably arise with home weddings, allowing you to focus on the happiness of this time.) Review traffic patterns through the house and gardens; anticipate where people will gather. Have an alternative bad-weather plan: One farsighted bride had the pergola by her pool fitted with canvas panels, which offered guests relief from the sun and, if rain had appeared, would have provided ideal shelter.

Decide early on what improvements you are prepared to make. Bear in mind that your guests will be blinded (to a touch of faded paint or a worn floorboard) by happiness for you and your groom.

In lieu of formal flower arrangements, invest in land-scaping ~ flowering shrubs, abundant window boxes and planters ~ all with bridal-white flowers. Work with your florist to design the flowers to look homey.

Rent a tent to add to the reception space; customize it with a grand crystal chandelier and an oriental rug. Rent an icemaker, an extra refrigerator, some gas grills. If you don't have a dishwasher, this is a good time to install one. Rent coat racks and hangers in case of a cold or rainy day. And rent a generator in case electrical needs overwhelm the system.

Empty the garage and put in sufficient lighting and worktables for caterers, florists, and other vendors to use.

Arrange major cleaning, including windows, the day before the wedding, and the day after the wedding, too.

Ribbon off private quarters. If you are renting portable bathrooms, keep units convenient but out of primary view.

Hire help to keep bathrooms tidy and to collect empty glasses and replace dirty ashtrays with clean ones.

Some pets are easily overwhelmed by large parties, and it's kinder to ask a friend to house them for the day.

If parking is limited, have a van or bus ferry guests from the church or a local parking area. If the grounds are large, hire a valet service or college students to direct traffic. It's a good idea to notify the local police of the wedding, too.

One last tip for the perfect home wedding: Just before the ceremony, turn off the phone, the fax, and the answering machine, and ask someone to stand at the front door (or in the lobby of your apartment building) to hold late-arriving guests, so that nothing will interrupt your vows.

If your reception will be outdoors, be prepared for rain showers or relentless sun. Have at hand a dozen or so double-size umbrellas, either in white or a color from your wedding palette. And to prove that even the ordinary can be made lovely, collect them in a vintage shopping basket caught up in a silk organza bow.

WEDDING CONSULTANTS

*I*magine having the perfect wedding but without endless meetings, negotiations, and searches for the right setting, menu, and flowers. Sound tempting? Then hire a good wedding consultant. Troubleshooter, organizer, fiscal wizard, and diplomat, a consultant will get to know you and your groom and your wishes, then bring your fantasy to life. Out-of-town brides, busy career couples, and those hoping to control expenses without sacrificing style should all consider the benefits of hiring a consultant.

A consultant can design an impressive affair that is true to your personality and original in spirit. Most consultants are skillful negotiators with access to business-to-business discounts; because she (yes, the overwhelming majority of wedding consultants are women) is a professional wedding planner, vendors are especially eager to retain her goodwill. A wedding consultant has access to the best suppliers and the ability to anticipate and sidestep problems and plan backups; she isn't flustered by mishaps, and keeps you blissfully unaware of minor glitches.

Most consultants are problem solvers by nature and will act as emissaries, inspecting the reception room in advance and seeing to the smallest details. After the event, the consultant can arrange for return of rentals, settle any breakage charges, and ensure that your cleanup is efficiently handled. A consultant may be booked to orchestrate an entire event or by the hour as a wedding-day coordinator ~ a valuable extra pair of hands when they are needed the most. She can be as involved or as uninvolved as you desire.

Be sure the consultant you hire has solid experience and positive references (ask if the bride would hire the person again). You will want to know she has managed a wedding of your size, has no schedule conflict, and will be in attendance on your wedding day if you desire.

Your consultant will keep your day on schedule. She will make sure everyone involved has vital maps and contact numbers and be in constant communication with all your vendors, heading off potential glitches and relieving you of those concerns. Arrange a final run-through the week before the wedding to confirm the final timing and to be sure that nothing has been overlooked.

CATERING SERVICES

The most basic component of a caterer's service is food and its presentation, but many caterers are in effect full-service party planners who create an entire event from tenting and lighting to music and flowers. Once you know your date, venue, and approximate guest count and have a broad idea of the service you want ~ a sit-down meal, cocktail party, or clambake ~ interview several caterers.

There are basically two types of caterer: On-site caterers are based in one location ~ a hotel, restaurant, or country club ~ and it is virtually impossible to hire another caterer to work in their space. An off-premise caterer operates as a traveling road show, bringing everything ~ even a kitchen ~ to a site.

Plan to meet at least three times with your caterer. At the preliminary meeting, broadly discuss your celebration. Walk through the location, and the space will suggest a style, a mood, a menu. Request to see the caterer in action for a true sense of the crew's merits. A superior caterer will work hard throughout the event, keeping buffets looking lavish even toward the end of the meal and tables well bused.

Based on your thoughts and budget, the caterer will present a proposal. The pricing will reflect the number of guests, your menu, and the range of amenities. This first proposal is only a suggestion, and the caterer will expect you to request changes. Meet a second time for a tasting, when tables will be set according to the proposal.

A finalized head count is due about two weeks before the event, when you and the caterer will meet for the third time. Now the caterer will confirm the final price based on current market costs. Expect to pay a fifty percent deposit, with the balance due at or before the wedding. Overtime rates, damage allowances, and wait staff attire should also be agreed upon beforehand and included in your contract.

Tell your caterer about your budget realities; it is part of his or her service to work within these limitations. The best budget stretcher I know is to base your menu on foods that will be at season's peak when you marry. In place of an expensive seafood appetizer, serve chilled cucumber soup, which is both pretty and tasty. Serve less-expensive poultry in lieu of red meat, and offer a fruit and cheese course to round out the meal ~ very elegant, very economical. Notice also how a fruit garnish and a dusting of powdered sugar can beautifully finish any dessert.

PARTY RENTALS

An astonishing number of weddings today involve rentals of some kind. Of course, the all-important foundation pieces ~ glassware, table settings, tables, and chairs ~ are the items we most commonly think of as rental goods. Beyond these is a world of artifacts you can rent for this one day: Ionic columns, canopies, tents. There is a world of heirloom pieces: Victorian table linens, vintage dishware, elaborate silver serving pieces. And there is a whole other world, of the utilitarian foot soldiers that make weddings comfortable: space heaters, high-power lights, generators, icemakers, coatracks, and, yes, portable toilets.

Visit the showroom to look at the items you're considering. Trust the formulas developed by rental services for ordering adequate supplies ~ they're the experts.

Your rental proposal will list every piece you might rent, outlining each item and its price, and the terms of delivery and pickup. The contract should also detail delivery and setup fees; the delivery date and time and location; the cancellation policy and a damage allowance.

Whenever I first talk with a bride and groom about the reception look they want, I think immediately of the types of "props" we can rent, because these pieces add more atmosphere than any other element. For more exotic pieces, I scour antiques shops, prop houses, specialty showrooms, landscape nurseries: I may want white clapboard birdhouses for centerpieces, a pair of grandfather clocks to frame the entryway, a wrought-iron garden bench to dress with flowers. I have rented trees; I have rented marble statues; I have rented carousels ~ chances are, if you can find it, you can rent it. Just keep in mind that most establishments will require a deposit that covers the full price of the items, and you should appoint someone to oversee delivery and return.

Rental items should be delivered early in the day or the night before the wedding ~ if you are planning a home wedding, save your sanity and insist that all rental goods be delivered at least six hours before the wedding. Everything should arrive ready-to-use: linens laundered, starched, and pressed; silver perfectly polished; dance floors gleaming; tents clean, showing no repairs. If you will be using a tent, have it set up the day before to avoid any last-minute hassles. Have a friend check off delivery orders as they arrive to make sure you receive the correct amount. Allow at least four hours for the caterer to dress the rental wares. After the wedding, equipment should be stacked ~ not cleaned ~ and wrapped as it was delivered, to be picked up by the rental agency.

The Perfect Wedding

INVITATIONS & STATIONERY

ENGRAVED In this most formal stationery style, the letters are raised and a bruise from the pressure of the press is apparent on the reverse of the paper.

THERMOGRAPHY Looking very much like engraving but less expensive, thermography is slightly shiny with a raised texture.

BLIND-EMBOSSING This inkless raised-impression style is created from a die and is appropriate for monograms and return addresses on envelopes.

LETTERPRESS This look is created by an old-fashioned printing machine with movable squares of type and will accommodate textured, handmade papers.

PRINTED In this method, offset or laser printing deposits ink onto the surface of the paper.

CALLIGRAPHY Either printed, engraved, or hand-done with special pens, this style of elegant penmanship with fanciful flourishes is labor-intensive. Most invitations feature type styles that re-create that look.

Engraved panels of ecru bond, envelopes lined with marbled tissue, handmade papers with custom watermarks ~ more than a mere request for attendance, your wedding invitation is a very personal messenger.

Invitations rely on a few appropriate words to succinctly verse a request and communicate important information about the event. For the purist among us, there is an etiquette of phrasing; meanings are inferred as much by what has been omitted as what is printed. A good host will balance etiquette with courtesy by including all the important specifics in print. Stationers have style books to address every situation.

About three months before the wedding, place your order. A well-designed invitation will include an R.S.V.P. card (with a stamped, self-addressed envelope) to speed a confirmed guest list. Optional inserts include an at-home card, listing your new address and date in residence, and a within-the-ribbon card, specifying seating for special guests in the first few ribboned rows of the ceremony. To make wedding day travel more felicitous, you might print up a local map, travel information, and, for out-of-town guests, possible lodging suggestions.

ORDERING YOUR STATIONERY

Be guided by the tone you have set for your wedding: For the most formal invitation, turn to an engraver; the informal affair, on the other hand, allows greatest creativity. Semiformal yet nontraditional invitations rely on elegant details to add a formal finish ~ hand-printed papers unfold to reveal an engraved request with gold embossed monogram; satin ribbons secure enclosures.

For an informal invitation, commingle symbols that represent passions you share ~ a baseball, a jazzy saxophone, a Monet ~ or, if you plan a home wedding, ask an illustrator

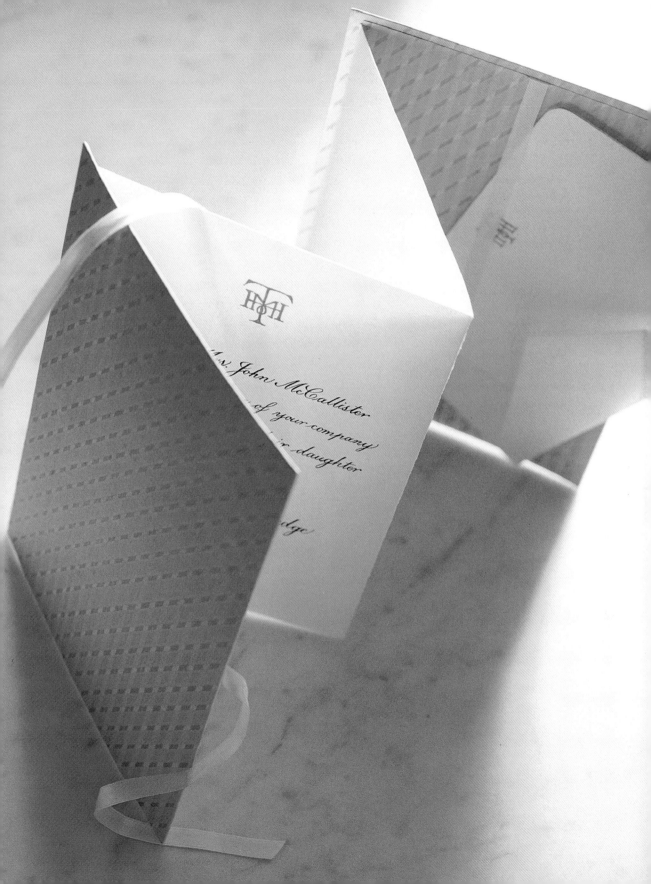

A graphic design studio or letterpress operation can create any of these magnificent invitations. The cut-out wedding cake *(right)* is a blank mass-produced card available in most stationery shops. If you wish to send announcements of your wedding, they should be styled as invitations, but without the specifics of place and time. Have these addressed and waiting; ask a friend to post them the day after your wedding.

to sketch your house. Computer graphics can help you create truly unique invitations: One bride I know was lucky to find the invitations of earlier generations in both her family and her groom's, and reproduced these in an accordion fold, beginning with her great-grandparents' invitations from the 1800s and ending with her own. To underscore the less-conventional nature of informal invitations, use alternate papers and envelopes ~ translucent glassine and brown kraft paper are my favorites.

Order invitations per household, not per guest, and include everyone in the wedding party and their families, as well as your officiant. As a rule, about twenty-five percent of a couple's list will be unable to attend, so you might want to invite a few more people than you would ideally enter-tain. Gauge your list, then order extra invitations to cover for mistakes in addressing and for keepsakes, to press or to frame, perhaps as gifts to your parents.

Address and mail the notes six weeks before the wedding, from a master guest list double-checked for accuracy in spelling and zip codes. (Save this same list to mark off confirmations and regrets; to confirm your guest count, you may have to telephone those who have not replied.)

Never use abbreviations; formal titles, not first names, are appropriate on the inner envelopes. The invitation is placed in an ungummed inner envelope with the response card sitting above it, the type of both facing the flap. Formal requests include a square of printer's tissue ∼ to protect against smudges ∼ and this tissue should be placed immediately over the invitation.

The envelopes of formal invitations are addressed by calligraphers, and the style of the calligraphy should match the lettering on the invitation. Invitations are never addressed by typewriter or computer, only by hand and preferably with a black fountain pen.

Updated twists on classic designs: marbled paper lines envelopes with gilt deckle edges; vellum overlays are printed with unusual shades of ink *(left)*. **One way to truly personalize your stationery while not straying too far from what is expected is to ask the calligrapher for an additional flourish; many have portfolios of stylized ornaments such as roses, cupids, and hearts which can be added with watercolor. Graphic artists can also design novelties such as these wedding day coasters** *(right)*.

PHOTOGRAPHY & VIDEOGRAPHY

A tender embrace, a joyful grin, a tearful toast, a dash through a shower of rice ∼ the entire day is full of memorable images. Long after the flavors of the food have faded, the images caught on film will remain. A good photographer should be adept at the candid, spontaneous shots: the flower girl who fell asleep, the grandparents holding hands, scattered flower petals on the vestibule floor. Sometimes the photos that are the least obvious can create the strongest impression, preserving the essence of the entire affair.

THE PERFECT EYE, THE PERFECT MEMORY

Try to interview a few prospective photographers, searching for the artistic perspective that suits you best. Of course, finished photos should be beautifully printed ∼ a professional photographer relies on a meticulous lab ∼ but it's the eye of the photographer that is the real value.

Ask to see entire, unedited shoots of complete weddings, not just final prints. Look for a point of view, a sense of romance, and a sense of humor. The photographer may also show you contact sheets of film negatives. A good photographer will capture the important story-telling moments; he or she anticipates without upstaging the scene. A great photographer appreciates available light and keeps moving, never relying on one static angle. Invite the photographer to shoot some of the pre-wedding festivities; this will make you more comfortable together and even help you to forget there's a camera about.

Be prepared to negotiate the fine points with your photographer. Most charge a daily rate and may pass along film and processing costs (important if yours has a journalistic approach and shoots over a thousand photos). A number of finished prints may be included, but this should be specified, as should the cost for extras. Photographers expect to be

Formal portraits are noted for perfect, even lighting. More than one light source is necessary to accomplish this masterfully; umbrellas soften the bounce, fill in shadows. Professional photographers can create a photo studio in any location. Try to shoot formal portraits directly after the ceremony or during the cocktail hour, and keep the session under thirty minutes, so that your guests do not have a drawn-out wait for your entrance.

Soon after you return from your honeymoon, your photographer will present you with proofs ~ one photographer I know ties stacks of quick prints together with a ribbon and presents them to the bride in a keepsake box with a window to highlight one great shot ~ or contact sheets to review. A magnifying glass and china marker will come in handy as you make your final selections.

reimbursed for anything beyond incidental travel costs, rental of any special equipment, and the daily rate of any assistants. If the photographer suggests a contract, read it carefully, particularly any discussion of ownership of negatives and the right to reproduce photographs. Ask for a clause that will pass the negatives to you after a number of years, or in the event the photographer dissolves his or her business.

CAPTURING THAT MAGIC MOMENT

Your photographer will want to know the details ~ daylight or evening, formal or informal, color or black-and-white (I prefer black-and-white, because it truly resonates with the beauty and emotion of the moment). Especially important is the number of guests: There is a great difference between recording an event with one hundred guests and one with three hundred. I once saw a wonderful photographer who knew exactly whom to shoot by watching the couple's reaction to the people on the receiving line. Whoever got the longest hugs and most enthusiastic handshakes found their way into the most shots. Provide the photographer with a shoot list and ask a good friend to stick with the photographer to point out important people.

Some couples now place a disposable camera on each table at the reception; it helps to break the ice among guests and can provide a serendipitous photo or two.

Expect to receive a proof box or enlarged contact sheets soon after the wedding to choose wedding photos. Proofs are quick prints, and they have not been perfectly printed or color-corrected. Edit the photographs to tell a story; balance portraits with candid shots, mood photographs, and sweet, telling details. Contrast tight shots with full-length perspectives, add still-life details, pair color with color, black-and-white with black-and-white. Consult with the photographer for the best selections; he or she will know which shadows can be erased in printing and which exposures will look better when enlarged.

Archival experts believe black-and-white photos hand-printed on fiber paper will last longest. Beautiful photographs

A beautiful album or folio is the best way to showcase your precious photographs. A bookbinder custom-made a folio for me (left)**. It is hand-crafted from silk and handmade papers. Hand-tooled leather albums** (right) **~ with acid-free pages and tissues ~ are a handsome alternative. Ask your bookbinder or stationer to emboss the cover or spine with your initials and wedding date.**

should be stored well and elegantly: Request albums with acid-free tissues and papers. Custom bookmakers can create photo folders lined with silk, hand-tooled leather albums, and hand-sewn paper albums, which should always be crafted with archival materials.

⌇ MOVING MEMORIES ⌇

Nothing brings a moment back to life like a videotape ⁓ a photograph captures the moment, film captures the energy. A good video is a melange of delightful sequences. You can't re-create the day, but you can hire a good videographer.

Photographers can suggest videographers, but don't take their recommendation as a requirement; review reels. You should have an emotional response to the work of the videographer. If you are watching a reel he or she has taken of another wedding, you should be thinking to yourself that that is exactly the way you want your wedding captured.

As with photographers, you should have a contract outlining the agreement you have reached with the videographer. Specify the date and time of your wedding, and the aspects you want included on the video. I've watched many, many wedding videos, and regardless of how elaborate a wedding is, the best videos are edited to five to ten minutes and layered with music. If you have your video edited down, remember to save the extra footage, as everything from the day is worth keeping.

A videographer should rely heavily on available light whenever possible. This is more natural-looking, less staged ⁓ the way the event was meant to look. Even when shooting outdoors at night, available lighting is best. A rule to film by is, "If you can see, you can shoot."

Sound can be picked up from the evening as well, but this exposes the tape to all the ambient noise ⁓ the chitchat at the tables, the banging of chairs, and so on. Talk with the videographer about dubbing the tape with appropriate music, even your wedding song.

Beautiful details are the trademarks of good bookbinders. A handmade cut-out heart stitched with gold threads is delicate and feminine. An unusual handmade spine features the threads that anchor the pages in the book to create a smart embellishment. Soft suede and beautiful marbled paper are another elegant alternative. Remember, bookbinders also custom-make boxes to hold your videotape, too.

Dressed to Perfection

*D*o you imagine yourself gliding down the aisle in frothy tulle skirts and Alençon lace? Or will you say your vows fitted in a smart suit and clever hat? What about your mother's wedding dress ~ can it be refitted for you? You may think you will never be able to choose among all the gowns you see, but you will; there is one just right for you. Before you begin looking, decide what month your wedding will be and if it is formal or informal, in the afternoon or evening. Then, in this chapter, read how to prepare yourself to shop; how to spot the signature of a great dress, and how to select one that flatters your figure and coloring. You'll also want to pair your gown with accessories, including beautiful wedding shoes, and take steps to ensure that you will look healthy and glowing, at your very best. Your choice of fashion will set the style for the others', from your attendants' to the grooms' and ushers'. This chapter will also show you how to pull all this together, right down to the men's cufflinks. There is advice on how to dress perfectly, and tips on what to carry with you so that you are carefree throughout your celebration. And you will learn how to maneuver full skirts with finesse, how to be utterly glamorous, whether kneeling at the altar or dancing in your husband's arms.

WEDDING GOWNS

*B*all gown or sheath? Sweetheart neckline or wedding-band collar? Off-the-shoulder or cap sleeves? So many choices . . . The names of the fabrics intoxicate: silk faille, gazar, cloque, moiré, chiffon, shantung; the laces enchant: Alençon, Chantilly, Honiton. For a gown this important, you must deal with someone you trust utterly ∼ a bridal salon, an heirloom restorationist, a private designer ∼ or you may make your gown yourself. Wherever you begin your search, think of four elements: silhouette, color, formality, and quality.

THE MOST BEAUTIFUL GOWN

The most universally flattering dress shape I know is the princess-line gown, with a skirt that falls softly from a shaped bodice without a defined waistline. A ball gown, with its full, feminine skirt, is a sentimental favorite. The sophisticated bride may prefer a sheath, a narrow gown whose delicate, deliberate movements are more appropriate to formal weddings. Whichever silhouette you favor, check your gown for practicality. If you must kneel during the ceremony or if you plan a long sit-down dinner, a fitted sheath may not be comfortable. If you will be outdoors in a garden, an ornate full skirt with elaborate details may be too fragile. If you chill easily or plan a winter wedding, choose a gown with long sleeves, or purchase a separate jacket or cloak.

Look for a gown that flatters your best features and camouflages any problem area. For instance, dresses cut with elongated torsos and waistlines that finish in a V or Basque waist at the front are slimming. If you have a full bustline, avoid three-dimensional details above the waist. For less amply endowed brides I recommend corset-styled bodices with an inner lift built right into the dress, or a neckline edged with flowers to discreetly enhance the figure. A beautiful neckline is flattered by off-the-shoulder sleeves.

A luxurious silk charmeuse underdress cut on the bias is draped with a fluttering breeze of chiffon and defined with a column of guipure lace. While this dress is suitable for any time of day, it is, by virtue of its bareness and its chiffon fabrication, best for semiformal summer weddings. In lieu of a veil, a long scarf of chiffon would be a perfect finish.

A sumptuous ball gown is the quintessential bridal silhouette, a lace bodice with full skirts of silk satin creating a regal presence. Long gloves are the perfect accent to sleeveless gowns for formal affairs. The chapel train is appropriate for the formal wedding. This gown is of shantung silk fabric, with a bodice of Alençon lace. Gloves add an appropriate degree of formality to a sleeveless gown. Wear a long layered veil to add more coverage for a religious ceremony.

White is the classic bridal hue, but be careful to choose the right shade for your skin color. Creamy-hued whites, often described as candlelight or silk-white, favor blondes, redheads, and fair-skinned brunettes. Bright white looks good on women with dark complexions and hair. White with an underlayer of pale pink or coral flatters everyone.

With the preliminary planning of your wedding, you have probably decided how formal it will be:

FORMAL AND VERY FORMAL Select a gown cut from rich fabrics such as lustrous satin for winter or ethereal silk chiffon for summer. It will be full-skirted, with a train: the longer the aisle, the longer the train; a chapel train is one yard, and a cathedral train is longer. For the most formal effect, cover your arms with long sleeves or gloves and wear a headpiece with a veil. If you prefer, a long veil may replace a train.

SEMIFORMAL Choose a gown that is floor length or has a train that just sweeps the floor. Bared shoulders and skirts of billowy tulle or crisp taffeta are fine all year round. I like a splash of delicate color ~ maybe a pastel sash at the waist that knots into a soft bow at the back and then cascades into a sweep train, or a neckline of blushing silk roses. A headpiece is optional, but a veil is typically worn to fall just below the shoulders or to the fingertips.

INFORMAL You have the widest choice with an informal gown: It may be floor length or ballerina length, a short chemise, even a pale dressy suit. If you are marrying informally yet want to wear a long gown, eliminate or streamline the accessories for the right balance.

THE SALON EXPERIENCE

Most brides do choose their gowns at a bridal salon. Good research beforehand will repay your efforts later: Ask friends and colleagues in detail about their experiences. Was the salon professional, were appointments honored, was the salon elegant, were sample gowns handled tenderly? Ask also if the alterations were impeccable, if the fittings lasted until the

bride was satisfied, and if the dress was delivered on time. Service is the trademark of the best salons: Their mission is to sell a great dress, ensure that it arrives on time, fine-tune the fit for you, and deliver it perfect for your wedding.

Call the salon for an appointment and expect to step into a world of service and one-on-one attention. Allow two or three hours for your visit, and be prepared to discuss the details of your wedding ～ season, time, location. By all means, bring a friend if you wish. Dress to undress, with a strapless bra, control-top pantyhose, and pumps. Even though these won't necessarily be the items you wear on your wedding day, they will help you visualize the finished look, making it easier for you to decide as you try on a variety of styles.

Virtually all bridal gowns are cut to order for your measurements by the designer, and most salons ask for a fifty percent, nonrefundable deposit when you place your order. A series of fittings ～ perhaps raising the waistline so that it sits

This sensuous dress *(above left)* **is of an exquisite lace that happens to be machine-made. It is sewn so that the seams are invisible, giving the illusion that the dress is one fluid, incredible length of lace. I think a lace veil becomes superfluous with a lace dress; instead look for a contrast, in this case an organza wrap that adds an urbane luster. A curvaceous crepe with a webbed yoke and cuffs** *(above right)* **is dramatic by virtue of its innate simplicity. Add a few vintage velvet leaves to your hair and keep your back bare of veiling to emphasize the lines.**

perfectly or taking in the seams to accommodate last-minute weight loss ~ will make sure that your gown fits beautifully. The salon will charge one fee for fittings, regardless of how many are required. Alterations, on the other hand, are more drastic adjustments to the design of the gown ~ replacing cap sleeves with long fitted ones, changing a drop waist to a normal one. Alterations have to be made by the designer of the gown and if available may increase the cost substantially.

Unless you have had a lot of experience with custom design and are comfortable with the design process, I think you will be more relaxed purchasing a gown from a sample that you can actually try on before placing an order. Yet, if you want a gown that's truly one-of-a-kind, cut from a fabric that's hard to find, this can be an exciting option. And while it may take about three months to actually produce the dress, be prepared for the design process to take even longer to unfold.

THE HEIRLOOM GOWN

Vintage boutiques are yet another fashionable resource for brides. Many turn-of-the-century cotton lace and Irish crochet lawn dresses survive and are surprisingly sturdy. Silk and tulle dresses are by nature more fragile and may have become brittle with age. Most heirloom dresses need to be reworked to fit contemporary figures, often adding fabric through the back of the dress and refitting the sleeves. Good retailers will carry vintage fabrics to match their gowns.

To revitalize a family heirloom, you'll need a seamstress with experience restoring old gowns ~ costume institutes and historical societies are a good place to start. You may want to use just part of a gown: One bride I knew despaired when she could not have her great-grandmother's dress altered to fit her, but she was thrilled with the dressmaker's suggestion to trim her new gown and veil with the antique lace. Other possibilities are to make a detachable train from retrieved panels; have cuffs or a fichu collar fashioned from bits of the silk and lace. When you have an old gown altered, watch

This trio of graceful gowns features the most flattering necklines and fluid skirts. At left, a modified bateau satin tank with an elongated waist has layers of tulle skirting. In the center, a short-sleeved lace bodice with a gentle scoop balances the softest chiffon skirts. At right, a skillfully sculpted geometric satin bodice with a crepe skirt has an organza train bustled into a feather-light bow.

for keepsakes ～ a charm, a ribbon, a wisp of hair ～ that may have been, many years ago, sewn into the bodice or hem.

Brides in untraditional dress count on accessories to add bridal esprit to a basic dress. There is nothing simpler than a sleeveless cotton piqué sheath (above), **here paired with lace mules, white gloves, and a wide-brimmed straw hat.**

The wedding suit is an honored tradition, especially for civil weddings. Whether by design or coincidence, wedding suits seem more sophisticated than short dresses. Accessories can transform a smart suit into a wedding ensemble (opposite), **here with a matching ice-blue marabou boa, satin bag, and pearl drop earrings.**

THE HOMEMADE GOWN

Yes, it's a romantic fantasy, lovingly stitching the beautiful dress in which you will marry. Please be warned: Only the bravest bride, with solid sewing experience, should attempt to execute her own gown. Even a simple column of silk from an easy pattern requires skill beyond that of the average home sewer, in addition to hours and hours of hard work.

But if you are determined ～ or if your sister or mother is an accomplished sewer who has offered this marvelous prize ～ invest in a dressmaker's dummy in your size. Make a test dress in muslin, to serve as a working sample. Once the fit is right, use the sample as a pattern. Choose only the finest-quality fabrics and notions, and work in an immaculate environment. Cover floors with white cotton sheets and keep walls and furniture well dusted. Install a three-way floor-length mirror and merciless lighting to inspect the workmanship as the construction proceeds. Take extra care with pressing and storing: Stuff your dress with tissue and pack it safely away when you are not working on it. Allow at least three months for the sewing and fitting.

WEARING YOUR GOWN

Manage your skirts with the ease of royalty, on stairs, in a limousine, or anywhere. Lifting your skirt is important: Gracefully bend just a little at the knees and softly pinch ～ never grab a fistful, as you don't want to wrinkle the fabric ～ a bit of skirt in each hand. Lift your skirts off center from the front of your thighs. With very full skirts and a train, never walk or step backward; instead, spin around, delicately lift the back of your skirts with one hand ～ always keep your elbow slightly bent for grace ～ and as you drop your skirts behind you, a breath of air will fluff the skirts as you step. A little practice will make each gesture a polished maneuver.

CHOOSING A GOWN

*E*ven if cost is no object, inspect any gown you are considering for quality. The best gowns are impeccably finished and look as great on the inside as on the outside. Understand the difference, too, between a slightly shop-worn sample and a poorly finished gown: The fundamental quality of your gown will not differ significantly from the sample. A salon that is concerned with presenting well-maintained samples can be trusted to take good care of your gown. Once you have made your selection, ask for a swatch of fabric for matching with shoes and other accessories.

THE FINE POINTS

SEAMS need to be smooth, with fabric evenly matched. The stitches should be tight and uniform, with no needle marks in the fabric or hanging threads. The fabric edges should be topstitched or wrapped with seam binding.

LININGS must be sufficiently heavy to conceal mid-layers, inner seams, boning, and undergarments, but light enough to protect the integrity of the top layer. Interfacings are never fused to the outer layer.

HEMS of heavy fabrics like satin are banded with at least two inches of horsehair to lift out the skirt. Skirt layers are sewn individually to the waist of the dress and are shortened or lengthened from the waistline to preserve the hemline and skirt motifs.

ZIPPERS should be hand-sewn. If a gown has back buttons, there should be a zipper under them for an extra-secure fit. Dresses with no buttons need invisible zippers. The zipper should extend to the widest portion of your hips to prevent tears.

CLOTH-COVERED BUTTONS are of the same fabric as the dress. Fastening loops should be secure, with just enough give for the button to slide through. Extra hooks and eyes are sewn into common stress points ~ waist, neck, bustles ~ for support.

BEADS and lace appliqués are secure, with pearls and beads individually stitched in place. Appliqués and all-lace bodices preserve design motifs and beautiful scalloped edges; lace seams are invisible.

BRIDAL HEADPIECES

*y favorite part of advising a bride on her ensemble comes when the gown has been selected and it's time to design the accessories that will make her uniquely beautiful and unforgettable. I always recommend choosing a headpiece just after the gown, then working on the shoes, gloves, flowers, and jewelry.

A crown of fresh flowers or a garland of silk ones, a fat satin bow or a rich velvet headband, a tiara of sparkling crystal or a barrette of baroque pearls ~ whatever headpiece you choose should be flattering, feel secure, and be easy to wear. Hats of all sorts, from brimless pillboxes to broad-brimmed sun hats, are elegant options. And delicious veils cut from netting or tulle add a wonderful measure of froth to a bridal ensemble. Length is the descriptive distinction of a veil:

CATHEDRAL is four yards long. This is the very formal veil.

CHAPEL is two and a half yards in length.

WALTZ AND BALLERINA lengths end just above the floor.

FINGERTIP extends to . . . your fingertips.

FLYAWAY is several layers and falls to the shoulders; it is great for informal gowns with back details.

MANTILLA is circular, attached to the top of the head and worn usually without a headpiece. Classically, it is all lace, but today it's just as often tulle edged with lace.

BLUSHER is worn over the face.

Wait until the first day of your fitting to order your headpiece. Bring a few hairpins and combs along to experiment with ways to wear your hair and to help anchor the veil. A headpiece is really only an accessory, and should never overwhelm. Strike a balance between your headpiece, veil, gown, and shading. Compare your gown and the headpiece in natural light to be sure they are the same shade. If your dress is beaded, appliquéd with lace, or edged with a particular flower, use one of these elements in the headpiece.

For a fresh, light adaptation of the ancient bridal head-dress of herbs and flowers, florets of hydrangea and brodiaea, daisies and hyacinth *(above)* **are wired together to make a bridal tiara. A more formal interpretation of the headdress, lightweight gilt blossoms are dotted with pearls** *(opposite)***. To balance such an important crown, silk ribbon edges the fingertip veil.**

The Perfect Wedding

Even simple veils are frothy and gossamer when cut from multiple layers. You may want to add definition with ribbon or with rolled or pearl-trimmed edges. Very long veils will hold their place and defy the gyrations of static electricity with the added weight of lace appliqués or a scattering of pearls across the edges of the tulle.

If you prefer a hat, a good milliner can show you the best brim for your features. One that turns down will add mystery and hide any tear you might shed, while a jaunty upturned brim will reveal your face. A perfect hat should sit securely but not tightly about the widest point on your forehead.

Consider your comfort before you opt to wear a grand hat on your wedding day. Has your groom ever kissed you while you wore a brimmed hat? Practice the moment ~ particularly if your groom is much taller ~ or you can be sure the hat will end up at your feet. Also, if you expect a long

For a garden wedding with elegance, wear a beguiling hat. One example is this insouciant straw hat with its bold gauze of evergreen. Because the hat makes such an emphatic statement, it needs an understated counterpart: a tailored silk gown with only a parade of back buttons for ornamentation. If you choose a color for your headpiece, echo that color in your bouquet, in a bow on your shoes, or in your bridesmaids' gowns.

receiving line, you can count on lots of hugs, and a broad-brimmed hat may be a good deal harder to manage than the narrow-brimmed boater or bowler.

Women with very fine, short, straight hair might want a headband style; those with long hair should consider wearing a French braid with a bow securely clipped to it. If you have full-bodied or curly hair, you will look well groomed and elegant in a chignon or French twist. Bear in mind there will be precious little time to primp at your reception. Wear your hair up and back from your face, and a light spritz of hair spray will help keep you photo-ready at all times.

Fresh flowers are a bridal favorite. A wreath or crown of fresh-cut flowers is best nestled in your hair or along the hairline; avoid wearing flowers across your face or rustling against your ears or neck, all of which can be irritating and distracting. Scatter individual florets through your hair for a sophisticated and fresh look. Individual buds of baby's breath

A bride's hat should sport some sort of trim ~ a silk flower, a touch of lace, or a fabulous bow of tulle, grosgrain, or silk. These small-brimmed hats are softened with, from left, bows of tulle, silk, and chiffon. While one often associates bridal hats with street-length dresses and suits, they can be surprisingly beautiful when paired with gowns, especially those that are more tailored. The secrets of a good match are a repeating element ~ a flower or bow on hat and dress ~ and continuity of tone.

will look like so many pearls sprinkled through your hair. Clip the stems short and tuck them into your finished hair. Hair spray, lightly applied, will help anchor each. For larger flowers, have the individual buds wired on short stems; wire a few together about a comb or place them singly in your hair with pins. Add a veil on a comb for a perfect finish. Always style your hair completely before adding flowers ~ and practice once or twice before the wedding.

TO ATTACH YOUR WEDDING VEIL

After you have dressed, secure your headpiece and veil with a series of overlapping bobby pins. Starting with a strand of hair at the point where you want to attach your headpiece, twist and twirl the length of hair into a small circle against your scalp. Crisscross several bobby pins (choose ones that match the color of your hair) through this circle of hair into an X-shape. Use this spot as an anchor for combs or more bobby pins; small elastic loops sewn on the underside of the headpiece will accommodate the hairpins or combs. Rest heavier headpieces at the top of your head.

Milliners have a simple trick they use to center the blusher veil on the bride's brow: during the fitting, the netting will be perfectly placed and a red basting thread loosely stitched through the exact front center of the veil. When the bride dresses on her wedding day, the thread acts as a marker that is pulled free once the veiling is in place.

Wear the veil over your face until you stand with your groom at the altar. Immediately after the ceremony, check in a foyer mirror to see that the veil is neatly arranged around your head. Leave the veil in place at least until you've had your first dance with the groom (drape a long veil gracefully over your arm); by this time, your photographer will have captured you in all your bridal finery. A detachable veil is smart: Snaps or Velcro quickly release from a headpiece without pulling the hair. And a veil on a separate comb can pull free effortlessly.

A headpiece should complement your gown's style and degree of formality, but beyond that there is enormous choice. Take, for instance, this simple princess-line gown of white satin banded with sandy beige. It pairs equally well with a brimless hat dotted with silk roses *(top left)* **and a petite cloche fashioned as a bouquet of silk roses caught up in a bit of Russian veiling, which is the open-weave coarser net that typically veils the eyes only** *(top right)*. **In the same vein, a debonair gown with a back waist flutter of silk flowers demands an equally soigné hat. One supremely sophisticated choice would be an ultra-fine, wide-brim straw hat knotted with an exquisite satin bow** *(bottom left)*. **A sleek gown of silk charmeuse with an organza overshirt is more beautiful with a simple layered flyaway veil on a comb** *(bottom right)*. **One of the reasons this is so successful is that the veil draws the eye to the gown's bodice detailing and dramatic button cuffs.**

FASHION ACCESSORIES

Embroidered gloves, heirloom pearls, a crystal pavé necklace: A bride's accessories should be emphatically luscious; if they are vintage, too, so much the better. In the display case of one shop *(opposite)*, delicate gloves are embroidered across the top of the hand with silk to resemble a leaf pattern. The choker with its heart pendant is made of embroidered jacquard ribbon. Because of its width, the pearl necklace *(above)* is called a dog collar. The estate Irish claddagh heart ring topped by a crown and vintage pavé earrings would work well with a simple ivory silk gown.

*N*o bridal ensemble is complete without accessories. Spend the time to seek out the treasures you'll wear: your mother's ~ or his mother's ~ cultured pearls, or custom earrings that pair your birthstone with your groom's. I like a triple-strand choker of seed pearls with a sweetheart neckline, a vintage locket on velvet ribbon for an heirloom gown, or no necklace at all for a dress with a beguiling décolletage. But be modest: Too many accessories, or the wrong ones, can detract from the beauty of the gown.

Make final decisions wearing your ensemble in front of a floor-length three-way mirror. Take off your watch, for such a utilitarian object has no significance on this special day. Try on the earrings and necklace with your headpiece, and add a bracelet, gloves, shoes, a purse. Then remove one or two elements, until the balance is perfect.

CHOOSING YOUR WEDDING SLIPPERS

Though they are not as immediately noticeable as the veil and headpiece, your wedding shoes will get just as much attention. And they should: Most shoes designed especially for the bride are exquisite works of sumptuous satin, and the styles are as varied as the gowns they accompany, from stately heels to flat skips to lace-up boots.

Look for shoes that have a balance with your gown in terms of design and delicacy: A bow at the back of your waist may be echoed on the toe of each shoe; a ballerina tulle skirt is complemented by a slender demi-heel. Open-toe pumps are really too casual for a bride. If you want an airy look, you could choose a sling-back or, if you are wearing a short dress, lacy mules. If part of your wedding is outdoors, wear flat or squat heels that will not sink into the ground. For long receptions, a back-up pair of shoes with a lower heel is essential ~ trust me. The best investment of all may be

Fabulously feminine bridal heels are covered in silk or satin ~ not leather ~ but the ornamentation can be dramatically different: sling-backs with bows, buckles, and a row of miniature rosettes *(above left)*. **For an indoor wedding, consider a spiral of pearls on the heel** *(above right)*. **If you have a gown with a sprinkling of tiny bows ~ or a great puffy bow at the waist ~ look for a shoe with a trio of simple satin ties** *(opposite)*.

inexpensive white satin or kid ballet slippers. To make them more festive, sew double-face satin ribbon streamers two or three feet long to the sides of the slippers; crisscross the ribbons about your ankles and tie them into sweet bows.

Comfort is the priority. You will wear your wedding slippers for six to twelve hours, and painful, even mildly uncomfortable, ones will be unbearable. Why risk suffering through this heavenly day because of shoes? One- or two-inch demi-heels will be more comfortable than high heels, flats more comfortable than either. Purchase wedding shoes a half size larger than usual; with all the time you'll spend standing and dancing, your feet will swell.

Take a swatch of fabric from your gown when you shoe shop. For a true match, I always compare fabrics in natural daylight. Silk or satin shoes that are a lighter shade of white should be dyed to match your gown. Contact a specialist shoe dye shop or the manufacturer of the shoes for advice here.

To avoid being uncomfortable in your shoes, wear them around your home as often as possible before your wedding day. Remember, however, to wear them on carpet so that they remain pristine. Sand the soles with very fine sandpaper to abrade the smooth finish, as highly polished marble and wood floors can be slippery.

BEAUTY & HEALTH

*L*ooking radiant on your wedding day is the inevitable result of following a regime you've begun months ahead. We all know that regular exercise helps maintain our best weight, but its primary benefit may be that it combats stress and increases our level of energy. One bride confided to me that she considered her workouts a "sanity saver" that had turned her pre-wedding jitters into abundant positive energy. If you have specific goals, see a nutritionist and a trainer.

❧ FRENCH TWIST OR SOFT TENDRILS ❧

Do you want a new hairstyle? If so, start working with your haircutter four months before the wedding, or as soon as you have your headpiece. If you want a radical new look, cut your hair in stages. Schedule a final trim two weeks before the wedding, so that your hair will look natural, not brand new.

Discuss hair color ~ whether to remove gray, intensify your tone, add a few highlights ~ and plan to make these changes, too, well in advance of your wedding day. (As tempting as it might sound, a drastic change is by nature high-risk, and your wedding is not an occasion when you want everyone whispering, "What has she done to her hair?") Schedule a final treatment two weeks before the wedding. Ask for conditioning advice to keep hair manageable, not limp from over-conditioning or brittle from too little.

Hold a dress rehearsal with your haircutter and headpiece. Your stylist may be available to assist you on your wedding day, but if not, ask for a referral. If you do your own hair, have a style that will be easy for you to manage. Unless yours is a geometric or short cut, wear your hair up on this day ~ you'll immediately look more elegant, and with just a touch of hair spray you'll be able to forget about your hair all day. Brides who are determined to leave their hair down must remember to brush it frequently to keep it camera-worthy.

Wedding-day beauty is created with the same tools you use every day, just with more care. If you are not working with a makeup stylist, treat yourself to new pots and applicators of makeup. Compared to all your other wedding expenses, this is a modest luxury, so invest in the best. For brushes, natural bristles work best; nail color in the faintest pastel is most becoming; and waterproof mascara ~ definitely use waterproof mascara.

Begin your wedding toilette with a luxurious soak ~ you'll probably be too excited to relax, but the bath will be soothing. Turn on gentle music, draw a warm bath, and pour in your favorite oil. In these last few moments of your life as a single woman, you'll find this pampering therapeutic. Moisturize with a scented lotion that matches your fragrance. The smartest indulgence on your wedding day? Put yourself in the hands of an expert makeup and hair stylist.

❧ THE WORLD OF BEAUTY CONSULTANTS ❧

Before you evaluate your makeup, you'll want your complexion to look its best. Please avoid tanning salons and the beach; ruddy skin doesn't look more beautiful than the real you. Meet with a beauty consultant, either privately or at a department store or beauty salon. Have a facial and waxing ten days before the wedding.

Describe your plans to the consultant, and include details about lighting, photography, and videography that may affect the shading of your makeup. Invest in a line of products that closely matches your own coloring for foundation, a palette of neutral, matte shadows, and a waterproof mascara.

You'll have plenty of people asking to see your ring, so look closely at your hands. Begin a series of weekly manicures several months before your wedding, so that you'll have strong, healthy nails. Avoid nails that are too long, and shun polish in vibrant colors. Pale beiges and blush pinks are universally flattering.

LINGERIE & UNDERPINNINGS

iscreetly hidden under your billowy bridal gown is the all-important foundation that will enhance your figure and improve the fit of your dress. The best underpinnings are exactingly precise yet utterly beautiful; after all, the wedding day is followed by your wedding night. But the most alluring lingerie will be irritating if it is too constricting and if it pinches rather than embraces your body.

A good bustier, I have found, is the best investment for any bride wearing a full ball gown. A corset is a strapless bustier with a long line that fits down to your waist; a merry widow has a longer line and is gartered to accommodate stockings. Though lingerie is cut by design to be admired, it should never show through your gown. Choose white, a very pale pastel, or a skin-tone color and tailoring that will disappear under your dress.

Buxom brides may need a corset specially sized for extra support, and a lingerie boutique is a good source for one. Less-endowed women will be pleased with the natural augmentation of a good lift, and more padding can be easily sewn into the cups. Be sure to have your bra at all your fittings, since it will affect the final fit of the gown.

Bridal gowns with voluminous skirts need a healthy petticoat to give the best shape. Salons carry a variety, and you can ask the salon seamstress to sew a pair of petticoats together for just the right amount of fullness. Narrow sheaths and delicate chemises need minimal undergarments ~ a body suit, a straight, long slip, or merely seamless pantyhose. Purchase an extra pair or two of hosiery as smart insurance for your wedding day.

I know some designers who craft their wedding gowns with a corset and petticoat sewn right into the dress. The designer of this kind of built-in security knows the value of the right underlying elements.

A ready-made back-lace-up bustier *(opposite)* **should be worn under a gown that has enough layers or is made from a heavy enough material to prevent the laces from bulging through. The silk tulle underskirt was found in a vintage shop. A beribboned garter** *(above)* **should be worn just above your knee. For a special keepsake, trim yours with heirloom lace and embroider your initials within the folds of silk lace.**

CARE & PRECAUTION

*S*oon your gown will arrive at your home, perfectly pressed and stuffed with sheets and sheets of tissue to hold its shape. Ask the salon for specific advice (have your maid of honor listen, too) about the gown, including dressing and bustling tips. Before you wed, find a good cleaner for the gown. Then arrange to have your dress sent to the cleaner as soon after the wedding as possible. Store the clean gown in sheets of acid-free tissue (not plastic bags) and an acid-free box in a dry, moderate space. Air the dress and inspect it annually and refold it along different lines to prevent permanent creases.

THE FINE POINTS

HANG your gown and headpiece in a safe spot, from a secure light fixture or coat hook. Gently remove the garment bag and slip a clean cotton sheet under the skirt. The weight of heavy fabrics like satin will pull most wrinkles from the gown.

PRESS the gown, if necessary, with a pressing cloth using a dry, clean, smooth iron on a low setting. Do not use steam, as water can spot fine silk.

HOLD the petticoat inside your bridal gown and step carefully into both; to avoid make-up smears, do not drop your gown over your head. Cinch your dress at the waist with your hands while your bridesmaid fastens the zippers, hooks, and buttons.

FINISH makeup and hair touch-ups with the skirts of your gown pulled over a stool or chair back. When traveling, pull the fullness of the skirt behind you, and sit forward to limit wrinkling.

PREPARE an emergency kit to keep on hand at the reception: clear polish for hosiery runs, white chalk to conceal dirt smudges, small scissors to trim loose threads, a needle and thread to match your dress for a tear, a silk flower as camouflage for a larger spot.

MAID OF HONOR & ATTENDANTS

Attendants' gowns need not be pastels; even warm-weather weddings can embrace gowns in colors like deep forest green *(opposite).* **Mid-brim hats are uniformly becoming, especially for an afternoon ceremony. Wrist-length gloves are pretty with bare arms, and crocheted gloves are nice for garden weddings. The bouquet is a mix of clematis, pansies, lemon balm, miniature geraniums, snow dwarf roses, Japanese anemones, and white forget-me-nots. As a gift to each attendant, a crystal heart framed with gold** *(above)* **is a lovely selection.**

*W*hen you have chosen the bridal gown, focus on the dresses for your attendants; the gowns should echo the bride's and complement one another. It's not unusual for salons to need three months or more to deliver the dresses and, of course, there will be fittings.

You may want the attendants to dress alike, which is the convention and allows a pretty, pulled-together look. Shop with one or two bridesmaids to minimize debate, and be aware of the delicacy of your position. Try the dress on yourself to appreciate how your friends will feel in it. Bear in mind the different body types this gown must flatter.

Today there are wonderful options for attendants ~ little black dresses or chiffon blouses worn with full taffeta skirts ~ that are easily rewearable. I have never felt that the women have to wear identical dresses; there is a tangible energy from attendants dressed in a variety of colors and shapes. But there are some rules, even to nonconformity: If the colors are different, the silhouettes should be similar. If the styles are different, the fabric should be from one harmonious palette. Each woman should select a gown that flatters her and works with her features, so that everyone looks her loveliest.

If dyeable shoes will be worn, have them all tinted at the same time and place, because dye lots can vary. Attendants' shoes need not match, but they should look coordinated. In that case each would be free to select whichever heel ~ of white or black, silk or satin ~ is most appealing. Be sure to review selections before purchases are made. Bouquets and jewelry should also be similar. To be sure your attendants' accessories are exactly as you wish, prepare and label individual packages with everything they'll need for the wedding ~ hosiery (include an extra pair), jewelry, gloves, tissues, purses, and nail polish. And please ~ ask attendants to leave their watches and handbags at home.

Enjoy special moments with your friends and sisters by dressing together. Lingerie should be hopelessly sumptuous: Petticoats of stiff net work best under gowns with fuller skirts, and strapless bras are essential under illusion necklines or any line where the straps would normally show. If you hire a stylist to do your makeup and hair, have someone available to minister to your bridesmaids ~ and your mother ~ too. Fill your dressing rooms with fresh flowers, perfumed air, and a couple of disposable cameras to record the joy of being with your favorite women.

FLOWER GIRLS

Precious smocked dresses with ribboned sashes and silken florets *(opposite)* **are appealing to child and bride alike. When accessorizing young attendants, consider pretty little gloves and perhaps some delicate flowers for their hair. Bouquets, baskets, garlands, wreaths, pomanders ~ whatever your flower girl carries should be sized for her small hands. Petite pearl-handled posies** *(above)* **filled with cyclamen and hydrangea with lamb's ears, caught up with bright white silk ribbon, are especially easy to carry.**

*C*harming, vivacious, adorable ~ flower girls are flattering attendants indeed. Children are able at even a young age to grasp both the solemnity of the ceremony and the gaiety of the reception. Typically, flower girls and ring bearers are at least four years old, so they can be reasoned with, are not easily distracted, and are able to appreciate the importance of their role in the ceremony.

The dresses of flower girls (and the ring bearer, who may be a young girl, too) should echo yours, but you needn't choose dresses that are miniature replicas of the bridesmaids'. Full skirts that fall to mid-calf are classic: These little gowns might be white organza or taffeta, to wear any time of the year; navy linen with sailor collars topped with pinafores of white organdy or floral chintz for warm weather; deep jewel-tone or black velvet gowns for autumn and winter weddings.

Keep accessories manageable. For hair, halos of fresh flowers, fat satin bows, and brimmed bonnets are delightful. Ballet slippers and Mary Janes are appropriate shoes, worn with white tights or anklets. Everything should be easy to wear, to avoid fidgeting over uncomfortable garments.

SUPPORTING THE CHILDREN

Rehearse the ceremony with children so that they can practice their parts. Keep responsibilities and instructions simple. For long ceremonies, permit children to sit with their parents. Young attendants should be dressed close to the time of the ceremony. Hire a babysitter to assist with the young ones before the wedding and throughout the reception. Seat their parents on the aisle in a front pew, as an encouragement for success, but allow young participants to have stage fright. If your flower girl feels unable at the last minute to precede you to the altar, ask the sitter or an usher to whisk her up a side aisle so that she may sit with her parents.

THE GROOM & HIS MEN

*C*lothing options for grooms have a far more contained tradition than those for brides, and tend not to follow fashion to quite the same degree. But with their snappy navy blazers and white trousers at summer weddings and their white tie and tails at the most formal city wedding, men can achieve every bit as much sartorial splendor as the bride and her attendants. Whether he chooses formalwear or suits, the groom and his men should dress alike (I often suggest that each of the men in the bridal party wear different but coordinated ties at semiformal and informal weddings ~ a striking, debonair look).

VERY FORMAL Weddings that take place in the morning are considered very formal, and accordingly the groom and his men should wear a morning suit, noted for its long jacket, gray waistcoat, and striped trousers. Fully dressed, these men will also sport dove-gray top hats, gloves, and spats, and they may carry walking sticks. Modern fellows will swap the traditional ascot or striped four-in-hand tie for a complementary silk tie.

For the very formal evening wedding, white tie and tails is appropriate. The swallowtail coat and trousers are black, worn with white piqué vests, shirts, and white bow ties. Top hats and white gloves are dapper additions.

FORMAL Weddings that occur after noon see the groom and his men in classic black tie, or tuxedo. White or ivory dinner jackets are an appropriate option for evening and are worn with black pants that are trimmed with grosgrain or satin ribbon, bow tie, and vest or cummerbund.

SEMIFORMAL Formal dress is appropriate, with jaunty accessories: bow tie, cummerbund or vest, even suspenders may be of a contrasting color.

INFORMAL A suit is a fine option. A navy or dark gray suit is the more formal choice, and casual options include a navy

The white jacket is, traditionally, an evening look for warm weather ~ May 15 to September 15. Formalwear departments stock these handsome jackets, as do many good vintage clothing shops. Such a shop may be a great place to pick up a truly smart and one-of-a-kind jacket, which is perfectly fine for the groom alone to wear. Since the white jacket is a very formal look, it should really be paired with formal black trousers and black accessories.

Ties are the pivot pieces in formalizing menswear. A silver tie *(opposite)* makes the dark navy suit more formal, a brightly patterned one less so. A morning suit *(above left)* is also made more casual with a boldly striped tie. Traditional black tie *(above right)* is in this case given a twist with a black-on-black bow tie, which has its own witty elegance.

blazer with white trousers, cotton in summer, flannel for fall. Then white bucks or saddle shoes are a good match. Almost any tie is fine, but its colors should harmonize with the bridesmaids' gowns.

Groomsmen traditionally cover the cost of their formal wear or suiting for the wedding day, but a generous groom will offer to cover exceptional expenses such as custom-made shirt studs or cufflinks. All kinds of formalwear can be rented, but I think that any man with more than one formal occasion on his calendar in a year should invest in his own black-tie dinner suit: he will feel more elegant each time he wears it, and its cost will be repaid surprisingly quickly.

If formalwear is rented, it should be fitted to the mea-

surements of each man. The hem of the tuxedo or suit jacket should be no longer than the middle of the man's longest finger. The sleeve of the jacket should skim the top of the hand; the cuff of the shirt should extend no more than half an inch beyond the jacket sleeve hem. Trousers should extend to the shoe's heel in back and break slightly over the top of the shoes in front.

Men are generally more casual than women about wedding preparations. They should have a haircut two weeks before the wedding, and a manicure the day before. Shoes should be well heeled and immaculate.

A ring bearer wears shorts or long trousers, and a jacket that corresponds to the groomsmen's attire: navy or white jackets with white trousers for summer; black velvet or wool for winter. Shorts are worn with white knee socks and white shoes. Pages wear knickers with a white dress shirt, white knee socks tucked under the knickers, and black dress shoes.

Consider gentlemen's wardrobes as foundations for accessories. One look involves richly patterned ties (above left)**, cufflinks, and antique silver pocket watches. For dapper formality** (above right)**, silk grosgrain slippers, cufflinks of broken car glass wrapped in silver, a gingham houndstooth check silk bow tie, and a dove gray top hat are all handsome options. Rich gold** (opposite) **is never incorrect. The wedding bands, cufflinks, and basketweave tie are set off by boutonniere of pastillage, a special request filled by the baker.**

*M*en appreciate some pampering, too; treat your groom to a relaxing massage the morning of the wedding. A groom and his men will appreciate the chance to dress together to celebrate friendship, and it's a great way to ensure that all the men are accessorized uniformly. Suggest to your groom that he and his groomsmen leave at least one hour to prepare themselves before the ceremony. This should allow plenty of time to address any last minute loose ends that might arise. Also have on hand a light buffet of sandwiches and cold soft drinks ~ as well as someone who is an expert at achieving a neat bow tie.

Romance in Full Bloom

*I*f you carry roses as you walk down the aisle, roses will ever after whisper to you of your wedding. A flower, nature's eternal symbol of joy and hope, is at the heart of the wedding celebration, and whether you create a bouquet of hundreds or prefer one tender bud, this is a potent sign of your love. From your bouquet to the centerpiece on each table, you want flowers that are magnificent, that are unforgettable. But there are too many choices; the cost is sobering. The solution? Find an imaginative, highly recommended florist who understands your wishes and respects your budget. A good floral designer is an artist with a profound appreciation of each flower and an understanding of the delicate process of combining one with another. A true professional florist works in a reassuring number of budget ranges, and most relish the creative challenge a modest budget offers. Make an effort to establish a rapport early on, and you will be repaid handsomely. Use the ideas in this chapter as a starting point for discussion with your florist, adapting the table bouquets and boutonnieres, the wreaths and garlands, to your personal style. Revise, refine, negotiate, and, ultimately, decide on what you yourself are comfortable with. After all, you want to be enthralled on your wedding day.

BOUQUETS, TINY & GRAND

An early summer bouquet *(opposite)* **combines the right mix of seasonal fresh flowers ~ fragrant garden roses, tendrils of bleeding heart, scabiosa, and lisianthus. But the real key to its success is controlling the intensity of colors: All the flowers, regardless of their color, have the same degree of tone. A pale composite bouquet** *(above)* **appears to be one giant rose, but instead it has been delicately wired together from hundreds of perfect rose petals.**

A bouquet of demure lilies of the valley and starry stephanotis caught up in a delicate ribbon of organza is the quintessential bridal accessory. But a fabulous bouquet can be created with any flower, and your options are limited only by the availability of the flowers, your imagination, and the skill of your florist.

The style of your wedding and your gown will guide your selection. A signature element ~ a creamy hydrangea, a stem of white lilac ~ should appear in all the other flower work, from attendants' bouquets to boutonnieres to ceremony arrangements and centerpieces at the reception. This will lend a sense of cohesion to the entire affair. Begin by discussing the kind of look you want to create, then narrow the options to the flowers that will be in season and that you adore. Your floral designer should work with these to develop suggestions for your bouquet and those of your attendants.

FORMAL AND VERY FORMAL bouquets are always all white, of one type of flower or a mix of just two or three different elegant flowers ~ roses, calla lilies, orchids, gardenias, stephanotis, and lilies of the valley are the most formal; tulips, freesias, lilacs, peonies, and hydrangeas are modern alternatives ~ fashioned into a nosegay or cascade and trimmed with pearly satin or sheer white chiffon and organza ribbons for a dramatic finish.

SEMIFORMAL bouquets are colorful but traditionally shaped nosegays and arm bouquets. My rules for combining flowers successfully: I mix muted pastels ~ smoky lavender lisianthus, dusty pink astilbe, powdery blue delphiniums ~ or crisp, bright hues ~ hot orange zinnias, rich plum scabiosa, fiery dahlias. Or I combine flowers of the same tone ~ blushing serena roses, pretty pink bouvardia, and hot-pink sweet peas. If you prefer all-white flowers, lend a touch of contrast with a gilt or softly hued ribbon.

A profusion of flowers ~ lavender, lily of the valley, bougainvillea, star of Bethlehem, scabiosa, lisianthus, sweet William, and French roses ~ is beautiful to behold. Such an elegant hand-tied bouquet should be exquisitely finished: Here a gilt mesh ribbon is French-braided to smartly conceal the stems ~ which also makes the bouquet easier to hold. More ribbon is looped into a great bow.

INFORMAL bouquets offer brides many more options. Often smaller bouquets or posies, they can be lively and unexpected ~ for instance, a handful of daffodils tied with a silk polka-dot ribbon, or a great pouf of garden-grown baby's breath. But informal doesn't mean unsophisticated: Consider a pomander of cymbidium orchids or a bouquet of gently green bells of Ireland, viburnum, and lady's mantle.

❧ SHAPES AND SILHOUETTES ❧

BOUQUETS are clusters of flowers that are either hand-tied together at the neck of the stems (florist tape binds all the stems, ribbons conceal the tape) or anchored in the water-soaked base of an oasis hidden in a bouquet holder. Primarily defined by structure, the shape of the bouquet determines the best flowers for each design. Many florists wire stems to improve the manipulation of fragile flowers, but most bouquets are groupings of stems left natural.

NOSEGAYS are round, densely packed bursts of blossoms about eighteen inches in diameter. Showy, round flowers like roses, hydrangeas, and peonies work well in this shape.

POSIES are petite nosegays, and here tiny buds like serena roses and grape hyacinths are ideal.

BIEDERMEIER NOSEGAYS are tightly packed concentric rings of flowers in various hues. Often the flowers are wired, and to underscore the repeating pattern of circles visually, each ring includes only one type of flower.

TUSSIE-MUSSIES are tiny bouquets carried in silver cone-shaped holders. To truly reflect the Victorian period style, use flowers that correspond to traditional meanings, which you can read about in facsimile books such as Kate Greenaway's *Language of Flowers*.

CASCADE bouquets are nosegays that gracefully extend tendrils of greenery and blooms from their bases.

COMPOSITE bouquets are single faux flowers created from individually wired flowers or petals. A glamelia, for example, is one fanciful flower made from dozens of individual

gladiolus florets wired to resemble a dramatic, fluffy camellia.

POMANDERS are blossom-covered globes. They are suspended from and held by a loop of ribbon.

BREAKAWAY bouquets have two sections, with a smaller bouquet nestled into a larger one. This enables the bride to toss one bouquet while saving the other.

❧ BOUQUET WISDOM ❧

Beautiful bouquets are the result of well-planned design, but you need not be an expert on flowers to carry one. Your florist will have plenty of suggestions, but do some homework first to have truly personal flowers.

CHOOSE FLOWERS IN SEASON. The best and most affordable are those in bloom locally. These can be cut close to the moment they'll be used, they have less distance to travel, and they are hardier than forced hothouse flowers.

My favorite bouquets combine unexpected elements. The result? The most amazing bouquets. Predictable pretty sabrina roses nestle against a cluster of quirky lotus pods ~ the combination of hard and soft is delightful ~ a harvest of premature hydrangeas and bouvardia add an ethereal quality, and lively yellow pansies splashed with aubergine brighten the mix.

I know many floral designers who are great fans of local farmers' markets and nurseries, where they buy in volume the same flowers you and I do. Don't overlook neighbors with good gardens who'll often happily contribute buckets of flowers for your wedding. Old-fashioned homegrown roses, blowsy and utterly innocent at the same time, are wonderful variations on the commercial hybrids stocked by florists.

FINISH BOUQUETS PROPERLY. Find the most beautiful satin or organza ribbons to lace up your bouquet. Ribbon can be breathtakingly expensive, I know, but relatively little is needed for a bouquet and ～ trust me ～ you won't regret this extravagance. Your florist may have limited supplies, but a milliner or notions boutique or mail order company is a good resource for an unusual fabric. Combine textures and complementary hues. Knot an organza ribbon with a wired silk ribbon, and together they become more memorable. Scour antiques shops and flea markets for vintage ribbons and notions. Instead of a paper doily collar to conceal the typical plastic bouquet holder, look for a fine mesh wire

Why settle for a bouquet of one type of flower when you can have a gardenful? A hand-tied bouquet *(above left)* of hydrangeas, viburnum, peonies, asters, feverfew, Virginia roses, and campanulas is wrapped with a charming candy-pink-and-white ribbon. Fragrant tiny petals of common herbs ～ silver thyme, lemon balm, and miniature geranium ～ are enchanting in a nosegay with rambling roses, jasmine, and clematis *(above right)*.

The words "graceful" and "lush" define the perfect bridal flowers. But the beautiful bouquet must also be practical, easy to hold, and not too heavy. A pomander is one of the cleverest devices ~ a heavenly globe of flowers clasped by a braided ribbon. This unusual bouquet must be composed of long-lasting flowers such as cymbidium orchids, which will flourish for hours without a water base.

cone or basket that can be easily fashioned into a bouquet holder. Love knots, favorites of the Victorians, are a sentimental finish. For good luck have at least three thin satin tendrils of knotted ribbon cascade from the bouquet or its stem. Hand-tied bouquets look more formal with ribbons elegantly French-braided to cover the stems.

BOUQUETS AND BOUTONNIERES SHOULD BE HARMONIOUS. Bridesmaids' bouquets should echo the hue and style of the bride's, though they should be smaller. Identical bouquets are the formal choice. Similar mixes of the same flowers or same-hued nosegays each of different flowers are just right for semiformal events. For informal weddings, have each bridesmaid carry a nosegay of her favorite flower ~ narcissus for one, sweet peas for another, and tulips for the maid of honor.

Lapels of grooms, ushers, and fathers of the bride and groom will be ornamented with boutonnieres. Years ago, a boutonniere, the little floral lapel pin each man in the wedding party sports, was likely to be a single carnation. Now, happily, it is more often a sublime grace note composed of flowers, herbs, leaves, and more. Boutonnieres are not corsages and should not be very large. Any flower is appropriate, but choose one that lasts well on the lapel. It's smart to opt for a hearty blossom and sprig of foliage not easily crushed. Many beautiful blooms are too tender, wilting quickly out of water, to be good choices for a lapel. Orchids, roses, eucalyptus berries, and clover are good possibilities. Pocket squares may be worn with boutonnieres, but they should be discreet, not extravagant puffs of fabric.

One adventurous florist I have worked with has made something of a specialty of creating boutonnieres that contain no flowers; instead, he works with fleshy sedums, silvery leaves of sage or dusty miller, berries, even lotus pods. More conventional boutonnieres feature a delicate version of the wedding's signature flower ~ a rosebud, stephanotis trumpet, or delicate floret of hydrangea, for instance. When you order flowers for the men, include your fathers.

If any flower can be said to be the bride's favorite, it must be the rose. This fragrant flower lasts well, dries beautifully, and is available all year. Hothouses keep florists well stocked in winter, but my favorites are ordinary garden roses; they mix beautifully with bushy stems of creamy hydrangeas into an easy-to-carry nosegay. Handsome ribbons are the best finish, and the creative twist is to combine complementary styles such as a wire ribbon with gold edge and a gilt jacquard ribbon.

KEEP BOUQUETS LOOKING GREAT. Flowers should be delivered well misted, wrapped in cellophane, and nestled in tissued boxes. Assign someone to receive and inspect the flowers. Never place waiting flowers near a heat source or in direct sun (they'll wilt). Before distributing bouquets to the wedding party, be sure stems are dry. Look over each bouquet and snip or pinch out bruised or crushed flowers. Some bouquets benefit from a light, quick fluff ~ a few flowers may have settled in transport ~ and ribbons from a gentle puffing.

IF YOU DO YOUR OWN FLOWERS, choose hearty varieties like roses, sweet William, lisianthus, and hydrangea. Make bouquets the day before the wedding and store with the stems in fresh clean water. Place them in a cool, shaded area like a garage or basement. Finish the bouquets with ribbons on the day of the wedding.

CARRY YOUR FLOWERS SMARTLY. Like a new pair of shoes, a heavy bouquet can only become more uncomfortable during the day. If you want to look as happy as you feel, caution your floral designer to avoid oversize bouquets that might be overwhelming. Hold a nosegay with two hands, centered just below your waist. Rest an arm bouquet along the lower half of your free arm, as if you were holding a football; the best side should face up and away from your body. Holding the bouquet too close against your body will crush it and may leave pollen on your gown.

CREATE A BRIDAL KEEPSAKE. It's possible to dry and preserve your bouquet. Though dried flowers generally will not last more than a few years, they nevertheless possess their own poignant beauty.

To be handsomely preserved, a bouquet needs attention immediately after the wedding. Order one bouquet to throw, one to save. Have a friend hang yours (and your husband's boutonniere) upside down in a dark, well-ventilated spot. Alternatively, untie the bouquet and air-dry flowers or embed in silica gel for potpourri; press petals and buds from the bouquet in your wedding album or in thank-you notes.

Many hothouse flowers lack any scent, but naturally pollinated garden blooms are heady. A posy of tiny stems of sweet-scented freesia, lilies of the valley, and bouvardia is wrapped with a striking silk and organza ribbon *(below left).* **A tussie-mussie of lilies of the valley, andromeda, and rambling roses** *(below right)* **is tucked into a reproduction of a Victorian posy holder, perfect for a bride wearing an heirloom gown or for her flower girl.**

FLORAL ACCESSORIES

Luscious blooms have been the bride's signature forever. Carry a bouquet, to be sure, but what could be better for a garden wedding than brimming your bonnet with sunflowers, amaranthus, zinnias, and slender stalks of wheat and a bow of chiffon *(opposite)*, **or adorning sleek silk slippers ~ a pair that closes with an organza ribbon is easiest to ornament ~ with a tiny posy of brodiaea, peppergrass, and bellflowers** *(above)*. **Pair fresh blooms on your toes with skirts that sweep your ankle or are shorter.**

Though bouquets are traditional for brides, there are other possible floral accents: a regal garland of flowers atop your head, single sprigs of baby's breath or stephanotis woven through your hair, or a fabulous broad-brimmed hat with dozens of flowers. Some brides strive to break from convention. More unusual accessories I've seen are a necklace of tiny orchid blossoms, a boa of creamy roses and astilbe, a pocket posy (perfect for a suit) of heather and cornflower, a tiny knot of grape hyacinth and ivy to trim the toes of bridal shoes, or a wrist cuff of gladiolus flowers. And at a recent wedding, the bride had two fresh pink rosebuds stitched to the bodice of her gown as a symbol of her love for her daughters.

If you choose to wear a boa or lei, a bouquet becomes superfluous, but flower-trimmed shoes and garlands of flowers are nicely balanced by bouquets. I like to tuck sprigs of white tuberose into the neckline of a gown with good décolletage, but just as easily any bride can wear a fabulous, perfect, fully open rose on a satin choker. Because these blooms have no water source, you'll need hearty flowers ~ orchids, herbs, asters, and stephanotis are all good.

Creating floral accessories demands a certain degree of stem manipulation, and wiring the stems is the best way to shape them gracefully. Your florist should be sure to remove any scratchy bits and use enough flowers to make a lush look that doesn't appear or feel too heavy. If you are ordering something the least bit out of the ordinary, I recommend having the florist create a prototype; plan this for a special evening, when you can fully enjoy the flowers and at the same time get a sense of how easy it will be to handle them.

Whatever they are composed of, floral accessories are beautiful. Adorn all parents, grandparents, and siblings with leis or necklaces of your bridal flowers, or corsages and boutonnieres, as symbols of unity within your new family.

The Perfect Wedding

WORKING WITH
A FLORIST

*P*art decorative artist, part botanical specialist, a talented florist brings more style and panache to your wedding than any other person. A florist who is also a party planner will be invaluable. Hire someone who is highly recommended, receptive to your ideas, and smart enough to work within your budget.

THE FINE POINTS

 BOOK busy florists up to a year in advance (a deposit is necessary to hold a date firmly) but wait until three months before the wedding to start discussing the actual look. Finalize the details three weeks in advance.

 SCHEDULE a meeting with your florist during off hours. Be prepared with details of the event and specifics of your dress. Visit locations together, then agree on an overall vision.

 DISCUSS loves, hates, wishes. Bring along visual references from books and magazines. Understand that flowers are a perishable product and not always available. Your florist should suggest compatible alternatives.

 ORDER a sample bouquet or arrangements for pre-wedding parties. Besides being lovely in themselves, samples are constructive tools for refining ideas.

 EXPECT a proposal with an outline of options including types of flowers, decorative accessories, costs. For major weddings, a visual presentation is expected. Refine all your ideas before signing the contract.

CENTERPIECES & DECORATIONS

Voluptuous flowers
(opposite) **have an uncanny
harmony with weathered
and rustic elements: An iron
chandelier is trimmed
with lengths of grapevine and
hydrangeas, garden roses,
champagne roses, and
smilax. For delicate sheen,
the pillar candles have been
smudged with gold paint.
Don't overlook architectural
elements, also great foils
for floral decorations.
A garland** *(above)* **of heather,
eucalyptus, hydrangeas,
sedum, boxwood, and roses
bemuses a stone maiden.**

lowers, with all their winsome charm, bring gaiety to the commonplace and make grandeur less imposing. Whether you'll marry in a great cathedral or in a cozy home, the key to successful decorating is the same: Take your cue from the space. With churches, the most ornate interiors look best with a single large design at the altar or twin arrangements on either side of the aisle, where lighting is focused. As one or two major pieces are more effective than a dozen smaller ones, your florist should be working with imposing branches and boughs of evergreen, not short-stemmed buds.

When designing a huppah, I like to soften its architectural elements with romantic flowers ~ Queen Anne's lace, Casablanca lilies, lilacs, tulips, anything with tendrils, and, for greens, asparagus ferns and variegated ivy. At home, in smaller rooms, more personal arrangements are better suited to the scale. For an outdoor ceremony, a garden in bloom really needs no embellishment; but if your space is rather plain ~ a meadow or field ~ have a pair of flowering trees in pots brought in to form a sheltering space for you and your groom to exchange vows.

The atmosphere you create at your ceremony should carry over to the reception that follows. Walk through the locations for both the ceremony and reception several times. Have your florist and consultant join you; their experienced eyes can quickly evaluate the space. Consider your overall point of view: If garden style is your choice, eschew hothouse flowers in favor of loose arrangements of seasonal ones. But those formal arrangements of classic white flowers are perfectly suited for a grand ballroom.

Beginning with the entryway, identify eye-catching spots ~ in the church: the foyer, the altar, the front pews; at the reception: an entrance, an arch, any columns, hearths, grand gilt mirrors, a sweeping staircase, balconies, a chandelier.

On these early visits, play with the lighting to cultivate the mood you seek: Use softer lightbulbs or candlelight, close curtains, block poor views with bushy plants. Embellish candelabra with tiny flowers like astilbe or azalea blossoms. If you are hosting your reception in a tent, you will have to organize in advance of erecting the tent. My first step is to cover the bare poles: I drape them with white cotton fabric or muslin, then cinch the fabric to the pole with a white cotton napkin. My florist is standing by with fresh-cut peonies, tulips, or sweet peas in water picks (little plastic holders containing water) to insert among the folds of the napkin. A more dramatic alternative is to secure flowering branches ~ magnolia or dogwood ~ to the poles and finish with raffia or vines.

❦ DECORATING BY DESIGN ❦

Beautiful decors are no accident, and even simply decorated spaces are always calculated. Flowers are the chorus line behind the bride, reflecting their light on her. Remember there will be other elements at work ~ lighting, containers, linens ~ and the eye is overwhelmed if it must take in too much. Instead, stagger the placement and the proportions of decorations. Cleverly sited floral arrangements will draw attention toward something you want to emphasize as they distract you from a mundane area, and you will get more mileage from your decor when people actually see what you want them to see.

But this kind of "set decoration" is really one part inspiration, nine parts execution. Whenever I am invited to a wedding in late winter or early spring, I think back to one of the most memorable weddings I have ever attended. Though the temperature outside was brisk and trees not yet in bloom, the bride and groom had forced hundreds of flowering bulbs ~ pot after pot of hyacinths, grape hyacinths, tulips, daffodils. These they arranged throughout the reception: on tables as centerpieces, across windowsills, alongside

A floral centerpiece on every table is a bridal hallmark, but far too often these are stiff and identical down to the last petal. I use common elements like similar flowers and vases, but I love to vary them. In this case, a bride's collection of Lalique crystal rose bowls (opposite) **is filled with a seemingly spontaneous handful of pink garden roses. A benefit of rose bowls: They are just right for dining tables, where guests need clear views. Another approach is a homey porcelain pitcher** (above) **with summer flowers: Queen Anne's lace, asters, viburnum. More flowers float on a platter around the base of the pitcher. This taller grouping is best for a place card table.**

To hold floral bouquets at a home wedding, open the cupboards and enlist offbeat containers ~ mason jars, water pitchers, tin cans with labels removed, cobalt glass, enameled milk buckets, blue-and-white teapots. A vintage basket with yarrow, asters, Johnson grass, sunflowers, Queen Anne's lace, and crab apple blossoms greets guests.

the guest book, and in the powder rooms. Guests were captivated by the combinations of bulbs and enchanted by the guileless simplicity of it all. That day flowering bulbs became the couple's signature, and friends have ever since presented them with unusual bulbs, keeping alive the joy of the wedding. If you want to force bulbs, be sure to buy ones that have been precooled. Allow about nine to ten weeks for flowers to appear. Once in bloom, these last one to two weeks. Want quicker results anytime? Plant small rose pots with ornamental wheat grass seed, place in a sunny spot, and in about three weeks you'll have a nice crop and a great alternative to the expected glass bowl of flowers.

THE ART OF THE CENTERPIECE

All weddings have one thing in common ~ tables. There are tables for buffets, dining, and cocktails; there are entry tables, side tables, gift tables, and even a table for the guest book. A good centerpiece will be important over and over again. There are two broad categories of centerpiece, one that people are expected to sit around, and another that is more of a landmark and may be placed near a wall or in the center of a table that people will walk around. The basic difference between the two is scale: When seated, guests should always be able to see one another, and centerpieces must never obscure the view. In large ballrooms, rely on elevated centerpieces, which lift the burst of flowers above eye level to match the grandeur of soaring ceilings.

Coordinate the flower container to the space and tablecloth. Masterful arrangements can be created in a wide variety of vessels. Talk with your florist about incorporating personal or family collectibles, a wonderful (and cost-free) way to add character to your wedding. Porcelain pitchers, Venetian glass, any of the American art pottery vases such as Rookwood and Weller, Victorian epergnes, Lalique crystal bowls, transfer-ware teapots: If it can hold water, it's a natural. If it can't, it may still be a possibility. Use a glass insert to hold

water and flowers or slip a potted flowering plant into the container, and remember to vary shapes and sizes of flowers and pots to animate the design.

A good florist will automatically contrast textures and stages of flowers for a lively mix. Expect immature buds and full-blown blooms in your arrangements; the most vibrant centerpieces rely on a variety of shapes and lengths. Stems will freely bend and twist and buds will open toward the light, just as they should, for asymmetry is a true reflection of nature.

Calculate the impact of color. Flowers are available in every palette to coordinate with any scheme, but your choice should also reflect available light and season. Evening or low-light weddings seem more luminous if you use white or pale flowers, and then gilt accents like burnished leaves and

Another unconventional option found in most homes is an ice bucket. Similar in shape, a sterling silver trophy bucket is a handsome container for a cheery bouquet of garden roses, feverfew, astilbe, and ivy.

Art pottery collectibles such as McCoy (opposite) **and Roseville are fetching vases. Emphasize the eclectic spirit of groupings with pieces of all sizes, and fill with different flowers in your favorite palette: here, astilbe, peonies, roses, sweet peas, azaleas. Take a cue from the color and shape of the vase when designing the bouquet: a top-knot of roses and fresh grapes** (above) **is dramatic in a spry stem vase. The lime green vase is made of case glass, a popular flea market collectible made by fusing the green glass between layers of clear glass.**

berries add sparkle. Sunny-weather events warm to bursts of colorful flowers that won't wash out in bright light.

Meet with the florist and caterer to orchestrate floral decorations for the food. If you are having a cocktail hour with hors d'oeuvre service, consider garnishing each tray with a calla lily or hydrangea or a sprig of lilac and ivy, anchored with florist putty. Larger buffet table trays call for more imposing arrangements, but the flowers should never compete with the flavor or aroma of the food. All varieties of eucalyptus, for example, share a distinctive fragrance that few of us consider compatible with food.

Rely on the season's bounty for raw materials. Walk through nurseries, gardens, fields, and flower shops at the time of year you'll have your wedding. Evaluate all your local flower choices ∼ it may seem romantic to have pitchers of languid, blowsy peonies, but in autumn this is a prohibitive and risky venture in North America. Expensive shipments from faraway may be able to provide enough flowers but if they do arrive intact, they'll never be as hearty or as fabulous as the local dahlias. Look beyond flowers; there are branches ∼ golden leaves of maple in the fall, flowering limbs of cherry in spring ∼ stalks of wheat and berries, fruit, stems of peppers, braids of garlic, lengths of grapevine ∼ all flowers of the earth and fabulous contenders for any arrangement. Some of the elements in centerpieces I've tried and admired are grapes with roses; a combination of wheat, winterberry, and bittersweet; fruit baskets of polished apples or lemons; a pile of white pumpkins and other autumn gourds.

⧼ THE HOME WEDDING ⧽

There are two important caveats if you plan to design your wedding flowers: First, your own wedding should not be your debut experience with floral arranging. This is truly a tremendous undertaking and some past experience in this medium is almost essential. Second, your wedding should be a small to mid-size event late in the day. This will allow you

Flowers can draw guests'
attention to tables set with a
guest book and place cards.
Here a burnished crushed silk
cloth *(opposite)* is swagged
with medallions of roses, bells
of Ireland, and eucalyptus.
Atop the table, a centerpiece
of garden roses, pink delphiniums, chocolate cosmos,
perilla, Queen Anne's lace,
dahlias, and eucalyptus stands
in welcome. Some flowers
serve no purpose other
than adornment. At the entry
to a formal reception *(above)*,
a gilded chair has been
fitted with a plump cushion
of hydrangeas and trimmed
with variegated ivy. The
bouquet is roses, hydrangeas,
and trumpet vine.

the latitude you will need to pull the event together in a timely fashion. In fact, approaching a florist for help is still a good idea; while you focus on the decor, your florist can create all the bouquets and boutonnieres.

The logical starting point is the entry, where you will want to issue a hearty welcome. Fill a half-dozen watering cans and galvanized pails with fresh-cut flowers and arrange them along the front walk or on either side of the porch steps. Hang a fresh flower wreath on the front door. Inside, station a guest book table in the foyer and dress it with an urn of flowering branches: in spring, quince or cherry blossom; in summer, viburnum; in fall, red and gold maple leaves; and in winter, a mass of evergreen branches or even a group of live potted spruces. Often the entryway has some strong focal element ~ an arch or a niche that makes placement of decorations easy to determine. If not, check local prop shops and antiques stores for architectural elements that you can rent ~ columns, trellises, sculpture, urns, even picket fencing. Nurseries, too, will rent trees and topiaries and flowering shrubs that you can site around an otherwise modest space. Since your guests will travel through this area quickly and move on, one good statement is sufficient.

If temperatures will be warm for your wedding, employ homey details such as weathered picnic benches, which are great surfaces for pots or vases of flowers. Arrange one by the back porch, another along the breezeway. Place benches under a great oak or at the corner of a deck. Top these with clay pots filled with miniature sunflowers or daisies. Create odd-numbered groupings of threes and fives, varying the sizes and styles of the pots: It's fine to include the ones with broken edges, too. Tuck torn sections of sheet moss between and around the pots to create a cheery vignette.

When everything is in place, you will find you have produced a romantic fantasy. To keep the fantasy alive after your last dance, arrange to have flowers delivered to a local nursing home or hospital.

Simply Splendidly Married

A wedding ceremony at its simplest is a basic question and answer. But just as no two couples are alike, no two ceremonies have to be identical either. Though a religious ceremony follows a sequence passed down from earlier generations, there is room for personalization in the service, the music, or the decoration. You and your groom may prefer a brief, quiet exchange of traditional vows. On the other hand, you may be extroverts, eager to share with everyone the exuberance of your commitment. Whatever your disposition, invest yourself fully in these few minutes; treat them with all the gravity and sincerity and good intentions you will bring to the marriage itself. If you write your vows, aim for a straightforward, humble tone, and do not shackle yourself with a long speech to perform during this charged time. Attend to the details: the musical orchestration, a rough seating plan, briefing the ushers. Anxiety increases with the unresolved, so write out a schedule that is carefully timed and allows for the flat tire and the late-arriving relative. And on the great day, give the drama its due. Shrug off any blips in the vow-taking; far more often than guests realize, the bride or groom misspeaks and no one is the wiser nor is the ceremony any less meaningful.

PERFECT TIMING

*M*ost weddings follow a similar organization of order: prelude, processional, welcome, readings, benediction, charge, vows, ring exchange, blessing, and recessional. On average, a ceremony is about thirty minutes' duration. The well-synchronized wedding depends on a sound schedule. List the sequence of events and assign someone to be the expediter, in charge of having guests seated as the ceremony is about to begin and keeping them moving through the reception line afterward. A good rehearsal on the day before the ceremony will help everyone relax.

THE FINE POINTS

GATHER the ushers at the ceremony site one hour before the wedding. Prelude music to welcome guests can begin about thirty minutes before the ceremony.

WIND DOWN the prelude music a few minutes before the processional. If the bride is running late, the prelude music should continue until the entire wedding party is in attendance.

SIGNAL that the wedding party is ready to proceed by seating the mother of the groom. Once the mother of the bride is seated, ushers unfurl the aisle runner. The clergy walks to the ceremonial spot and is joined immediately by the groom and his best man.

STRIKE UP the processional hymn; ushers walk to the front followed by bridesmaids. Attendants are paired for formal weddings; less formal weddings with few attendants will have them walk singly or escorted by ushers. (Ushers may also enter from the chancery with the groom.) The maid of honor is next; child attendants follow. Jewish processionals have the cantor and rabbi enter first, then grandparents, ushers, the groom escorted by his parents, bridesmaids, and finally the bride escorted by her parents.

COMMENCE the bridal march once all the attendants reach their places. Have a friend give the bridal train a final fluff, and take a deep, calming breath. On the arm of your escort, proceed toward your groom.

Marriage Certificate

This Certifies
that

Ms. Mary Ann Springer

and

Mr. Edward John

THE CEREMONY

Compared to wedding
certificates from the
nineteenth century, today's
marriage records are
disappointing indeed. But
you can have your own
illuminated wedding
certificate created by a
calligrapher and then signed
by the officiant (*opposite*).
For late-afternoon and
evening weddings, stake a
row of torchères (*above*)
along the path to the
ceremony site ~ use glass
hurricane lanterns to
protect the flames from wind.
Decorate the torchères
with gay satin ribbons in
white or the color of
your attendants' gowns.

*R*ich with drama and romance, a wedding celebration moderates the seriousness of the ceremony with the happiness you all feel. As the true heart of the celebration your vows merit as much planning and thoughtfulness as any other aspect of the day. Begin by reviewing the service with your officiant several weeks before the wedding. Some rites strictly adhere to conventional nuptials and others encourage individualization. Inquire about readings; some of my favorites are "The Passionate Shepherd to His Love," by Christopher Marlowe; "Eve Speaks to Adam," by John Milton; Anne Bradstreet's "To My Dear and Loving Husband"; "Song," by William Blake; and "Love Tells Us Who We Are," by Donald T. Sanders. Perhaps you want to introduce a cultural element ~ readings in more than one language, jumping the broom, or a unity necklace, which is popular in Latin cultures.

Beyond writing the exchange of vows itself, there are innumerable ways to personalize a ceremony. Just for the marriage rite, you may wear a crown of olive leaves or evergreen; you might give each person at the ceremony a single flower, a tulip or poppy or thornless rose. You could ask guests to gather at your home and walk to the ceremony with you. You could release, just moments after your marriage, a pair of doves. I witnessed a touching gesture at the wedding of a dear friend: Alongside her own bouquet, the bride carried two delicate posies of lily of the valley, meaning happiness, and ivy, for fidelity. Just before joining her groom at the altar, she paused to give them to her mother and her groom's mother as a symbol of all they would now share.

A wedding program is a thoughtful keepsake for each guest, and for anyone who is unable to attend. Begin with a poem or thought of thanks and love. Describe the ceremony, and list the prelude and ceremonial music, too. Compose a description of any significant personal rituals, and notes on

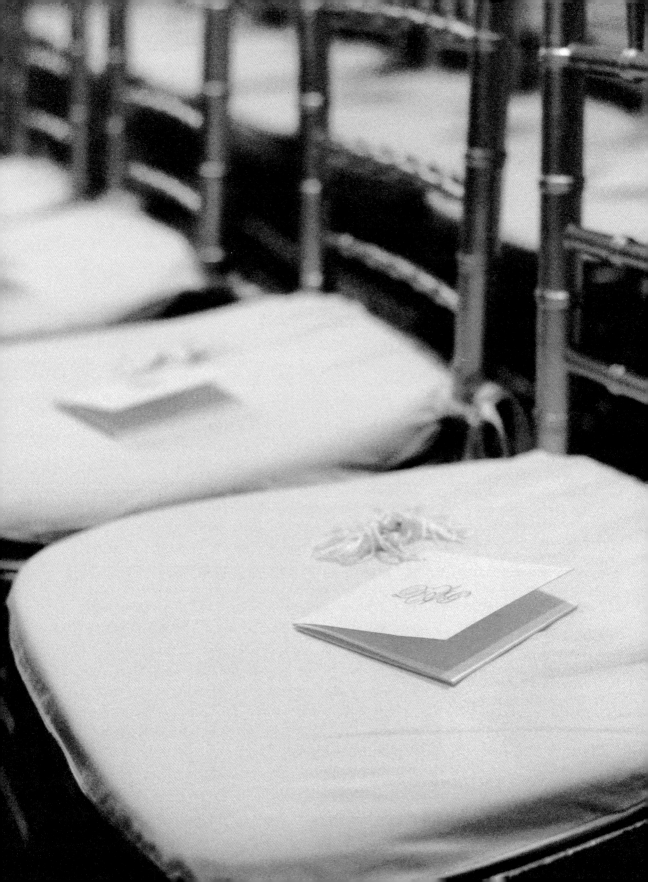

the location and your personal vows, and finish the program with the names of the wedding party and the officiant. Design the program to suit the formality of your ceremony.

If you are marrying after sunset, request a candlelight ceremony. A very moving new ritual I like also involves candles: Just before the vows, the bride and groom each carry a lit candle to the altar, where they light a unity candle with their flames. Or you may place a candle with a paper collar at each seat. After lighting the unity candle, the newlyweds proceed to light the first candle in each row; as their candles are lit, guests share the flame with their neighbors.

HERE COMES THE BRIDE

One of the most satisfying elements of any wedding is planning the music, a pleasant task that can be performed months ahead. Listening with your fiancé to a variety of selections and choosing those you want to have performed at your own marriage is one of the more fanciful obligations of the engaged couple. Music ~ soothing, inspirational, and emotionally charged ~ is the great communicator. Serenade guests with a pianist, a chamber ensemble, or an a cappella quartet as they wait for the wedding to begin. The range of all the arrangements should be compatible, never too loud, and exquisite to the ear. For a thirty-minute prelude, five to eight selections are needed. I am always moved by "What a Wonderful World," by George David Weiss and Robert Thiele, "Always," by Irving Berlin, "Canon in D Minor," by Pachelbel and Bach's *Brandenburg* Concerto Number 2. For the processional, consider "Trumpet Voluntary," "The March," and "Wedding March" from *The Marriage of Figaro.*

Do include music during the ceremony itself. A good friend who is a vocalist or instrumentalist might offer a solo performance after the vows: "Ave Maria" or "The Wedding Song." Choose the right tempo for the recessional, upbeat and triumphant ~ "Molto Allegro" or "La Réjouissance."

Handmade or engraved with a monogram and bound with tassels, wedding programs *(opposite)* **escort guests through the ceremony and are taken home as keepsakes. Chamber musicians** *(above),* **with their classical appeal, are entirely appropriate for any wedding ceremony. Before the ceremony, you might ask them to play Vivaldi's** *Four Seasons.*

Begin your wedding with a memorable first impression, a jubilant welcome for your guests. Stencil your new monogram (use waterproof paint) on fifty small banners and stake them at regular intervals along a church walkway or driveway. Drape a garland of roses across the front gate of the churchyard or, for a civil ceremony, an estate. Swag yards of white tulle along any fencing. Hang giant wreaths of grapevine and berries on the front of a house or barn. Just inside, stand an antique easel with a calligraphed sign illuminating your names and the wedding date with gilt floral flourishes. For evening or holiday weddings, string lengths

Public gardens, country estates, even landscape nurseries have enchanting grounds for outdoor weddings. But you want to impose some structure to your meadow, field, or open setting. Look for unexpected, but highly effective, elements such as a handsome pair of french doors. Anchor these to square posts, add decorative finials, and top the posts with urns. Fluttering chiffon panels are an ethereal finish for the doors. Seasonal flowers such as these spring peonies and lilac always look best spilling over urns. As a final touch, weave branches of apple blossom along the lattice posts.

of miniature white lights on branches of trees or fixtures that line the entry. Check ahead to confirm the schedule and details of your decorations, and ask someone reliable to oversee their installation and removal.

Even a vest-pocket garden can be an enchanting wedding site. An ivy-covered wall offers a lush yet understated backdrop for vows. Flanking the couple, a pair of iron stands holds urns of fragrant antique roses, lilies, peonies, hydrangeas, delphiniums, and bouvardia. Graceful wrought-iron garden chairs, chosen to coordinate with iron stands, are "tied together" with blazing orange organza ribbons. Off to the side, iced Champagne and glasses await.

⇜ WHERE YOU WILL MARRY ⇝

If you are to be married in a civil ceremony, you may hold your wedding in any number of places ∼ at home, or in a town house, a garden, even a meadow. Your first step is to establish an appropriate space for the ceremony. Employ some architectural element to focus the attention on the bride and groom; at home this might be the fireplace, an elegant archway, or picture windows with a panoramic view.

A beautiful pool, with its reflective blue waters, is always romantic, but never more so than at dusk; set hundreds of flickering votive candles around the edge of the pool. If you are lucky enough to be near a lake, hold your ceremony at water's edge, on a dock draped with yards of white tulle and strung with twinkling white lights. A sandy beach, with its crashing waves and sparkling foam, needs no more than some sand torches and a pair of crossed oars.

Where there is no physical structure, you will have to create one. Rent a pair of stately columns and balance urns filled with trailing ivy on them. Decorate a latticed arch with climbing vines and seasonal flowers. An old-fashioned rose trellis, even if it has chipped white paint, is an unexpected touch of nature indoors. You might use two or four standing iron candelabra with dripping beeswax candles to frame the bride and groom.

⇜ THE JEWISH WEDDING ⇝

Jewish ceremonies are layered with rich tradition, of which the most prominent is the huppah, a structure which symbolizes the home and under which couples are wed. Some Orthodox temples will provide a prayer-cloth canopy, although frequently less strict congregations perform the

For a friend's late-spring wedding, I worked with an artist and a florist to create this huppah. After our first conversation, the artist sketched out some tentative designs; we agreed on alterations, and approached the florist with our final blueprint. The posts were cut from foam board, which was hand-painted in a fanciful trompe l'oeil pattern. The flowers, arrangements of fat roses and delicate asparagus fern, provide a soft counterpoint. A built-in shelf was provided for the wineglass.

ceremony under a huppah that is more decorative. The basic requirement of a huppah is that it have four posts; often, too, it has some manner of fabric covering at the top.

If you wish to design your huppah, speak first with your rabbi about any restrictions. Before commissioning the design, consider what aspect of it you would like to showcase: Will it have posts of rich, hand-carved wood; will it be draped with luxurious, hand-embroidered cloth; will it have fantastic arrangements of flowers climbing its legs toward a floral canopy at the top? Your carpenter and florist should collaborate closely, presenting you first with sketches, then with sample materials, and finally with a miniature mock-up. If you're having an outdoor wedding, choose water-resistant materials and waterproof cloth for the huppah's top, and have the huppah situated safely away from gusts of wind or glaring sun, both of which could devastate its flowers.

Showering brides and grooms with flower petals has been a beloved tradition for centuries. Today this custom makes even more sense, given that it poses no threat to birds (as rice does), and need not be swept up (as confetti must be). In summer, on the morning of the wedding ~ before the sun seeps into the garden, drying out the flowers ~ harvest petals from old-fashioned roses and peonies, both known for their large blooms and masses of showy petals. Fill a baptismal font, birdbath, or giant shell with the petals. Or have a calligrapher inscribe your first names and the wedding date on sheets of thick, deckle-edged paper. Twist the paper into cones and fill them with petals. Have the pretty cones waiting in a basket at the church steps so that guests can toss petals and take the cones along as keepsakes.

TRANSPORTATION

*I*mpose the same level of style on your transportation as you have on every other element of your wedding. Pair the location with an appropriate mode of transportation, and consider the best conveyance for the route ~ if you're driving several miles to the reception, a horse-drawn carriage is impractical. The traditional stretch limousine with a uniformed driver and enough space to accommodate comfortably you in your full gown, your attendants, and a bucket of Champagne is appropriately formal. An antique convertible is high-spirited fun.

THE FINE POINTS

MATCH your personality to a vehicle: formal and traditional, a limousine; old-world, a Bentley; fun-loving, a sporty convertible; for motorcycle fanatics, a sidecar for the bride; folksy, a horse and buggy; family-style, a double-decker bus for all.

ARRANGE transportation to convey the bride, her attendants, and her parents to the wedding and reception. To ferry large wedding parties, consider hiring a bus or passenger vans and festoon them with balloons or garlands.

PROVIDE accurate, printed directions to all drivers. Do not assume they will be familiar with the locations. Travel the scenic route between locations when practical.

CONFIRM rates, tips, extra charges, and method of payment with the driver. Book early, obtain an itemized contract, and reconfirm all the arrangements the week before.

INSIST that drivers be well groomed, uniformed to coordinate with the vehicles, pleasant, and prepared for rain with oversized, doorman-style umbrellas.

PLAN ahead for your drive from ceremony to reception by having chilled bottles of sparkling water and fruit juice or Champagne for refreshment.

the Toast
the Kiss
the Dance

A wedding reception is the ultimate party of life and love. You will revel in the magic of your own moment, knowing that you've found a great location and hired the right crew to orchestrate a perfect event. Now all your work, and the searching for the best suppliers and negotiating for just the right elements, is rewarded as your dream becomes reality. The tension that began to build before the ceremony will evaporate as the solemnity of the service gives way to elation and joy. Your guests are enchanted: "This is great fun" . . . "absolutely beautiful". . . "We're having such a good time." There are many demands on your attention, but don't keep guests waiting for your arrival. Avoid reception line bottlenecks, and remember thoughtful details such as having parasols available for sunny mid-summer afternoons. Perhaps the most crucial element is a timetable. Everyone in the wedding party, your parents, and each vendor, including the band, should have a copy. Be flexible: Even with detailed planning, there is bound to be some last-minute change or adjustment. Delegate a trusted point person to handle important decisions, then forget about any potential glitches and relax. A successful party should seem effortless and allow you and your husband to be "guests" at your own wedding.

THE RECEPTION

Set a table near the entry to display place cards directing guests to their seats *(opposite)*. This is a place for a bold, even over-the-top gesture. A dramatic container makes beautiful floral arrangements even more so. Coordinate the style of the container with other elements on the table ~ the asymmetrical lines of a whimsical vase are complemented by a calligrapher's spirited script, and the burnished hue of the vessel is echoed by the silk cloth. Another unusual piece is a sculpted iron centerpiece *(above)* with grapevine details, here on a buffet table.

The wedding ceremony that unites you as husband and wife may be disarmingly brief, but the happy celebration that follows unfolds over the course of an afternoon or even late into the evening. This, truly, is your time, when all your preparations come together for the delight of your guests.

FORMAL AND VERY FORMAL receptions, either at noon or late in the day, feature the grand traditions. Chamber music or jazz entertain as guests arrive, and later a live band or orchestra performs for dancing. Each table is formally set with a complete service of silver, crystal, place cards, and menu cards, together with a floral centerpiece and, for evening receptions, candles. Following a cocktail hour is a meal consisting of several courses. A very formal reception will include white-glove French wait service.

SEMIFORMAL receptions are also catered affairs. Food service may be seated or buffet or a bit of both ~ passed hors d'oeuvres preceding a buffet meal, followed by a served dessert. A seat should be available and a table assigned for every guest, with servers in attendance. Centerpieces may be floral or some elegant alternative, such as a crystal compote brimming with sugared fruits. Music is live, and a specialty group ~ strolling mariachis, trumpeters, or a pianist and flutist ~ welcome guests.

INFORMAL receptions are more intimate in nature and number: a Champagne and wedding cake toast in a hotel suite, a family-style home wedding, a cocktail party at a club, a buffet at a country inn. If you're serving only cocktails, limited seating is appropriate. Casual centerpieces echo the light mood ~ a profusion of flowering bulbs, a basket of field flowers, or a pile of autumn squashes. Music may be live ~ a bluegrass band for a barbecue ~ but prerecorded accompaniments are more typical.

This is worth shouting about! Since most guests arrive by automobile, I set a symbolic display at the parking gate: a banner that exhorts everyone to "Celebrate Our Joy!" is fun, or, for a more formal event, a pair of flags beautifully lettered with your monograms (for an evening reception, be sure they are effectively lit). Dress the entry points to your reception room with festive wreaths, garlands, ribbons, or pennants. Within, a stylishly draped table bears place cards and a spectacular centerpiece. For formal affairs, place cards in tiny ecru envelopes or classic tent cards are appropriate; for less formal weddings, I like to slip each card into a translucent glassine envelope. The cards or envelopes should be arranged alphabetically. A less formal but equally elegant approach is to display a scroll on an antique easel or along a table with everyone's name listed, along with seating information.

Very near the place card table, a similarly appointed table should display the guest book. A beautifully bound blank

Ballrooms are not just for nighttime parties. This sun-filled room shimmers with translucent pastel and gilt tones. The formally set tables have centerpieces of garden roses, each effortlessly arranged in one of the bride's Lalique rose bowls. Carrying out the theme, favors are Lalique figurines. A gilt iron numeral identifies the table. Uniform placement is the mark of a perfectly set table. Once all the elements are in order, stand behind each chair to center each plate, align the flatware and glassware, and arrange the napkin.

book is best, or one with pale lines on which to sign; a fountain pen makes any signature look more elegant. I have someone sign the first entry with a note of good wishes, as an encouragement for others to do the same.

Have a coat check facility. Guests should never be expected to tip for wedding day services, and to eliminate any doubt at the entryway, place a folded tent card that indicates gratuities are provided by the host.

❧ A SEATING PLAN ❧

The typical wedding reception requires guests to sit for about two hours, often longer. A wise host will seat everyone with a companion, keep couples together, and pair co-workers and other tight-knit groups. If you can't fill a table with guests who know one another, seat people who share interests and affiliations or children of similar ages.

Guests should not feel squeezed, but the table should also feel comfortably full. Sixty-inch round tables seat eight

For a summer wedding with refreshing charm, nothing surpasses crisp cotton lace overlays *(opposite)*. **A collection of twenty different patterns dresses every table, over pale lemon skirts. A profuse mix of peonies, astilbe, roses, and sweet peas fills a McCoy vase. Secured to each napkin** *(above left)* **with a wired ribbon are golden heart ornaments, keepsakes for guests. Table numbers** *(above right)* **are an opportunity for artwork; a silversmith and jeweler friend created this tripod frame to hold a sandblasted plate of glass ~ later, a photo.**

to ten; sixty-six-inch rounds seat nine to eleven. Request a floor plan, or sketch one out on a large sheet of graph paper. Your room's size is important; if the space is too big, section off a cozier portion with folding screens or billowing drapes of theatrical scrim. If the room is too tight, consider another location or see if you can use an adjacent room or terrace.

The newlyweds' is the first table; place it in a prime spot in view of all. A round table to match the guests' is best, but another option is a long head table, set on only one side with the wedding party facing the guests. So that guests can easily identify their places, tables should be clearly numbered with illuminated cards, or gilt, iron, or etched-glass numbers.

Welcome guests into your home for a sophisticated family-style reception; set the table ~ a long plank table and a squadron of Mission chairs are just right for a family gathering ~ with your favorite objects. Mix, don't match, your wonderful collectibles: one-of-a-kind flea market treasures of crystal and china with assorted silk napkins, fruits, and bud vases scattered about each place setting. The low centerpiece of garden flowers is of bouvardia, hydrangeas, chocolate cosmos, and campanulas; a formal silver candelabrum rests on a grandmother's favorite crocheted cloth.

✦ THE WEDDING AT HOME ✦

The charm of a home wedding is the more relaxed, familiar atmosphere. Keep the decorations and menu personal and homey: Wrap bows around pots of flowering plants and line the walkway with them. Run yards of tulle along fencing or from light post to light post. Overfill window boxes with assortments of white flowering plants ~ baby's breath, nicotiana, begonias, impatiens ~ and pale green leaf plants ~ dusty miller, artemisia, lamb's ears. Rent columns, trellises, or a canvas canopy to define a dining area outdoors.

To prevent breakage, your most valuable, irreplaceable possessions should be stored. Remove bulky sofas, armchairs, coffee tables, area rugs, and television sets. Rent ballroom chairs for seating, then soften rooms with favorite photographs from both your families; line mantels and bookshelves with vases of flowers; light rooms with candles.

Prepare family-style recipes ~ the dishes you love most ~ and present food on your own service pieces. Bring out all your heirloom china; rent anything else you need. If you have not hired a consultant, assign a reliable friend to coordinate with the kitchen for food service and to supervise the maintenance: ashtrays emptied, soiled glasses and napkins returned to the kitchen, candles replaced as needed.

HOME WEDDING TIPS

A well-conceived schedule is the key to maintaining your wedding-day sanity. Anticipate potential trouble areas ∼ parking, bathrooms, kitchen equipment ∼ and devise solutions beforehand. Enlist your most organized and diplomatic friend to supervise the setup of the celebration, including the floral decorations, tables and chairs, and centerpieces, and to inspect each finished table setting. Try not to assume any responsibilities beyond saying "I do." After all, you want to have plenty of time to luxuriate in your personal preparations and have fun at your own wedding.

THE FINE POINTS

 EVALUATE your home with a pro such as a caterer, or with a friend who hosts many parties; or book a few hours with a consultant for valuable advice on logistics.

 SKETCH a floor plan. Pencil in furniture and plan to move it or remove it to fit your needs. Avoid bottlenecks when determining placement for the guest-book table, the bar, and buffet and dining tables.

 DELEGATE responsibilities ∼ you'll need someone to greet and direct guests. Hire college students to help with cleanup and parking. Instruct them to wear pressed chino trousers and white shirts, and have a white cotton professional apron available for each.

 REMEMBER the mundane but critical ∼ stock bathrooms with plenty of accessible paper and toiletries; be sure plumbing and tanks are in working order. Spray outdoors to control pesky bugs.

 GET AWAY ON ∼ or near ∼ schedule, unless you're spending the night at home. Guests love to send off newlyweds and you won't want to miss this once-in-a-lifetime thrill.

HOLIDAY ROOMS

Low lights and a formal
setting embrace guests
with the luxurious ambience
that holiday celebrations
inspire *(opposite)*. A good
location with fine old-world
details is key for staging
this mood. Tapestries blanket
the walls with warmth,
and cloths of floral damask
richly drape tables. At
the table's center, an Empire
period epergne brims
with precious winter roses.
Limoges sets the table
(above left), votives smudged
with gold paint glow,
and even fork tines reveal
a tiny heart *(above right)*.

*B*urnished fabrics, gilt accents, and flickering lights are the telling tones of winter celebrations. Rely on these and all the other elements of the season to reinforce the festive spirit of your wedding. For a rich pine fragrance, carpet the entryway to your reception with a bushel or two of pine needles; drape staircases and mantels with garlands; wreathe doorways. The deep green palette of evergreens exudes a warmth that chilly days demand; by combining hollies, junipers, spruces, and cedars with fragile fresh roses, lilies, and hydrangeas, you'll also get a good deal more value from your flower budget.

Evaluate rooms for their view. Conceal barren lots behind draped windows, but play up those landscapes of snowy glades. Evergreens or moonlit terraces will become magical with a few well-placed outdoor decorations. String lengths of white lights along tree branches or zigzag them over a sleeping gazebo. Create clusters of rented potted evergreens strung with white lights. Line luminarias, flickering candles in pretty paper bags, along a balustrade or up a flight of steps.

The most formal holiday tables will be uniformly set, but creative license should rule the day. For instance, top undercloths of green velvet with overlays of silver mesh; pair mother-of-pearl butter knives with a traditional silver floral service. Choose crystal cake stands or mercury-glass bowls of different patterns and shapes to hold centerpieces of juniper or cypress and berries.

For less formal centerpieces, scatter the tables with clusters of antique ornaments or fill wide, low wooden bowls with assorted lengths of various metallic ribbons and toss with gold and silver pinecones. Metallic-leaf fruits such as pears, pomegranates, nuts, and tiny apples make a good mix. Apply the leaf unevenly ~ gold is my favorite, but silver and copper are wonderful, too ~ allowing about half the natural color of the fruits to show through. Simple centerpieces can be made of glass vases of cut amaryllis, white mixed with red winterberry, or red combined with branches of curly willow.

Warm an imposing stone mantel with a massive garland of silvery eucalyptus *(opposite)*. **Once the hearth is lit, hearty eucalyptus won't wilt from the fire's blazing heat. A handsome stone pedestal brims with scabiosa, spiral eucalyptus, schefflera berries, dendrobium orchids, wild grasses, persimmons, and Dutch roses. Tables are set** *(right)* **with gold-rimmed stemware and votives.**

DETAILS & ACCENTS

*I*t is always the thoughtful, judicious flourish that conveys the personal aspect that is so memorable at weddings. You will articulate the importance of this day with your attention to the details: The architectural features of your location, the parameters of the tables, even the guest chairs themselves are a canvas for creativity. The objective is not to overwhelm the senses but to create a few exquisite moments by layering a simple foundation with something lovely and unexpected.

❧ PLEASE BE SEATED ❧

Prime items for embellishment are easy to identify ∼ the tables themselves are most obvious. A properly set table begins with a circle of foam over the wooden top. First, a floor-length table skirt covers the foam. Then the overlay ∼ always shorter than the skirt and decorative ∼ is centered on the table. Now the elements of the setting: In the middle, of course, a centerpiece composed of flowers or fruit; votive or taper candles; place cards, salt and pepper cellars, and a table number are the common ones. For each individual place setting, a charger, napkin, flatware, water goblet, wineglass for each pour, and a bread plate.

Chairs are also appropriate for decoration. Rental chairs are routinely provided with seat cushions, and the rental firm will offer a variety of color and fabric selections. For an elegant yet unexpected dress, order the cushions in two colors, for instance, yellow and white or gold and silver to match your color scheme, or alternate a few subtle shades of pastel silks. For a small reception party, assemble a lively mix of vintage and antique gilt chairs.

Through the years I have worked with ballroom chairs, folding chairs, and upholstered side chairs, and my first decision is always whether or not to slipcover. The most formal option is to dress every chair. But bear in mind that it's perfectly fine

Swathe an ordinary side chair in yards of billowing bridal tulle. This fine net is an affordable, sensational draping with an utterly romantic presence. Anchor the fabric with a blooming cinch of roses, peonies, and graceful tendrils of ivy. A lavish bow of satin ribbon and a contrasting hue of gilt or vanilla net are equally magnificent. Frame the chair within a picturesque niche as a symbolic representation of your own bridal image, or actually use this elegant rest at your bridal table.

to dress just a fraction of the chairs in use. You might trim only the chairs of the bride and groom, or only the chairs at the bride's table. It's easy and quick to knot a simple fabric bow across the lower back of the chair. A more elaborate treatment involves draping a garland of garden roses across the chair back. Ballroom chairs are beautiful bared too.

⁓ A LITTLE NIGHT MAGIC ⁓

Never underestimate the importance of light. The most beautiful adornments will shrink from view without the right illumination to compel a closer look. A good lighting specialist will make the most of a sensational location and radically transform an ordinary one. A row of up lights (squat fixtures that direct light upward) can be placed to splash monuments with light or create a pattern of light on nondescript walls and hedges. Pin lights or spotlights installed on the ceiling can focus attention on tabletop centerpieces without tormenting eyes.

Even simple adjustments with a dimmer switch can have an impact. For a home wedding, tape down the light switch of any glaring overhead fixture so that no one accidentally turns it on; replace bright bulbs with lower wattages. Daylight is beautiful and bright, but even it should be controlled: Shade too-sunny windows with simple rice-paper shades or scrim drapes. Ban any and all fluorescent lighting; it's just too clinical for a celebration.

Candlelight, utterly romantic and shamelessly flattering, is appropriate for celebrations after 5 P.M. Short and squat, votive candles are true workhorses; scatter them casually and liberally about, to line porch railings, windowsills, and brick ledges. Use them to flank low centerpieces, or create a votive centerpiece by filling a tiered pastry stand with the candles. Simple glass votives are fine, but I can't resist dressing them up ⁓ I knot a short length of ribbon around the glass, smudge or stripe the interior glass with gold paint, or wrap a galyax leaf about the glass and tie it with a bit of raffia or gold cord.

These are ballroom chairs fit for any bride: a scalloped slipcover of raw silk dotted with fat pearls *(top left)*; a simple organza skirt swagged with pale yellow gauze and knotted with a posy of bright yellow paper rosebuds *(top right)* or stitched with a sprinkling of vintage silk flowers *(bottom left)*; a handsome tasseled damask and a hand-painted organza that covers merely the chair back *(bottom right)*.

Tall candles may rest in short or tall candlesticks, and you'll want dripless tapers that will burn at least four hours. Choose holders that match the decor of the table, and avoid static uniformity when possible. Assorted candlesticks are handsome together, especially when they are all glass or all gold or silver. Dress each with a bobeche, the tiny saucer that rests around the base of the candle to protect the stick and the table from dripping wax. For the bridal table, look for a couple of candle bracelets, short lengths of links to circle the candle base, that have been detailed with crystal charms to refract and bounce glimmering light.

❧ A PROPER PLACE SETTING ❧

Crystal set alongside pure white bone china ornamented with silver, or blue-and-white spongeware pared with linen, or depression glass with bakelite ∼ the flatware, glassware, plates, and linens are important elements for setting a table. But the real story will come with the details you add. Every

The soft glow of flickering candlelight instantly adds a romantic note. Recycled glass cups banded with silver (above) **or wrapped in crochet covers beribboned with organza, and minia-ture porcelain flowerpots are ready-made options. For a beguiling twist, wire a petite rope of carousel, heather, sweetheart roses, and viburnum to a silver candle-stick fitted with a filigree shade** (opposite)**.**

Details should dress every table. I asked a talented baker to fashion these menus *(above left)***, which are scripted and illuminated with royal icing. The more conventional place cards were done with paper and ink** *(above right)***. The calligraphy is not the same on each but it is compatible, and thus achieves a consistent look. Marzipan fruits echo the brilliant colors of the menu to create a table treatment that's as lively as it is whimsical.**

place setting will include a cloth napkin, a natural focus for a personal touch. Tie up napkins with a variety of silken ribbons or braided cord ∼ knot each so that the bow or tie rests on the napkin and is easy to remove. Ribbons, frog closures, and various cords can be found at notion shops, vintage shops, and flea markets: Shop here for precious trinkets to tie into the ribbons ∼ decorative jewelers' brass ornaments, small plaster castings to hot-glue to a ribbon, vintage charms. Or you might prefer an element of nature: a single fresh flower or a graceful leaf, a lady's apple or double stem of cherries, a stalk of wheat or a curl of ivy.

If you assign seats to your guests, a simple ecru place card edged with a gold border or engraved with your new monogram and labeled with a fine script is the formal approach. But there are dozens of ways to add a decoration for less formal receptions. In the months preceding your wedding, press individual pansies, sweet peas, violets, or nasturtiums, or fronds of young ferns, in the pages of a book or a flower press. To make the place cards, affix a tiny flower or frond to each card with a dab of white glue. Or brush the card with watercolors to create a sunburst or other decorative ornament. Punch each tent card with a pair of small holes at the bridge of the card, then thread through a thin ribbon and tie it into a bow. For another look, use a gold marker to write the name of each guest on a single broad leaf of ivy and tuck this into a folded napkin. Victorian hang tags or medallions of handsome paper overlaid with a square of vellum tied with a silk cord are other alternatives.

Menu cards awaiting guests on their dinner plates are always popular. An engraved card that matches the place card is proper, but individual scrolls of handmade paper circled with a ribbon are appealing. Individual menus, de rigueur at formal events, should rest on the charger plate. If the menu cards are shared, rest one between every two plates or stand a pair back-to-back in the center of the table.

The easiest way to add a special look to your reception table is to tie the napkins with a decorative embellishment. Pretty vintage silk flowers *(below left)***, Mexican milagros ~ tin charms which depict a bride and groom ~ passementerie frog closures, a mother-of-pearl button secured with a twist of wired gold cord, molded sugar flowers and a monogrammed sugar bow** *(below right)* **are wonderful ways to set the table.**

MUSIC & ENTERTAINMENT

*N*othing so quickly establishes a mood and a celebratory tempo as music. Whether you hire a six-piece swing band, a reggae group, or a disc jockey, or you play your own recorded tunes, you must marry serenaded by your favorite music.

Musicians can make or break a party: A good live band communicates an energy that's palpable, and a successful disc jockey plays songs that always sound right. Choose music that starts lively but easy while people meet and mingle, cools during dining so that guests can talk with one another, then finally excites on key to draw everyone to the dance floor. Standards like "Time after Time" by Sammy Cahn and Jule Styne, "Isn't It Romantic?" by Rodgers and Hart, and Irving Berlin's "They Say It's Wonderful" are popular and stirring. Other favorites of mine are "Our Love Is Here to Stay" by George and Ira Gershwin, "My Romance" by Rodgers and Hart, and "All the Things You Are" by Jerome Kern and Oscar Hammerstein.

For your first dance together, "My One and Only" by George and Ira Gershwin and "At Last" by Harry Warren and Max Gordon are both unbeatable and easy to dance to. Your dance with your father will be poignant, but you can keep it from becoming teary with Cole Porter's "You're the Top."

Book musicians directly or through music brokers. One friend of mine called a radio station directly and hired her favorite radio disc jockey. Most musicians can provide you with a sample tape of their work, but you should always see them perform. Negotiate and sign a contract outlining the date and hours (allow time for setup), the location, the names of the performers and their instruments, the total fees, and a payment schedule. Be sure to provide your musicians with a list of songs you enjoy ~ and any that you hate. Tell them how you want them to dress; I think dark suits and white shirts for men and black dresses for women are always the best choice.

Every room has its own acoustics. A professional performance band will be deliberate about calibrating its sound to perfect pitch. Microphones and amplifiers should be adjusted periodically throughout the reception, as the noise level rises, to keep the volume right. Be clear beforehand about the acceptable band level; conversation should not be overwhelmed by music.

BUYING & SERVING CHAMPAGNE

Effervescent Champagne bubbles express the festive atmosphere of a wedding. Strictly speaking, true Champagne is available only from the Champagne district in France, but there are many other elegant varieties of this sparkling wine. Californian *méthode champenoise*, Italian *prosecco* or *Asti Spumante*, German *Sekt*, and Loire Valley *brut* are each suitable for wedding toasts. If you are not a Champagne connoisseur, a good wine merchant will help you narrow the choices to the type, label, and vintage that most appeal to you. A fine Champagne is well worth its cost for this, the most sentimental toast of your life.

THE FINE POINTS

TASTE the wines to find your favorite. Styles of Champagne vary considerably: Brut is the driest; extra-dry is less dry; sec is sweet; demi-sec is the sweetest.

ORDER enough wine to serve all the guests. For toasts only, a full bottle will serve five people; for cocktails, calculate one bottle for every three guests.

CHILL sparkling wines before serving. Submerge bottles to the neck in buckets full of ice cubes and cold water to reach forty-two to forty-seven degrees Fahrenheit. Allow at least forty minutes to cool the wine adequately.

OPEN pressurized bottles with care. Peel off the foil cap, then twist and loosen the wire muzzle. Slant the bottle away from people at a forty-five-degree angle and remove the muzzle. Hold the bottle firmly and slowly twist out the cork. Internal pressure will then push the cork into your hand ~ listen for a distinctive sigh, the sound of a properly uncorked bottle. Pour a small amount into a glass, allow it to settle, then fill to two-thirds.

SERVE the wine in traditional Champagne flutes or tulip-shaped glasses. The slender silhouette maximizes but doesn't prematurely dissipate the bubbles; the best wines have more effusive bubbles.

TOASTS TO THE NEWLYWEDS

*T*he opportunity to thank loved ones publicly is a treasured ~ if jittery ~ moment of every reception. Tradition dictates that the best man offer the first toast, followed by the groom, his bride, and the couple's parents. The maid of honor may wish to share the toasting duties with the best man. Stand to give a toast and remain seated to receive one. Once a toast is made, the toaster will raise his or her glass, signaling all to join in a celebratory sip. If you are being toasted, do not raise your glass, but wait to take a sip once the hurrahs are complete.

A good toast will never be too long or formulaic. Polished speechmakers know the value of brevity and the appeal of sharing personal ~ but not private ~ anecdotes. A little advance preparation will ensure that this important moment is resonant and seems effortless. I like to convey a genuine sentiment with some humor, affection, and reflection. Begin with a brief anecdote of how you met. When I married, I described my husband's awesome first introduction to my parents and all of my ten brothers and sisters. Write out your toast in advance and recite it a few times to be comfortable, but never read from your notes: Your thoughts should seem spontaneous.

Begin the toasts when the reception of guests is complete, or, for seated dinners after the cocktail hour, once the guests are seated. Before a toast is offered, music should stop. All important toastees should be present, and each guest should have a glass. Champagne, the appropriate cheer for toasts, is available in traditional bottles of 750 milliliters, but when serving large groups pour from more impressive magnums, the equivalent of two bottles; immense jeroboams, the equivalent of four bottles; or even the giant Methuselah, the equivalent of eight bottles. Children and adult guests who prefer soft drinks should be offered sparkling water or ginger ale.

"To you!" ~ everyone wants to raise a glass in celebration of your union and the tender sentiments that embrace the day. "May you have many children," and "May the wind always be at your back" ~ like these old Irish adages, many ancient toasts look ahead, wishing you long lives and happy children.

DINING & RECEPTION MENUS

Pass bite-sized appetizers *(opposite)* **for cocktail hour ~ saffron and black sesame crepes filled with a julienne vegetable curry, zucchini and parmesan galette, seared tuna on a potato crisp, and grilled lemon-ginger shrimp with avocado salsa. These appetizers are substantial enough to suffice for a stand-up reception of hors d'oeuvres, Champagne, and wedding cake. Even after a cocktail hour, plated meals begin with an appetizer, a tasty starter like saffron and spinach ravioli filled with lobster and asparagus** *(above)*.

I think preparing a good menu is akin to staging a theatrical production. The overall look should excite and compel a taste; the food itself should be savory and not overwhelmed by the scenery. A sense of drama is communicated with meticulous, sumptuous presentations that whet the appetite. Perfectly matched wines sustain the tempo, and a tantalizingly sweet finish is a captivating denouement. A caterer's forte is orchestrating the right look and flavors, and many caterers specialize in a single style.

～ FOOD & BEVERAGES ～

A formal dinner is always preceded by a cocktail hour. Passed hors d'oeuvres are traditional; appetizers should be bite-sized and easy to handle. As a three- or four-course meal follows, allow two to four servings per guest; a caviar station and vodka bar are a glamorous backup. Serve Champagne and have a full bar available. Dinner will be seated. In an effort to appeal to all guests, some caterers suggest you offer a choice of entrees, but I find this just too cumbersome and unnecessarily fussy. Instead, vary the courses to please a variety of palates. A dessert course is expected, and so is a wedding cake.

Buffet service is often perceived as cost-cutting, but in reality the savings may be negligible, if any. Buffets need all the same elements of a served affair ~ china, silver, tables and chairs, a wait crew to serve the buffet and to clean up ~ and more food choices are offered. Any more than twenty guests requires two buffet entree tables and additional buffet tables for other courses: appetizers, a raw bar, salads, and desserts. If you expect young ones, provide a children's buffet ~ mini-pizzas, peanut-butter-and-jelly finger sandwiches, chicken tidbits. Entrees should be easy to self-serve with one hand, but at least one waiter should assist at each buffet table: most important, to serve meat and fish. Extra waiters should

police the dining tables to remove used dinnerware, serve water, and otherwise assist diners.

Early afternoon breakfast or brunch receptions may be seated or buffet service. Begin with mimosas, bloody Marys, and fresh juices. Egg dishes are traditional ∽ eggs Benedict, frittatas, or omelettes to order ∽ but recently I have enjoyed two festive brunch receptions, one with a crepe station and another with dim sum.

Teatime is 2:30 to 4:30 P.M. This is a wonderful opportunity for a smaller guest list. Begin with a series of finger sandwiches ∽ cucumber, salmon, chicken ∽ followed by scones and wedding cake. By all means, serve Champagne.

Cocktail parties in the early evening are less typical for receptions. (Your invitations should be specific so that guests may plan their day accordingly.) Providing a full bar is fine, or you may serve only Champagne and sparkling water. Offer eight to ten types of hors d'oeuvre, and allow two or three of each per guest. Have stations of cheeses and breads and cookies and chocolates, and serve wedding cake.

Family-style receptions are perfect for gatherings at home or any informal outdoor location ∽ the beach, a park, or the tennis club. Passing large plates of food is typical, but Tex-Mex barbecues, clambakes, and picnics are appropriate, too.

The greatest budget inflations are special food items and guest counts (remember your staff, including the band and photographer, although they don't need to share the same menu). You can control costs by scaling down guest lists and serving only cocktails and hors d'oeuvres. Or you can work with less expensive ingredients; you might, for instance, serve a pasta dish or a rich risotto instead of a meat-based entree. At a more casual wedding, eliminate an additional dessert course and finish the dinner with wedding cake.

If you're like me you'll eat little or nothing at your own reception, so have your caterer box up a selection to take away with you, including a bottle of Champagne. Arrange to have leftovers donated to a food bank.

Good caterers know that a perfect meal combines taste and style. A Napoleon of wild mushrooms drizzled with basil oil is more dramatic-looking than its elements would suggest ∽ triangles of puff pastry layered with mushroom filling and stacked capriciously promise a meal that is delicious but not to be taken too seriously.

WEDDING CAKES

Place regal wedding cakes where they'll command the attention of every guest. Elaborate ones like a fondant tower piped with swags and bows of royal icing and decorated with pastillage flowers (*opposite*) **should be simply presented. Drape a round table with a beautiful cloth and line up silver forks precisely for the most elegant display. Southern custom calls for a groom's cake in addition to any other dessert that might be served. This luscious chocolate groom's cake** (*above*) **with chocolate-dipped strawberries can be served alongside the more traditional cake.**

When you enter the reception, do you look first for the wedding cake? Many of us do, and when I think back on all the weddings I have attended, one constant is the ecstatic, eager children swarming around the cake ∼ with its tiers of buttercream piped with swags, profuse with molded flowers ∼ towering above them.

Though most bakers and bakeries have a limited capacity to produce extravagant confections, unless you're marrying at a very busy time of year you may begin the search for your cake three months before the wedding. Make an appointment to meet and review the baker's portfolio. No matter how fabulous a cake looks, it must be delicious, and most kitchens (which are always in the process of baking) will offer a taste of their various cake/filling/frosting combinations. Always sample the elements of the cake before you commit.

Wedding cakes are priced per slice: Less ornamental cakes in buttercream will be the best value, exquisite adornments of pastillage more expensive. An average three-tier cake will serve fifty to a hundred guests; five-tier cakes may serve about two hundred guests. My baker friends warn against cakes of more than five tiers, which are very heavy and difficult to maneuver. For larger guest lists, serve the remaining slices from extra cake kept in the kitchen.

Fine bakers will always mix textures ∼ tender cake and smooth filling, royal icing over fondant, marzipan to decorate buttercream ∼ for the most inspired creations.

BUTTERCREAM is my favorite for taste; it is smooth and creamy without being too sweet. In addition, it takes well to a wide variety of flavorings from the fruit juice to liqueurs. The icing remains soft, so it cuts very easily; the basketweave, swags, and fleur-de-lis are signature buttercream flourishes, as are the rosettes. One inspired baker I work with combines several shades of color in her pastry bag to pipe lifelike

variegated flowers. Real buttercream is made with butter only and may be temperamental in heat and humidity. (For this reason, it should never be left in the sun, or in an over-heated room.) Though a baker may want to include vegetable shortening for stability, that is not necessary for anyone working in air-conditioning, and you should confirm with the baker that your buttercream will be all butter.

ROYAL ICING is the cake decorator's highest expression. This soft paste is piped from a bag and dries quickly. It's ideal for creating latticework, cages, stringwork, beading, over-piping, and flowers. Once dry, the surface is hard and brittle.

ROLLED FONDANT is a pliable mixture of sugar, corn syrup, glycerin, and gelatin. A sheet of fondant can wrap each cake tier. I love it because the smooth finish is a wonderful base for pastillage flowers, royal icing details, and an unlimited variety of architectural designs. However, a fondant cake cannot be refrigerated, so filling choices are limited.

Fondant literally wraps a cake and is an ideal canvas for decorative flourishes. Piped royal icing stems of lily of the valley *(opposite)* **bloom on low tiers as molded figurines of sugar waltz around the top tier, crowned with a molded sugar floral fan. Molded pastillage flowers** *(above left)* **planted in a flourish of buttercream wrap a low cake and crown its top. An individual serving of a three-tiered cake piped with royal icing and set with pastillage roses is a petite treat** *(above right).*

Decorations are expected for wedding cakes. A repeating motif of silver pearl dragées studs each tier of buttercream topped with a crown of fondant *(opposite)*. A grander alternative *(below left)* features distinct but similarly decorated tiers tinted in different pale pastels with whimsically detailed pure white fondant and royal icing. The silent bride and groom make the traditional topper *(below right)*; seek out vintage sets or have one created of pastillage to mirror your own wedding-day appearance, right down to the gown.

WHIPPED CREAM is a luscious soft frosting. As with buttercream, you should confirm with the baker that your cake will have only real heavy cream ∼ with no extenders or stabilizers. Whipped cream does not like heat and humidity, and it must be refrigerated until just before serving.

PASTILLAGE (or gum paste) is a paste of sugar, cornstarch, and gelatin that dries to a porcelain finish. It is used to mold realistic flowers and fruits that are edible ∼ though not very tasty ∼ and will last for years.

MARZIPAN is a malleable paste of ground almonds, sugar, and egg whites. Often it is rolled in sheets, like fondant, as an icing, but it molds beautifully into fruits, seashells, and flowers, which can be painted with food dyes to seem quite realistic.

SPUN SUGAR is actually pulled strands of caramelized sugar. I'm in awe of the magic the fast hand of a pastry wizard creates: effortlessly spinning bird's nests, domes, and bows. Sadly, spun sugar will not withstand extreme humidity and heat.

Most cakes are delivered on standard cardboard rounds, but I prefer a more decorative base. Use an heirloom cake stand or have one made to measure by a potter or silversmith with your joint monogram in the center. Provide this to your baker in advance to fit the cake. Or supply your baker with a wood cutting board with a beveled edge and ask him to cover it in fondant or marzipan, to match your cake.

Display your cake for all to admire. Dress a table just for the cake with a special cloth ~ perhaps one from your mother's wedding, or her wedding veil over an undercloth ~ or use an overlay different from your other table skirting to create a showcase. If your cake and cloth are both simple by design, swag the table with a garland of variegated ivy and clusters of fresh flowers or sugared fruits.

CUTTING THE CAKE

When you're ready ~ don't make it too late into the reception ~ your consultant or a bridesmaid should cue the band to play a brief fanfare to alert the guests. Cut the first slice of cake with your groom for luck, with your right hand on the handle of a sharp knife and your groom's hand over yours. Pierce the bottom tier of the cake with the point of the knife, then carefully maneuver the knife through the cake. Remove a slice. Tradition has the groom and bride feed a bite to each other before offering slices to their parents. Then the cake service is taken over by your caterer, who may move the cake to another room for plating. If you choose, fresh berries or ice cream can be served alongside the cake.

Tradition has it that the top tier of a wedding cake is saved to be enjoyed on the first wedding anniversary. The caterer will remove the tier and cover it carefully with plastic wrap and aluminum foil, then box it. Still, most cakes will not withstand a year in the freezer, so I recommend you enjoy your cake on your first month's anniversary.

Bakers are sugar artists who create sculptural wonders. For a beachfront wedding, a fondant cake *(above)* is awash with pastillage seashells. Contrasting tiers of pastel pink-and-white buttercream flourishes *(opposite)* feature different pretty cakes: Perched at the top is a delicate layer covered with dotted swiss; beneath that is a cake ribboned with columns; resting below the columns there is a layer dappled with rose-buds; and on the bottom, a foundation of lace filigree. The bow at the top of the cake is wired ribbon.

FAVORS & KEEPSAKES

Appealing favors: an intriguing
handmade box *(above left)*
yields a hard sugar rose ~ a
token of love ~ to keep
always. A miniature silver
basket *(above right)* filled
with iced almonds is a sweet
offering of good luck. I
had an inexpensive but lovely
sandalwood fan from
Chinatown in San Francisco
(opposite) personalized
with the couple's names
by a calligrapher. The paper
is trimmed to cover the
top blade of the fan,
then glued in place. A wired
ribbon is the finish.

*O*ffering a token of affection to each of your guests is a symbol of your thanks, a tiny treasure by which to remember the day. My ideal favors are ones you create or at least decorate yourself. The touch of your own hand makes the gift all the more meaningful. Choose something simple: vintage holiday ornaments, iced heart-shaped cookies. Blind-emboss kraft paper or glassine packets with your wedding date and monogram and fill them with flower seeds. Embroider linen handkerchiefs with a pair of tiny hearts; technique is not important so long as one can tell they are hearts. If you live near the ocean, fill pretty shells with beeswax and a wick. When the wax is cool, wrap the candles in fishnet and tie the net with pretty ribbons.

Circulate with your groom offering your favors from a garden basket, leave a keepsake at each place setting, or position a table with charming parcels near the exit as a fond farewell. Whatever you offer, be sure to keep one or two for your very own, as well as for anyone who could not attend.

Credits

A page-by-page listing of each product and provider featured in this book follows. Once you determine the identity of the item photographed, use the resource list (where services and products are listed alphabetically by category) to obtain the contact number for every listing.

HALF TITLE PAGE: hand-painted sign, Marc Musters. **TITLE PAGE:** satin princess-line gown with celery-hued back bow and banded sleeves, Vera Wang, at Stanley Korshak; photographed at the Hotel St. Germain, Dallas. **COPYRIGHT PAGE:** astilbe, peonies, and sweet peas in assorted McCoy vases, floral design, vases, and embroidered cotton tablecloths by Florals of Waterford. **PAGE 9:** *top, top to bottom:* sapphire cabochon bezel set in 18k gold ridged shank, Jenny Lessard; yellow sapphire cabochon bezel set in gold band, Gloria Natale; blue sapphire cabochon bezel set in finely granulated split gold shank, Jenny Lessard; square champagne diamond bezel set in brushed 22k granulated gold band, Gloria Natale; oval citrine bezel set in sterling, Marcia Lorberfeld; band of blue sapphires bezel set in 22k gold to resemble third-century Roman wedding band, Gloria Natale; flower stem of white penstemon by Christopher Bassett. *middle:* wedding chapel cake designed by John Auburn and Mike McCarey of John and Mike's Amazing Cakes; photographed at The Beverly Hills Hotel. *bottom:* handmade paper box, Judy Ivry; silver ribbon, Vaban; feather boa, Adrienne Landau Designs, Inc. **PAGE 10:** *top:* invitation, calligraphy by Margaret DiPiazza Ink. *middle:* centerpiece of roses and hydrangea, Valorie Hart Designs; pedestal, Brian Windsor Art, Antiques, Garden Furnishings.

bottom: calligraphed place cards, *top to bottom:* Heather Belle McQuale; gilt edge, Marjorie Salik; grape detailing, Heather Belle McQuale; cupid letter press, Claudia Laub Studio; calligraphy, Stephannie Barba; heart detail, calligraphy, Stephannie Barba; monogram, calligraphy, Heather Belle McQuale; floral detail, calligraphy, Maria Thomas, Pendragon Ink; envelope, Ellen Weldon. **PAGE 11:** *top:* hand-thrown, inscribed porcelain pots, G. Wolff Pottery; engraved stone, Stoneworks; plantings, Florals of Waterford; guest book, Two Women Boxing, Inc.; pen and ink, Prometheus. *middle:* pastillage roses, Deborah Kaplan and Liz Cushman; fondant-draped cake, Deborah Kaplan, Sud Fine Pastry. *bottom:* formal place setting, plates, crystal, flatware, linens, Party Rental Ltd.; table design by Susan Holland & Company.

PAGE 12: *top:* grapes, roses, lilac arrangements, Florals of Waterford; pastel candles, Zona; crystal candlesticks, Florals of Waterford; crystal, Party Rental Ltd.; plates, Mottahedeh; hand-painted tablecloth, Kimberly Soles. *middle:* flowers, Laurie Stern; parasols, Elaine Bell Catering. *bottom:* cake, Margaret Braun; hand-painted tablecloth, Carla Weisburg. **PAGE 13:** *top:* dried botanical heart ornament, Deborah Shapiro. *middle:* hand-painted tablecloth, Kimberly Soles; floral design, Florals of Waterford; plates, Mottahedeh; glassware, Party Rental Ltd. *bottom:* Elaine Bell Catering. **PAGE 14:** *top:* handmade keepsake box, Talas Inc; place card calligraphy, Marjorie Salik; kid leather gloves with vintage floral trim, Shaneen Huxham; lace handkerchief, Eve Reid Inc; pearl necklace, Mikimoto; wedding photographs, Tanya Malott Lawson; program,

I.H.M. Systems. *middle:* silk princess-line gown, Donald Deal; silver mesh neck scarf, Debra Moises; cotton canvas umbrella, Mespo; model, Zornista Kamenova, represented by Elite Models; hair and makeup, Brian Marryshow, Lachapelle Representation. *bottom:* buttercream cake resembling a stack of blooming garden boxes, designed by Diane Jacobs, The Cakeworks. **PAGE 15:** *top:* flower girl dress, Nancy Tollin, dress at Marina Morrison; silver thyme, lavender rose, wild sweet pea, and pansy posy by Devorah Nussenbaum at Verdure; photographed at the Haas-Lilienthal House. *middle:* model, Jaycee Gossett, represented by Elite Models; hair and makeup, Barbara Fazio, represented by Lachapelle Representation. *bottom:* hand-decorated mints, Jan Kish—la petite fleur; vintage plate, Golyester Antiques.

CHAPTER I

PAGE 16: *a:* gilt-painted wood tray, Zona; gold-banded dessert plate and fork, The Four Seasons Hotel, Los Angeles; chocolate scripted proposal, Donald Wressel, Pastry Chef, The Four Seasons

Hotel, Los Angeles. *b:* crystal candlestick, Baccarat; candle bracelet, Visual Design; candle, Creative Candles. *c:* porcelain gift box, Tiffany & Co.; fringed silk scarf, Departures from the Past; gift card, Mrs. John L. Strong at Gump's. *d, bottom to top:* 22k gold band, Darlene De Sedle at Stanley Korshak; iolite cabochon anchored in crown-shaped bezel setting, tourmaline cabochon in bezel setting detailed with a circle of leaves, and heart granulated old band, all by Temple St. Clair Carr, Stanley Korshak; crushed silk table square, Ann Gish. **PAGE 18:** silver ring boxes, sapphire and diamond ring, Camilla Dietz Bergeron; diamond ring, Van Cleef & Arpels; pearl ring, Angela Cummings; embroidered tablecloth, MU | H Inc. **PAGE 20:** *left, top to bottom:* sterling silver "truth" and "respect" ring, Meryl Waitz for The Loom Company; heritage ring from a personal collection; pair of sterling silver bands, Brenda Schoenfeld; ribbon, Vaban. *right, top to bottom:* etched and granulated gold crown band, Meryl Waitz for The Loom Company; gold band, Cartier; custom-cast gold

band granulated with personal hieroglyphics, Coffin & King; hand-cast four knot gold band, Angela Cummings; 18k yellow gold twist band, Jenny Lessard; fluid-leaf gold band, Elizabeth Rand; rings on back of gilt hand mirror by Coffin & King. **PAGE 21:** sterling silver bands, top one ribbed and granulated, bottom one detailed with hearts, clubs, and spades, Meryl Waitz for The Loom Company; ribbon, Midori Inc. **PAGE 22:** *top to bottom:* emerald-cut diamond with baguettes, round diamond flanked by tapered baguettes, emerald-cut diamond flanked by trillions, oval diamond flanked by tapered baguettes, marquise diamond flanked by six individually set round brilliants, all set in platinum, Van Cleef & Arpels. Rings rest on bow detail of blue silk handbag by Nancy Bacich for Showroom Seven. **PAGE 23:** *top to bottom:* channel band of round diamonds, band of individually set marquise diamonds, half-band of individually set emerald diamonds, band of individually set diamonds, channel band of square diamonds,

all in platinum, Van Cleef & Arpels; resting on glove with silver lace and knot detailing by Reem Acra/Reem Bridal. **PAGE 24:** men's suits, Barneys New York; boutonnieres, Judith Brandley Florist of Sierra Madre. **PAGE 25:** bridesmaid's gown, Barneys New York, Los Angeles Bridal Salon; bouquets, Judith Brandley Florist of Sierra Madre. **PAGE 26:** *left:* assorted frames, Gill & Lagodich; embroidered gold organza by Ann Gish. *right:* perfume bottles by Rose Tattoo; calligraphy by Stephannie Barba; silk ribbon by Midori Inc. **PAGE 27:** *top right to bottom left:* snap-together cufflink, ABC Carpet & Home; crystal cufflinks, Baccarat; pinecone cufflink, Mish Jewelry; carnelian cufflink, Lisa Jenks Limited; button cufflinks, Camilla Dietz Bergeron; white piqué French cuff, Ike Behar. **PAGE 28:** scissors, William-Wayne & Co. **PAGE 29:** *top to bottom:* type on vellum ribboned to card, Blue Marmalade; nautical, Heather Belle McQuale; heart, Prose & Letters; apple tree, The Printery. **PAGES 30–31:** plate,

handkerchiefs, flea market collectibles; quilt, ABC Carpet & Home; silverware, pitchers, flowers, all by Florals of Waterford; napkin pins, Meryl Waitz for The Loom Company; place cards, Cari Ferraro of Prose & Letters; glasses, Party Rental Ltd. **PAGE 31:** Shaker basket, Canterbury Woodworks Inc. **PAGE 32:** calligraphy by Stephannie Barba; silver caddy, Tudor Rose; teacup, saucer, Golyester Antiques; teaspoon, The Four Seasons Hotel, Los Angeles.
PAGE 33: vases, flowers, Florals of Waterford; table runner, Kate Morrison.
PAGE 34: flowerpots, Design via Carioca; tools, seeds, potting soil, Smith & Hawken; note card, 100th Monkey Productions.
PAGE 35: gift card, Mrs. John L. Strong, crystal, china, flatware, all at Gump's, San Francisco; organza ribbon, Vaban.

CHAPTER 2

PAGE 36: *a:* slices of cake, Diane Jacobs, The Cakeworks; *b:* custom hand-tinted, handmade invitation, fan favor, Arak Kanofsky Studios; *c:* cameras, equipment, Terry de Roy

Gruber Photographers; folding chair, Party Rental Ltd.; *d:* floor plan, The Pierre Hotel Grand Ballroom, New York.
PAGE 39: Custom pillow, ribbon, MU|H Inc.; gold bands, Barneys New York.
PAGE 40: location, Otto Kahn Mansion; gilt vase, Coffin & King; flowers, Stacey Daniels Flowers; quilted tablecloth, Nancy Angel of Angel Threads; place cards, Stephannie Barba; stone chair, ABC Carpet & Home; tables, Party Rental Ltd.; rear table-cloths, Ann Gish. **PAGE 42:** *a:* iron gate, Hotel St. Germain; floral heart-shaped wreath, Two Design Group; *b:* townhouse's central staircase, The Pratt Mansion. *c:* The Grand Ballroom, The Pierre Hotel; flowers, Christian Tortu at Takashimaya. *d:* pavilion, flowers, Florals of Waterford; custom awning-stripe drapes, Nancy Angel of Angel Threads; tables, tablecloths, ballroom chairs, Party Rental Ltd. **PAGE 44:** penthouse suite, catered tea, The Stanhope Hotel, New York; wedding cake, Gail Watson Custom Cakes; bridesmaid's gown, Carolina Herrera; usher's morning

suit, Lord West; tie, Gene Meyer; flowers, Blue Meadow Flowers. **PAGE 46:** vases, Room Service; floral design, Christopher Whanger; photographed at Old City Park, Dallas.
PAGE 47: cotton canvas umbrellas, Mespo Umbrellas; shopping basket, Florals of Waterford; ribbon, Midori Inc. **PAGE 49:** ribbon, Bell'occhio; cord, Hyman Hendler; bridal consultant, Marcy Blum Associates; place card, Ellen Weldon; sterling clip, Meryl Waitz for The Loom Company. **PAGE 50:** caterer, Elaine Bell Catering Company. **PAGE 52:** silver rental tray, water pitchers, Party Rental Ltd. **PAGE 55:** engraved invitation design, calligraphy, Ellen Weldon; accordion folder, Tactile Books. **PAGE 56:** *left:* letterpress invitations, folded card, Claudia Laub Studio; all others, Purgatory Pie Press. *right, top to bottom:* ribboned coral mono-grammed invitation and invitation or wedding pro-gram detailed with pair of engraved gilt doves, both by Ellen Weldon; vellum-covered invitation of stack letterpress cards tied together with silk ribbon,

SoHo Press; blank wedding cake cutout invitation or program, Kate's Paperie.
PAGE 57: *left, clockwise from top:* marble envelope and matching invitation, Marjorie Salik; lavender-hued bouquet invitation, Claudia Laub Studio; foliage flourish invitation, Twelve Dozen Graphics. *right:* letterpress coasters, Purgatory Pie Press.
PAGE 58: Fred Marcus Photography at The Pierre Hotel. **PAGE 60:** *left:* metal proof box, Sam Flax; photographs by Tanya Malott Lawson; ribbon by Midori Inc. *right:* contact sheet photographs by Ross Whitaker/Terry de Roy Gruber Photographers; magnifying glass, Tudor Rose. **PAGE 61:** *left:* handmade folio, Angela Scott; photographs by Tanya Malott Lawson. *right:* handmade tooled leather album, Daisy Arts; engraved invitation, acid-free photo corners, Kate's Paperie; wired organza ribbon, Vaban; chair, ABC Carpet & Home. **PAGE 63:** *top to bottom:* heart album, Kate's Paperie; album with threaded spine, Tactile Books; leather and mar-bleized album, Angela Scott.

CHAPTER 3

PAGE 64: *a:* bridal headbands, gloves, Carolina Amato; tiara, Yumi Katsura Bridal Collection; silk barrel clutch, Châlloner; photographed at Yumi Katsura Bridal Salon. *b:* dotted Swiss cotton over tulle petticoat, Sydney Bush; silk sling-backs, Claudio Merazzi, Stanley Korshak; photographed at the Hotel St. Germain. *c:* gloves, La Crasia; fragrance, Chanel No. 5. *d:* abalone saucer, ABC Carpet & Home; silk napkin, Nancy Angel for Angel Threads; jewelry, *left to right:* mother-of-pearl double hydrangea earring and freshwater pearl necklace, both by Angela Cummings; cultured pearl engagement ring in prong setting, Telepress; golden South Sea pearl necklace, Angela Cummings Boutique; cast gold engagement ring with cultured pearl in a bezel setting, Lisa Jenks Limited; granulated gold beads and pearl necklace, Jenny Lessard; South Sea pearl drop earring with gold vine stem, Angela Cummings Boutique; cultured pearl 9 mm necklace, Telepress;

cultured pearl necklace with cast gold clasp and seed pearls and cast gold drop earring, Lisa Jenks Limited. **PAGE 67:** bridal gown designed by and photographed at Yumi Katsura Bridal Salon. **PAGE 68:** gown by Amsale; gloves by Reem Acra/Reem Bridal, worn by Jaycee Gossett, represented by Elite Model Management; hair and makeup by Barbara Fazio, represented by Lachapelle Representation. **PAGE 69:** *left:* lace sheath by Manalé, worn by Lisa Uphill, represented by Click Model Management; hair and makeup by Mutsumi, represented by Lachapelle Representation; freshwater pearl necklace, Stephen Dweck; organza shawl, Adrienne Landau Designs Inc.; satin shoe, Peter Fox Shoes; photographed at The Central Park Conservancy, New York. *right:* two-ply crepe sheath by Inatome International, worn by Lori Herbert, represented by Elite Model Management; hair and makeup by Barbara Fazio, represented by Lachapelle Representation; earrings, Meryl Waitz for The Loom Company; silk velvet vintage leaves tucked

into coiffure, Carolyn Blazier. **PAGE 70:** *left to right:* satin tank bodice, drop waist, tulle skirt dotted with floral lace appliqués by Riccio; scalloped lace bodice, dropped waist, chiffon skirts by Helen Morley; satin bodice, crepe skirt, and organza train falling from silk flowers, gown by Wearkstatt; all gowns photographed at Marina Morrison. **PAGE 72:** cotton piqué dress, Michael Kors, worn by Evelynne; hair and makeup by Mutsumi, represented by Lachapelle Representation; straw hat, Lola Millinery; cotton gloves with satin bow, Reem Acra/Reem Bridal; peony, lilac, hydrangea bouquet by Blue Meadow Flowers; mules, Vanessa Noel; photographed at the penthouse suite of The Stanhope Hotel.

PAGE 73: pale blue silk suit by Nicole Miller, worn by Zornista Kamenova, represented by Click Models; hair and makeup by Brian Marryshow, represented by Lachapelle Representation; feather boa, Adrienne Landau Designs Inc.; silk handbag, Nancy Bacich for Showroom Seven; earrings, Mish

Jewelry; handmade shadow-striped white gift box by Judy Ivry; organza mesh ribbon, Vaban; groom's tuxedo, Paul Smith; photographed at The Central Park Conservancy. **PAGE 74:** silk cloque bodice and tulle skirt by Amsale, worn by Jaycee Gossett, represented by Elite Models; hair and makeup by Barbara Fazio, represented by Lachapelle Representation; floral headpiece, Reem Acra/Reem Bridal; earrings, Mish Jewelry; gloves, Reem Acra/Reem Bridal; screen, the Claiborne Gallery. **PAGE 75:** cowl-neck ball gown, Vera Wang, Barneys New York, Los Angeles. **PAGE 76:** gilt headpiece and veil, Paris Veils & Hats; chair, ABC Carpet & Home. **PAGE 77:** fresh floral tiara by Christopher Bassett; silk pillow, MU|H. **PAGE 78:** charmeuse gown, Carolina Herrera, worn by Lori Herbert, represented by Elite Model Management; hair and makeup by Barbara Fazio, represented by Lachapelle Representation; hat by Marina Killery Couture Hats; earrings, Meryl Waitz for The Loom

Company; lady's mantle bouquet by Miho Kosuda Ltd. **PAGE 79:** hats by Emma Carlow, Sandra Johnson Couture. **PAGE 80:** *a:* hat designed by Lola Millinery; bracelet by Mish Jewelry; empire gown by Richard Glasgow. *b:* hat with veiling by Lola Millinery; earrings, Meryl Waitz for The Loom Company; gloves, Reem Acra/Reem Bridal; handbag by Anya Hindmarch; gown by Richard Glasgow. *c:* charmeuse gown by Carolina Herrera; hat by Lola Millinery. *d:* sheath, Donald Deal; veil by Lola Millinery; shoes, Kenneth Cole; earrings, Fragments; all worn by Zornista Kamenova, represented by Click Models and photographed at Lola Millinery; all hair and makeup by Brian Marryshow, represented by Lachapelle Representation. **PAGE 82:** gloves by Carolina Amato; heart choker and pearl-handled silk purse by Homa; topper, headband, and other accessories, Marina Morrison. **PAGE 83:** woven South Sea pearl choker, Ezmaralda Gordon; ring, Tail of the Yak; earrings,

Joan Gilbert. **PAGE 84:** *left, left to right:* triple satin bow sling-back, satin side buckle, leather rosette sling-back, all by Vanessa Noel. *right:* satin pump with spiral pearl detailing by Christin Louboutin, Stanley Korshak; organza ribbon, Vaban. **PAGE 85:** shoes, Christin Louboutin, Barneys New York; gloves, Homa. **PAGE 86:** *a:* Clinique waterproof "black/brown" mascara. *b:* La Poudre de Chanel "light" Translucent Loose Powder; makeup brush, Boyds. *c:* assorted pale pink and beige nail lacquers by Sally Beauty Supply. *d:* Bobbi Brown Essentials lip brush and tissue with blot of carnation #12 Bobbi Brown Essentials Lip Color. **PAGE 88:** *left:* Jaycee Gossett, represented by Elite Model Management; hair and makeup by Mutsumi, represented by Lachapelle Representation; photographed at The Stanhope Hotel. *right:* velvet backpack, Châlloner, photographed in the Penthouse suite of The Stanhope Hotel. **PAGE 89:** tulle net petticoat, Sydney Bush; bra, La Perla, worn by Jaycee Gossett, represented by Elite

Model Management; hair and makeup by Mutsumi, represented by Lachapelle Representation; hanging embroidered bridal gown, Reem Acra/Reem Bridal; shoes, Vanessa Noel; photographed at The Stanhope Hotel. **PAGE 90:** corset, Poupie Cadolle, Paris, distributed by Milltex; petticoat, Jana Starr Antiques, worn by Jaycee Gossett, represented by Elite Model Management; hairpin, b j design; hair and makeup by Barbara Fazio, represented by Lachapelle Representation; earrings by Meryl Waitz for The Loom Company; chair, Amy Perlin Antiques. **PAGE 91:** silk garter by Karyn Sanders, Sweet Material Things. **PAGE 93:** emergency kit basic supplies: clear nail polish, white thread, safety pin, white chalk, scissors, silk flower. **PAGE 94:** heart pendant, Temple St. Clair Carr, Stanley Korshak; ribbon, Midori Inc. **PAGE 95:** dress, Dessy Creations, Marina Morrison; nosegay, Devorah Nussenbaum at Verdure; hat and gloves, Zazu & Violets'; ribbon, Hyman Hendler; photographed at the Haas-Lilienthal House, San

Francisco. **PAGE 96:** French silk rosebud peignoir, Sue Ekahn/New York, worn by Andrea Searcy, represented by Click Model Management; hair and makeup by Karen Bensimon, represented by Lachapelle Representation; pearl compact, Judith Lieber; cultured pearl earrings, Telepress; photographed at The Stanhope Hotel. **PAGE 97:** petticoats, Sydney Bush; strapless bra, Arlotta, worn by Andrea Searcy, represented by Click Model Management; short bra, La Perla, worn by Jaycee Gossett, represented by Elite Model Management; pearls, Judith Lieber; photographed at the penthouse suite, The Stanhope Hotel. **PAGE 98:** dress, Sandra Johnson Couture. **PAGE 99:** posy by TFS, photographed at The Beverly Hills Hotel. **PAGE 100:** jacket, Lord West; boutonniere, Alexandra Randall Flowers; iron chair, the Claiborne Gallery. **PAGE 102:** navy suit worn by Andrea Tamagnini. **PAGE 103:** *left:* stroller, Lord West; tie, Gene Meyer, worn by Tyler Ricci; dress, Carolina Herrera; photographed at The Stanhope Hotel. *right:*

tuxedo, Paul Smith, worn by Ken Kenitzer, represented by Boss Models; bouquet by VSF; photographed at The Central Park Conservancy. **PAGE 104:** bow tie, Carrott & Gibbs; wedding bands, Darlene DeSedle, Stanley Korshak; cufflinks and studs by Nancy & Risë; pastillage boutonniere, Frosted Art. **PAGE 105:** *left:* pocket watch, cufflinks, ABC Carpet & Home; bow tie, Carrott & Gibbs. *right:* top hat, ABC Carpet & Home; shoe, Cole-Haan; cufflinks, Steven Raspa; bow tie, Carrott & Gibbs. **PAGE 106:** formal wear and accessories, Lord West, worn, left to right, by Ken Kenitzer, Tyler Ricci, and Scott Goodrich, all represented by Boss Models; men's boxers, Paul Smith; men's slippers, Berk of Burlington Arcade; photographed at the penthouse suite, The Stanhope Hotel. **PAGE 107:** men's vanity set, studs, Departures from the Past; boutonniere, Anthony Albertus.

CHAPTER 4

PAGE 108: *a:* yellow-and-white awning-striped cotton drapes, sewn and installed by Nancy Angel of

Angel Threads; floral tie-back of peonies, clematis, columbines, oranges, lisianthus, roses, ferns designed by Florals of Waterford; ballroom chairs, tables, linens, Party Rental Ltd. *b:* nosegay of scabiosa, heritage roses, hydrangea, and phlox by Maria Giovanna Vella of Bomarzo. *c:* rose floral swag, Silver Birches Custom Design Floristry; photographed at The Beverly Hills Hotel. *d:* centerpiece of peonies, phlox, red grapes, and plums in a stack of mossy clay pots and wheat grass designed by Florals of Waterford. **PAGE 110:** nosegay by Zezé Flowers. **PAGE 111:** composite nosegay designed by Miho Kosuda, Ltd. **PAGES 112–113:** nosegay designed by Don Hathorn of Atelier A Work Shop; ribbon, Brimar Inc.; photographed at The Crescent, Dallas. **PAGE 114:** nosegay of lotus pods, hydrangea buds, sabrina roses, pansies, lady's mantle, and astilbe designed by Florals of Waterford; wire chair, Florals of Waterford. **PAGE 115:** *left:* bouquet by Christopher Whanger and Rubin Navarro; ribbon, chair, Room Service. *right:*

nosegay designed by Devorah Nussenbaum at Verdure; bench, Rayon Vert Extraordinary Flowers, Extraordinary Home. **PAGE 117:** pomander designed by Robert W. Dailey, Jr. and Todd Fiscus of Two Design Group; chair, Hotel St. Germain. **PAGE 118:** nosegay designed by Clifford Miller of TFS; ribbons, Vaban; hatbox, Manny's Millinery; photographed at The Beverly Hills Hotel. **PAGE 119:** *left:* posy designed by Charles Gonzalez and Robert Charles Smith of Laurels Custom Florist; ribbons, Midori Inc. *right:* tussie-mussie designed by Charles Gonzalez and Robert Charles Smith of Laurels Custom Florist. **PAGE 120:** hat designed by Clifford Miller of TFS; photographed at The Beverly Hills Hotel. **PAGE 121:** silk shoe, Peter Fox Shoes; posy of bellflowers designed by Christopher Bassett; ribbon, Midori Inc. **PAGE 122:** floral stock including roses, calla lilies, sweet peas, eggs, and baskets; photographed at Zezé Flowers. **PAGE 124:** floral candle chandelier

designed by Charles Gonzalez and Robert Charles Smith of Laurels Custom Florist. **PAGE 125:** Medici garlanded bust designed by Alexandra Randall Flowers; photographed at the Otto Kahn Mansion. **PAGE 126:** vases, Lalique floral design by Susan Holland & Company; photographed at The James Burden Mansion. **PAGE 127:** pitcher, floral design by Christopher Whanger and Rubin Navarro; photographed at Old City Park. **PAGE 128:** basket designed by Christopher Whanger and Rubin Navarro; photographed at Old City Park. **PAGE 129:** bucket designed by Christopher Whanger and Rubin Navarro. **PAGE 130:** arrangements and vases by Florals of Waterford. **PAGE 131:** topknot and vase from Florals of Waterford. **PAGE 132:** arrangement designed by Alexandra Randall Flowers; tablecloths, Ann Gish. **PAGE 133:** gilt chair, Gill & Lagodich; floral design by Valorie Hart Designs; pedestal urn, Brian Windsor Art, Antiques, Garden Furnishings.

CHAPTER 5

PAGE 134: *a:* illuminated monogram, hand-weathered paper, An Englishman in L.A. *b:* Victorian basket filled with roses, astilbe, eucalyptus, and hollyhocks, designed by Ron Wendt Design; stone chair, ABC Carpet & Home; photographed at the Otto Kahn Mansion. *c:* organ and music. *d:* hand-painted sign, Mark Musters; photographed at Old City Park.

PAGE 137: rose columns, The Garden Gate Creative Design. **PAGE 138:** marriage certificate, illuminated and calligraphed on hand-weathered paper, An Englishman in L.A.

PAGE 139: iron torches with glass hurricanes, The Garden Gate Creative Design; ribbons, C. M. Offray & Son, Inc.

PAGE 140: ballroom chairs photographed at The Pierre Hotel; wedding program, I.H.M. Systems, Inc.

PAGE 141: chamber musician from Curtis Music & Entertainment.

PAGES 142–143: floral finials and doors designed by Florals of Waterford; squared latticed columns from Florals of Waterford;

chiffon panels, Ann Gish; ballroom chairs, Party Rental Ltd.

PAGES 144–145: iron flower stands and arrangements designed by Robert W. Dailey, Jr. and Todd Fiscus of Two Design Group; ribbons, Midori Inc; iron garden chairs, flagstone courtyard, Hotel St. Germain. **PAGE 147:** trompe l'oeil huppah designed and installed by Geoff Howell; flowers designed by Zezé Flowers; ballroom chairs, Party Rental Ltd.; photographed at the Otto Kahn Mansion.

PAGE 148: baptismal font at the Swedenborgian Church trimmed with nasturtiums, filled with rose petals, designed by Devorah Nussenbaum.

PAGE 149: paper cones filled with rose petals, Margaret DiPiazza Ink.

PAGE 151: classic car, Mogel's Classic Auto; nosegay of dahlias, roses, hibiscus, and alstroemeria designed by Clifford Miller of TFS.

CHAPTER 6

PAGE 152: *a:* Wedgwood style cake with pale pastel tiers, Cheryl Kleinman Cakes. *b:* organza slipcover,

pale yellow gauze wrap designed by Nancy Angel of Angel Threads; yellow paper Mexican flowers, Tzin Tzun Tzan; chair by Party Rental Ltd. *c:* crystal candlesticks, Florals of Waterford; colorful candles, Zona. *d:* calligraphy by Maria Thomas, Pendragon Ink; flowers designed by Christopher Whanger; tablecloth, Room Service. **PAGE 154:** flowers designed by Stacey Daniels Flowers; vase, Coffin & King; tablecloth, Nancy Angel of Angel Threads; place cards, Crane & Co.; calligraphy, Stephannie Barba; chair, ABC Carpet & Home; rear tablecloth, Ann Gish; photographed at the Otto Kahn Mansion. **PAGE 155:** flowers designed by Stacey Daniels Flowers; grapevine iron flower stand, Mark Musters; party accessories by Party Rental Ltd.; photographed at the Otto Kahn Mansion.

PAGES 156–157: table and party design by Susan Holland & Company; photographed at The James Burden Mansion.

PAGE 158: crocheted linen tablecloth, Trouvaille Française; flowers and vase designed by Florals of

Waterford; engraved menu, Ellen Weldon; glassware, china, flatware, linen napkins, salt and pepper shakers, and ballroom chairs, Party Rental Ltd.

PAGE 159: *left:* ribbon, Vaban; gold heart, Deborah Shapiro; calligraphy, Ellen Weldon. *right:* table number frames, Meryl Waitz for The Loom Company.

PAGE 160: china, crystal, flatware, tablecloth, mission chairs and table, and silver candelabrum photographed at Rayon Vert Extraordinary Flowers, Extraordinary Home: floral design by Kelly Kornegay.

PAGE 161: Roman bud vase from private collection.

PAGE 162: chocolate groom's cake topped with pastillage bouquet of calla lilies, Katrina Rozelle Pastries & Desserts.

PAGE 163: all-white spring floral centerpiece, Devorah Nussenbaum at Verdure; vintage wire compote, Tail of the Yak; photographed at the Haas-Lilienthal House.

PAGE 164: nineteenth-century compote, Brant Laird Antiques; flowers designed by Robert W. Dailey, Jr. and Todd Fiscus of Two Design Group; table setting design, Claire

Heymann at the Hotel St. Germain. **PAGE 165:** *left:* votives, Two Design Group. *right:* table accessories, Hotel St. Germain. **PAGE 166:** table accessories, Champagne and wine glass, Stupell Ltd. Fine Gifts; napkin, Ann Gish; embossing, Judy Ivry; ornament, Deborah Shapiro; placemat, Angele Parlange; tablecloth, La Maison Moderne.

PAGE 167: garland, pedestal crowned with flowers and grasses designed by Christopher Bassett; iron candelabrum designed by Mark Musters; photographed at the Otto Kahn Mansion. **PAGE 168:** tulle-garbed bridal chair swagged with flowers designed by Joseph Maake Flowers & Decorative Accessories; photographed at the Otto Kahn Mansion.

PAGE 171: *a:* scalloped slipcover, Slips; straw hat, crocheted gloves, Zazu & Violets'. *b:* organza and gauze slipcover designed by Nancy Angel of Angel Threads; paper flowers, Tzin Tzun Tzan. *c:* organza slipcover wih silk flowers designed by Nancy Angel of Angel Threads.

d, left: brocade slipcover designed by Nancy Angel of Angel Threads. *d, right:* hand-painted slipcover designed by Carla Weisburg; sewn by Demi Adeniran. All chairs this page, Party Rental Ltd. **PAGE 172:** silver tray, Party Rental Ltd.; votives, *left to right:* metallic-edged votive, Ecologia; crocheted votive cover, Susan Schadt Designs; porcelain votive, G. Wolff Pottery.

PAGE 173: garland designed by Alexandra Randall Flowers; candle shade from private collection; tray, glassware, Party Rental Ltd.; candlestick, ABC Carpet & Home; tablecloth, Ann Gish. **PAGE 174:** *left and right,* marzipan fruits and menu, Jan Kish—la petite fleur; place card, Crane & Co.; calligraphy, Stephannie Barba; tablecloth, ABC Carpet & Home. **PAGE 175:** *left:* napkins, *left to right:* silk rose, Carolyn Blazier, wraps silk pleated napkin, Ann Gish; Mexican tin milagro, Tzin Tzun Tzan; ribbon, C. M. Offray & Son, Inc.; ties, damask napkin, ABC Carpet & Home; frog closure, Tender Buttons; linen napkin with pulled

work, ABC Carpet & Home; button, Tender Buttons; gold cord, Brimar Inc.; silk napkin designed by Nancy Angel of Angel Threads; pastillage flowers, Gail Watson Custom Cakes; trapunto linen napkin, ABC Carpet & Home. *right:* monogrammed napkin bow, Jan Kish—la petite fleur; napkin, Nancy Angel of Angel Threads. **PAGE 176:** Hank Lane Orchestra photographed at The Pierre Hotel. **PAGE 178:** stand, Florals of Waterford; Taittinger and Domaine Carneros by Taittinger, distributed by Kobrand. **PAGE 181:** Champagne flutes, tray, Party Rental Ltd. **PAGE 182:** ravioli, Creative Edge Parties; gilt-edged plate, Dan Levy Studio; brocade tablecloth, silk napkin, ABC Carpet & Home. **PAGE 183:** canapés by Creative Edge Parties; tray, Tudor Rose. **PAGE 185:** lobster Napoleon, Creative Edge Parties. **PAGE 186:** cake, Arturo Diaz of Frosted Art; table, Hotel St. Germain. **PAGE 187:** groom's cake, Arturo Diaz of Frosted Art. **PAGE 188:** cake, Cheryl Kleinman Cakes. **PAGE 189:** *left:* cake,

Rosemary Cheris Littman/Rosemary's Cakes; tray and server, Tudor Rose; ribbon, Vaban; chair, ABC Carpet & Home. *right:* cake, Cheryl Kleinman Cakes. **PAGE 190:** *left:* cake, Cheryl Kleinman Cakes. *right:* vintage brides and grooms cake toppers, ABC Carpet & Home. **PAGE 191:** cake, Gail Watson Custom Cakes; ribbon, Vaban; photographed at The Stanhope Hotel Penthouse Suite. **PAGE 192:** cake, Katrina Rozelle Pastries & Desserts. **PAGE 193:** cake, Paul Jerabeck Special Affairs Catering; chintz tablecloth, hand-painted folded chairs, Room Service; tray, Silver Vault. **PAGE 194:** *left:* paper box, Judy Ivry; ribbon, Vaban; pastillage keepsakes, Gail Watson Custom Cakes; gift card calligraphy, Stephannie Barba. *right:* basket, Tudor Rose; iced almonds, Jan Kish—la petite fleur.

PAGE 195: fan, Phoenix Imports; calligraphy, Stephannie Barba; ribbon, Vaban. **PAGE 208:** vintage auto, Mogel's Classic Autos; bouquet, Clifford Miller, TFS; calligraphy, Stephannie Barba.

The Perfect Wedding

*A*cknowledgments

I pen this page of thanks as this book is about to go to press. In order to create any book, the efforts of many are required. That is why these acknowledgment pages are so very important. Without nurturing and focused helmsmen, it would have been impossible for this massive undertaking to become a book. I thank Ella Stewart and John Smallwood for their foresight and wisdom, their stamina to edit with finesse, and above all, for elegantly guiding *The Perfect Wedding* to its completion. I thank Clayton Carlson of Harper Collins for his keen vision and his intuitive appreciation of the merits of this book, and Janis Donnaud for finding the perfect home for *The Perfect Wedding.*

I thank my very good friends Marili Forastieri, Tanya Malott Lawson, Alan Richardson, and Ross Whitaker for photographing my ideas so lusciously. A visual book such as this depends upon the masters behind the cameras to bring its pages to life. *The Perfect Wedding* is the embodiment of their great talent. Producing over three hundred photographs is no simple feat and many people are responsible for making it possible. My hearty thanks to my dedicated assistants Heather Prendergast, Maria Capatorto, Edina Sultanik, Cheri Crump-O'Donoghue, Cindy Phillips, and Jenny Nelson, who eagerly embraced every challenge and helped me rally for each deadline. I thank Linda Lachapelle and Cynthia Birdwell, who generously made available their talented hair and makeup crew, Karen Bensimon, Barbara Fazio, Brian Marryshow, and Mutsumi, whose meticulous hands graced each model in this book. I thank Boss, Click, and Elite Model Management agencies for their talent ~ Evelynne, Gene Garvin, Scott Goodrich,

Jaycee Gossett, Lori Herbert, Zornista Kamenova, Ken Kenitzer, Cassiana Mallman, Tyler Ricci, Andrea Searcy, and Lisa Uphill ~ who so elegantly animated these pages.

Much of this book was photographed on the road. Luckily, Ross Whitaker had the courage to travel with me and I had the good fortune to have crucial help in cities along the way to make my job feasible. I thank Jody Thompson-Kennedy, Beverly McGuire Schnur, and Robin Riddle for being my eyes and ambassadors to their home-towns. (Beverly and Robin's research came in very handy as they exchanged their own wedding vows during the course of this project.) I thank Nina Austin, Karen Metz, and Patti Miller, a triumvirate of bridal salon directors, for providing me with access to their impec-cable boutiques. Each director also introduced me to a few of their clients who in turn gave me the opportunity to photograph beautiful weddings. I thank Allison Kreitzburg and Andrew Ross (page 12, center); Rebecca Burnett and Christopher Price (page 137); Carolina Cruz and Andrea Tamagnini (pages 24, 25, 102), as well as Alice Wong and Hiro Clark Wakabayashi (page 42, top right), and Debbie Felberbaum and Glenn August (pages 42, bottom left, 58, 142, 176) for enthusiastically welcoming me into their wedding celebra-tions. Thanks also to Kimberly Paige and Patrick Fleming and Jeff Dunas and Laura Morton for allowing me to include photographs and contact sheets of their weddings.

I thank so many dear old and new friends for all their help: Mike and Katie Bartholome, John Meeks, Anthony Albertus, Kelly Kornegay, Devorah Nussenbaum, Todd Fiscus and Robert Dailey, Valorie Hart, Kimberly Soles, Amy Leonard, Terry de Roy Gruber, John Dolan, Ken and Lisa Gibbons, Junior Villanue, Laurie Stern, Miho Kosuda, Ron Wendt and Philip MacGregor, Beth Lipton, Clifford Miller, Charles Gonzalez and Rob Smith, Spruce Roden, Jack Follmer and Todd Rigby, Marc Musters, Geoff Howell, Sandra Johnson, Judy Ivry, Angela Scott, Meryl Waitz, Stephannie Barba,

Ann Fox Foley, Cathy Cook, Guy Wolfe, Gail Watson, Colette Peters, Jan Kish, Cheryl Kleinman, Ann Gish, Peter Meitzler, John Mayer, Sy Mogel, Carla Weisberg, Carla Rubin and Bob Spiegel of Creative Edge Parties, Alexandra Randall, Stacey Daniels, Tommy Tellas and Michael Mitrano, Nancy Angel, Christopher Bassett, Peggy and Zezé, Christopher Whanger, Katrina Rozelle, Donald Wressel, Diane Jacobs, Deborah Kaplan, Deborah Shapiro, Don and Nancy Hawthorn, Rosemary Watson, Betty von Nordstrand, Mike McCarey, Margaret Braun, Rosemary Littman, Marci Blum, Sunny and Michael Halperin, Ann Diamond, Amsale Aberra, Michal Rubinowitsch and The Stanhope Hotel, Mary Jo McNally and The Pierre Hotel, Susan Holland, Georgetta Lordi and The Otto Kahn & James Burden Mansions, Nancy Watson and the Haas-Lilienthal House, The Central Park Conservancy, Claire Heymann and the Hotel St. Germain, Terri Dishman and The Beverly Hills Hotel, Pat Hackman and The James Leary Flood Mansion, Lola Erhlick, Karen Saunders, Debbie and Bernie Toll, Frank Treviso, and Jonathan Bush. Each of you wholeheartedly made your talents, locations, and services available to me, and your generosity and enthusiasm are deeply appreciated.

Once the pictures were complete and the text written, it fell upon a small crew to complete the daunting task of structuring it all into a book. This book has a wonderful, captivating design thanks to the creative efforts of Susi Oberhelman and Pat Tan. Sarah Stewart managed to assist everyone and always knew how to solve the most stubborn problems. Leslie Sharpe smoothed rough copy edges and Jennifer Spirn, with her remarkable eye for detail, was invaluable and astounding; she made sure that nothing went unchecked. And the assistance of Rosalind Colman, Georgina Gustin, and Ken Velásquez was very helpful as we closed this book. I thank you all for your amazing efforts. This book is absolutely fabulous and a handsome testament to the talents of everyone.

Photography Credits

This book is my gift to you, to help you have the wedding you have always dreamed of. It contains three of the four elements you will need for your wonderful event: advice to guide you, ideas to inspire you, and the experts to help you execute all of your wedding plans. Now you must add the final element ~ your own personal style ~ to create The Perfect Wedding. With this book in hand, you are well on your way to a memory you will treasure a lifetime.

RESOURCES

Listed here are many of my favorite wedding providers ⁓ the vendors, artists, manufacturers, wholesalers, and designers hand-picked for the quality of their work, their reliability, and their commitment to service. Those marked with an asterisk are featured in *The Perfect Wedding*.

A few rules of thumb will go a long way in making this planning period an easier one for you. Remember always that you are the customer. Don't hesitate to discuss your tastes, needs, and budget requirements; many establishments offer additional options and custom details on request and will go out of their way to accommodate your wishes. If you don't find what you're looking for close to home, consider contacting businesses located outside your area; some vendors will travel or ship products to meet your needs. And don't be shy about asking for referrals before buying or hiring ⁓ reliable businesses are proud of their work and will happily give you the names of previous clients. Lastly, be sure to get written contracts and sales receipts for major purchases and services, with all important details itemized. ⁓

ACCESSORIES

NAME	PHONE	ADDRESS	COMMENTS
Adriana Caras	310.659.4768	Los Angeles, CA	handbags
Adrienne Landau Designs Inc.*	212.695.8362	New York, NY	feathers, boas, capes
Alençon	415.389.9408	318 Miller Ave. Mill Valley, CA 94941	custom veils and headpieces
Anya Hindmarch*	011.44.171.584.7644	91 Walton St. London SW32HP England	handmade handbags; call for local availability
Argentum-The Leopard's Head	415.296.7757	414 Jackson San Francisco, CA 94111	antique silver
Bell'occhio	415.864.4048	8 Brady St. San Francisco, CA 94103	vintage ribbon, silk flowers
Bella Donna	415.861.7182	539 Hayes St. San Francisco, CA 94102	
BJ Design*	212.744.1728	New York, NY	silver and gold hairpins, custom wedding bands; call for local availability
Bottega Veneta	415.981.1700 212.371.5511	108 Geary St. San Francisco, CA 94108 635 Madison Ave. New York, NY 10022	leather a specialty
Carey Adina	212.755.5234 800.466.6054	New York, NY	handbags; custom work; catalog
Carolina Amato*	212.532.8413 800.GLOVE.95	New York, NY	gloves; call for local availability
Carrie Forbes	310.448.1788	Los Angeles, CA	crochet evening bags; call for local availability
Châlloner, NYC*	212.274.1437	New York, NY	headpieces, gloves, handbags; call for local availability
Charles William Gaylord Antiques	415.392.6085	2151 Powell St. San Francisco, CA 94133	antiques

R E S O

Collective Antiques	415.621.3800	212 Utah St. San Francisco, CA 94103	antique and estate jewelry, furniture, linens
Coup de Chapeau	415.931.7793	1906 Fillmore St. San Francisco, CA 94115	millinery, veils, hats
David Luke	415.255.8999	773 14th St. San Francisco, CA 94114	antiques
Debra Moises Group*	212.496.6811	New York, NY	scarves, purses, gowns; custom; by appointment
Designs On You	415.956.0130	545 Sutter St., #304 San Francisco, CA 94102	gowns, veils, silk flowers, shawls, purses; custom
Eve Reid Inc.*	214.521.0391	Dallas, TX	hair accessories, lace a specialty; custom
Finale	516.371.1313	Cedarhurst, NY	gloves, hard-to-find cottons; call for local availability
Fogal	310.273.6425	439 N. Rodeo Dr. Beverly Hills, CA 90210	hosiery
Fownes	212.683.0150	New York, NY	gloves in all lengths; call for local availability
Fragments	212.334.9588	107 Greene St. New York, NY 10012	jewelry, gloves, millinery; call for local availability
Gallery Japonesque	415.391.8860	824 Montgomery St. San Francisco, CA 94133	Japanese antiques, dishware, ceramics
Great American Collective	415.922.2660	1736 Lombard St. San Francisco, CA 94123	antiques
Hanes Hosiery	800.342.7070		hosiery; available at department stores
Hollyhock	213.931.3400	214 N. Larchmont Blvd. Los Angeles, CA 90004	
Homa	201.655.1239	Montclair, NJ	veils, bridal accessories
Jasper Byron	415.563.8122	3364 Sacramento St. San Francisco, CA 94118	antique furniture, light fixtures

JS Suarez	212.753.3758	450 Park Ave. New York, NY 10022	handbags, fine leather a specialty
Judith Leiber*	212.327.4003	987 Madison Ave. New York, NY 10021	accessories including jeweled minaudieres, pearl jewelry
Kitty's Antiques and Collectibles	214.416.5160	Dallas, TX	
La Bagagerie	212.758.6570	727 Madison Ave. New York, NY 10021	handbags, leather a specialty
La Crasia*	212.594.2223	304 Fifth Ave. New York, NY 10001	gloves; custom design available
Lacis	510.843.7178	2982 Adeline at Ashby Berkeley, CA 94703	lace and textile, orange blossoms
Lady Primrose's at the Crescent	214.871.8333	500 Crescent Court Dallas, TX 75201	antiques
The Leg Room	212.861.5920	1058 Madison Ave. New York, NY 10023	hosiery
Lisa Nishi Couture	914.359.0813 902.945.2409	Tappan, NY Nova Scotia, Canada	floral neckware, millinery; call for local availability
Lovers Lane Antique Market	214.351.5696	Dallas, TX	
Maria V. Pinto Designs Inc.*	312.360.1330	Chicago, IL	silk stoles, scarves; call for local availability
McKinney Avenue Antique Market	214.871.1904	Dallas, TX	
Meg Cohen Design	212.473.4002	New York, NY	silk chiffon stoles, cashmere scarves; call for local availability; custom; by appointment
Mespo Umbrellas*	718.680.3601	Brooklyn, NY	black and white cotton; call for local availability
The Mews	214.748.9070	1708 Market Center Blvd. Dallas, TX 75207	antiques, furniture, sterling, candlesticks, linen
Nancy Bacich*	212.673.6068	New York, NY	custom evening handbags; call for local availability

Nicole Valenza, Ltd.	800.304.6393	164 Madison Ave. New York, NY 10016	hosiery
The Pavilion Antiques	415.459.2002	610 Sir Francis Drake Blvd. San Anselmo, CA 94960	country American, European antiques
Royal Appointments	847.501.3077	839 Elm St. Winnetka, IL 60093	Victorian accessories
	847.559.8111	2158 Northbrook Court Northbrook, IL 60062	
Saks Fifth Avenue	310.275.4211	9600 Wilshire Blvd. Beverly Hills, CA 90212	
	212.753.4000	611 Fifth Ave. New York, NY 10022	
Santa Monica Antique Market	310.314.4899	1607 Lincoln Blvd. Santa Monica, CA 90404	
Sew Sensational	310.928.3583	Downey, CA	ribbonry, vintage-styled jewelry; call for local availability
Shaneen Huxham*	212.944.6110	New York, NY	handmade gloves; call for local availability
Showroom Seven	212.643.4810	New York, NY	designer accessories; by appointment
Staccato	415.381.1746	30 Miller Ave. Mill Valley, CA 94941	
Suzanne Werson*	212.472.7392	New York, NY	custom handbags, satin pouches, silk flowers a specialty
Swarovski	212.213.9001	New York, NY	fine Austrian crystal, handbags, jewelry; call for local availability
Toujours	415.346.3988	2484 Sacramento St. San Francisco, CA 94115	bridal accessories, lingerie, hosiery, jewelry
Umbrella Shop	415.896.5856	San Francisco, CA	custom; mail order
Uncle Sam	212.582.1977	161 W. 57th St. New York, NY 10019	umbrellas, parasols
Whiting & Davis	212.736.5810	New York, NY	mesh handbags and scarves; call for local availability

Zazu and Violets*	510.845.1409	1790 Shattuck Ave. Berkeley, CA 94709

A L B U M S   A N D   J O U R N A L S

NAME	PHONE	ADDRESS	COMMENTS
Apiary Press	310.450.3681	2329½ 33rd St. Santa Monica, CA 90405	
Arch	415.433.2724	407 Jackson St. San Francisco, CA 94133	
Brett Landenberger	415.664.8015	2707 Judah St. San Francisco, CA 94122	
Daisy Arts*	310.396.8463	Venice, CA	hand-tooled leather; call for local availability
Flax	415.552.2355	1699 Market St. San Francisco, CA 94103	
Gump's	415.982.1616	135 Post St. San Francisco, CA 94108	
It's a Wrap!	214.520.9727	25 Highland Park Village Ste. 106 Dallas, TX 75205	
Kate's Paperie*	212.941.9816	561 Broadway New York, NY 10012	handmade papers, albums, custom invitations
Klaus Rotzscher	510.845.3653	2181 Bancroft Way Berkeley, CA 94704	
Kozo	415.521.0869	531 Castro St. San Francisco, CA 94114	
Oggetti	415.346.0631	1846 Union St. San Francisco, CA 94123	
Pine Street Papery	415.332.0650	42½ Caledonia St. Sausalito, CA 94965	

R   E   S   O

Soolip Paperie & Press	310.360.0545	8646 Melrose Ave. West Hollywood, CA 90069	
Strawbridge	415.388.0235	86 Throckmorton Ave. Mill Valley, CA 94941	
T. Anthony	212.750.9797 800.722.2406	445 Park Ave. New York, NY 10022	leather albums; catalog
Tail of the Yak	510.841.9891	2632 Ashby Ave. Berkeley, CA 94705	
Tiffany & Co.	415.781.7000 212.755.8000	350 Post St. San Francisco, CA 94108 727 Fifth Ave. New York, NY 10022	
Translations	214.373.8391	4014 Villanova Dallas, TX 75225	contemporary journals- and albums
Two Women	415.431.8805	San Francisco, CA	paper gifts; call for local availability
Two Women Boxing, Inc.*	214.939.1626	Dallas, TX	silkscreen journals, gifts; call for local availability

ARCHIVAL SUPPLIES

NAME	PHONE	ADDRESS	COMMENTS
Gaylord Brothers	800.634.6307		acid-free tissues, boxes; catalog; conservation hotline
Lacis	510.843.7178	2982 Adeline St. Berkeley, CA 94703	
Light Impressions	716.461.4447	439 Monroe Ave. Rochester, NY 14603-0940	photography presenta- tion supplies; catalog
Photographic Archives Lab & Gallery	214.352.3167	5117 W. Lovers Lane Dallas, TX 75209	acid-free tissue, boxes

| Talas, Inc.* | 212.219.0770 | 568 Broadway
New York, NY 10012 | custom boxes, albums;
retail and mail order |

ARTISANS

NAME	PHONE	ADDRESS	COMMENTS
Ashley Powell	610.593.2468	Christiana, PA	master thatcher for gazebos, cottages
Bobbie Lefenfeld	212.647.0722	New York, NY	beaded candle shades, frames; by appointment
Carriage House Papers	800.669.8781	Brookline, MA	handmade papers; catalog
Coffin & King*	212.541.9527	New York, NY	gilded decorative objects; custom, by appointment
Dari Gordon and Bruce Pizzichillo	510.832.8380	2690 Union St. Oakland, CA 94607	handblown glass vases, bowls
Dieu Donné Papermill	212.226.0573	433 Broome St. New York, NY 10013	handmade papers, natural fibers, custom watermarks
G. Wolff Pottery*	203.868.2858	New Preston, CT	horticultural earthenware; custom, by appointment
Gary Halsey	718.398.7521	Brooklyn, NY	decorative painter: trompe l'oeil, landscape, portraits, murals
Gill & Lagodich, Ltd. Fine Period Frames*	212.619.0631	New York, NY	gilders, frame restoration, period and vintage frames
Happy Martin	212.722.0867	New York, NY	decorative painter, custom projects
Hoboken Pottery	201.659.8965	258 Newark St. Hoboken, NJ 07030	thrown stoneware, handmade tiles
Jill Gill	212.362.8440	New York, NY	watercolor and ink illustrations, home portraits

Katie Winn and Woody Hughes	516.929.3418	Wading River, NY	custom majolica cake stands, serving pieces; mail order
Kim Kushner	415.388.4913	1001 Bridgeway, Ste. 560 Sausalito, CA 94965	custom gift wrap
Lynn Rubino	212.807.7525	New York, NY	custom illustrations; handcolored pen and ink miniatures
M. Balin Interior Art	707.539.4233	P.O. Box 9427 Santa Rosa, CA 95405	invitations, envelopes, place cards
Mary Nells/ Mary Anderson	212.865.8370	New York, NY	custom découpage with wedding photos; by appointment
Nancy Adams	415.488.4575	10 Creamery Rd. San Geronimo, CA 94963	
Natoma Ceramic Design	415.495.0440	P.O. Box 78093 San Francisco, CA 94107	ceramic tableware and art pieces
Pamela Hill	209.286.1217	P.O. Box 800 Mokelumne Hill, CA 95245	quilts
Patrick Clark	718.634.3397	Rockaway Park, NY	custom stained glass and glass sculpture; by appointment
Pawel Bendisz	415.566.7457	2665 Judah St. San Francisco, CA 94122	antiques, paintings, furniture
Pinson & Ware	818.359.6113	Monrovia, CA	
Richard Jordan	212.265.2556	New York, NY	decorative painter; tromp l'oeil, special effects
Slips	415.362.5652	1534 Grant Ave. San Francisco, CA 94133	custom slipcovers, pillows, furniture
Smyers Glass	707.745.2614	675 E. Hill St. Benicia, CA 94510	handblown glassware
Susan Eslick	415.255.2234	3120 20th St., Ste. 311 San Francisco, CA 94110	custom ceramics

Tom Penn	212.645.5213	Long Island City, NY	custom silversmith, jewelry, accessories, tableware
Wendy Lindkvist	415.381.3365	San Francisco, CA	custom-stained glass windows

ART SUPPLIES

NAME	PHONE	ADDRESS	COMMENTS
Amsterdam Art	415.387.5354	5221 Geary St. San Francisco, CA 94118	
	510.649.4800	1013 University Ave. Berkeley, CA 94710	
	510.946.9333	1279 Boulevard Way Walnut Creek, CA 94595	
Arch	415.433.2724	407 Jackson St. San Francisco, CA 94111	
Asel Art Supply Inc.	214.871.2425	2701 Theater Springs Dallas, TX 75201	
	817.335.8168	3001 W. 7th St. Fort Worth, TX 76107	
Baggot Leaf Company	212.431.4653	430 Broome St. New York, NY 10013	gilder's source, leaf, tools, instruction
The Bead Store	212.628.4383	1065 Lexington Ave. New York, NY 10021	
Binders Discount Art Center	214.739.2281	9820 North Central Expwy. Dallas, TX 75231	
Flax Art & Design	800.547.7778	1699 Market St. San Francisco, CA 94103	
Lee's Art Shop	212.247.0110	220 W. 57th St. New York, NY 10019	
Metalliferous	212.944.0909	34 W. 46th St. New York, NY 10036	decorative metallic supplies, tools; retail; catalog
Mill Valley Art Materials, Inc.	415.388.5642	433 Miller Ave. Mill Valley, CA 94941	

New York Central Art Supply	800.950.6111	62 Third Ave. New York, NY 10003	
Pearl Paint	212.431.7932	308 Canal St. New York, NY 10013	
Rubberstilzkin	510.440.9406	44384 S. Grimmer Blvd. Fremont, CA 94537	decorative rubber stamps
Sam Flax*	212.620.3010	New York, Atlanta, Orlando	call for availability
Sax Arts & Crafts	414.277.0722 800.558.6696	100A East Pleasant St. Milwaukee, WI 53212	Japanese lace papers, paper casting molds

BAKING SUPPLIES

NAME	PHONE	ADDRESS	COMMENTS
August Thomsen Corporation	800.645.7170		cake decorating utensils; catalog; call for local availability
Broadway Panhandler	212.966.3434	477 Broome St. New York, NY 10012	French bakeware, cake pans, decorations
Cake Art Supplies	415.456.7773	1512 Fifth Ave. San Rafael, CA 94901	
House on the Hill	708.969.2624	Villa Park, IL	mail order catalog
La Cuisine, The Cook's Resource	800.521.1176	323 Cameron St. Alexandria, VA 22314	mail order catalog, retail
Merchants Bakery Supplies Inc.	214.247.8282	3113-C Gardenbrook Dallas, TX 75234	to the trade
New York Cake Baking & Distributors, Inc.	212.675.2253	56 W. 22nd St. New York, NY 10011	
Parrish's Cake Decorating Supplies	310.324.CAKE	Gardena, CA	mail order

R C E S

Sugar Bouquets	201.538.3542 800.203.0629	Morristown, NJ	sugar molds and presses, instructional videos; catalog
Sugar 'n Spice	415.387.1722	3200 Balboa St. San Francisco, CA 94121	
Williams-Sonoma	800.541.2233		baking, kitchen supplies; call for local availability

BEAUTY

NAME	PHONE	ADDRESS	COMMENTS
Apothia by Ron Robinson	310.207.8411	Los Angeles, CA	beauty accessories, cosmetics, skincare; by appointment
Art Luna	310.247.1383	8930 Keith Ave. West Hollywood, CA 90069	full-service hair salon
Arté	212.941.5932	284 Lafayette St. New York, NY 10012	full-service hair salon, manicures
Bergdorf Goodman	212.753.7300	754 Fifth Ave. New York, NY 10019	cosmetics, fragrances
Bobbi Brown Essentials*	212.980.7040	New York, NY	cosmetics, supplies; call for local availability
Boyds*	212.838.6558	655 Madison Ave. New York, NY 10021	cosmetics, makeup artists
Brownes & Co. Apothecary	305.532.8784 888.BROWNES (for catalog)	841 Lincoln Rd. Miami Beach, FL 33139	plant-based skincare supplies, cosmetics, makeup applications; mail order
C.O. Bigelow Chemists	212.473.7324	414 Avenue of the Americas New York, NY 10011	T. Leclerc pressed pow- ders, skin care products
Catherine Fraser	510.526.2669	1632 Cornell Ave. Berkeley, CA 94703	

Chanel*	212.355.5050	New York, NY	cosmetics, fragrance, fashion; Frederick Fekkai beauty salon
Charles Ifergan	312.642.4484	106 East Oak Rd. Chicago, IL 60610	full-service hair salon, makeup
Clinique*	212.572.4436	New York, NY	cosmetics, skincare products available in department stores nationwide
Colours Salon	206.284.6041	Seattle, WA	hair salon, by appointment
Fresh	617.421.1212	121 Newbury St. Boston, MA 02116	skincare, body care, fragrance, scented candles
Garren at Henri Bendel	212.841.9400	712 Fifth Ave. New York, NY 10019	full-service hair salon
Guillaume Gignac	212.246.0321	54 W. 55th St. New York, NY 10019	hair salon
International Apothecario	401.849.9944 800.755.5252	13 Touro St. Newport, RI 02840	European soaps, toiletries; mail order catalog; retail
Kiehl's Pharmacy	212.475.3698 800.KIEHLS.1	109 3rd Ave. New York, NY 10003	hair and skincare products, cosmetics; retail, mail order; call for local availability
Kim Rozelle	214.363.9088	Dallas, TX	makeup artist; by appointment
Klaus Rotzscher	510.845.3653	2181 Bancroft Way Berkeley, CA 94704	
Lachapelle Representation Ltd.*	212.838.3170	New York, NY	hair and makeup artists' representatives; by appointment
Laura Geller	212.570.5477	1044 Lexington Ave. New York, NY 10021	hair and makeup artists
Let's Face It	212.219.8970	568 Broadway New York, NY 10012	full-service skin, nail and body treatments, facials
Lucy Peters	212.486.9740 214.486.9740 310.274.0454	New York, NY Dallas, TX Beverly Hills, CA	electrolysis

M.A.C. Cosmetics	800.387.6707		cosmetics; call for local availability
Makeup Center	212.977.9494	150 W. 55th St. New York, NY 10019	cosmetics, makeup artists; by appointment
Maria Russo Salon	617.424.6676	9 Newbury St. Boston, MA 02116	full-service salon
Mariana's Skin Care	508.922.0707	498 Elliot St. Beverly, MA 01915	facials, body treatments, makeup
Minardi-Minardi Salon	212.308.1711	29 E. 61st St., 5th Fl. New York, NY 10021	full-service hair and beauty salon specializing in hair color
Mister Lee	415.474.6002	834 Jones St. San Francisco, CA 94109	spa facilities
Noelle the Day Spa	404.266.0060	3619 Piedmont Rd. Atlanta, GA 30305	full-service spa, aromatherapy massages
On the Avenue	415.388.1126	167 E. Blithedale Ave. Mill Valley, CA 94965	
Peter Anthony Studio	801.649.9595	Park City, UT	full-service salon, hair, makeup, manicures, skincare
The Phoenix Salon	214.352.8411	5600 West Lovers Lane Dallas, TX 75209	hair and makeup artists; by appointment
Pileggi on the Square	215.627.0565	717 Walnut St. Philadelphia, PA 19106	full-service hair and beauty salon, massages
Ronni Kolotkin	212.388.0600	New York, NY	electrolysis; by appointment
Salon at the Mansion on Turtle Creek	214.521.4300	2821 Turtle Creek Blvd. Dallas, TX 75219	hair and makeup
Salon Cristophe	202.785.2222 310.274.0851	Washington, DC Beverly Hills, CA	full-service hair salon, makeup artists
Sally Beauty Supplies*	214.720.1910 800.284.SALLY	Dallas, TX	cosmetics, beauty supplies; call for local availability

The Sanctuary Day Spa	617.524.0707	38 Newbury St. Boston, MA 02116	
Scentiments & Essentials at Fred Segal	310.394.8509	Santa Monica, CA	beauty products, fragrances, cosmetics
Skin Care for the Nineties	415.285.4868	San Francisco, CA	makeup and skincare; by appointment
Strawberry Jam	215.862.9251	44C South Main New Hope, PA 18938	fragrances, cosmetics
Susan Ciminelli Day Spa	212.265.5080	106 Central Park South Ste. 14G New York, NY 10019	full-service spa; skincare, massages
Sylvie's	818.905.8815	17071 Ventura Blvd. Encino, CA	full-service skincare salon, manicures
Tail of the Yak	510.841.9891	2632 Ashby Ave. Berkeley, CA 94705	
Toni & Guy	214.696.3825	6030 Sherry Lane Dallas, TX 75225	hair and makeup
Tony Fielding Salon	214.522.9486	3617 Fairmont Rd. Dallas, TX 75219	full-service hair salon, makeup artists
Yosh For Hair	415.989.7704 415.328.4067	173 Maiden Lane San Francisco, CA 94108 240 University Ave. Palo Alto, CA 94301	
Valerie Beverly Hills	800.282.5374	Beverly Hills, CA	cosmetics, brushes, makeup artists

BOOKBINDERS/BOX MAKERS

NAME	PHONE	ADDRESS	COMMENTS
Angela Scott*	212.431.5148	New York, NY	by appointment

Apiary Press	310.450.3681	2329½ 33rd St. Santa Monica, CA 90405	
Barbara Mauriello	201.420.6613	Hoboken, NJ	by appointment
Dallas, TX School of Book Binding	214.241.5692	4115 Meyerwood Lane Dallas, TX 75244	
Henry Nuss Bookbinder Inc.	214.747.5545	2701 Main St. Dallas, TX 75226	
Jack Fitterer	518.325.7172	Hillsdale, NY	hand letterer
Judy Ivry*	212.677.1015	New York, NY	embossed albums; by appointment
Marjorie Salik*	212.219.0770	New York, NY	by appointment
Tactile Books*	212.242.4320 206.784.6063	New York, NY Seattle, WA	accordian invitations, folder frames; by appointment
Trade Bindery	415.981.1856	355 Fremont San Francisco, CA 94105	
Yesteryear	310.278.2008	8816 Beverly Blvd. Los Angeles, CA 90048	

BRIDAL DESIGNERS

NAME	PHONE	ADDRESS	COMMENTS
Alençon	415.389.9408	318 Miller Ave. Mill Valley, CA 94941	custom gowns
Alvina Valenta	516.661.0492	Babylon, NY	call for local availability
Amsale*	212.971.0170 800.765.0170	New York, NY	call for local availability
Bella Donna	415.861.7182	539 Hayes St. San Francisco, CA 94102	

Birnbaum & Bullock	212.242.2914	New York, NY	nontraditonal custom gowns; by appointment
Bob Evans	212.889.1999	New York, NY	custom gowns; by appointment
Bowdon Designer Fashions	707.525.8054	838 Fourth St. Santa Rosa, CA 95404	
Bravura	415.474.9092	2904 Octavia St. San Francisco, CA 94123	
The Bridal Diamond Collection	212.302.0210	New York, NY	traditional and contemporary gowns; call for local availability
Carmela Sutera	212.921.4808	New York, NY	bridal lingerie; call for local availability
Carolina Herrera*	212.944.5757	501 Seventh Ave. New York, NY 10018	custom gowns; by appointment; call for local availability
Christian Dior	800.340.3467		custom gowns; by appointment; call for local availability
Christopher Hunte	212.244.0420	New York, NY	custom gowns,by appointment
Designs on You	415.956.0130	545 Sutter St., Ste. 304 San Francisco, CA 94102	
Dessy Creations*	212.337.7911 800.52.DESSY	New York, NY	informal gowns; call for local availability
The Diamond Bridal Collection	212.302.0210	New York, NY	traditional and contemporary gowns; call for local availability
Dolce & Gabbana	212.966.2868	New York, NY	contemporary gowns; call for local availability
Donald Deal*	212.730.8835	New York, NY	contemporary gowns; call for local availability
Endrius	212.838.5880	New York, NY	custom couture gowns; by appointment

Gillian Swonnell	617.542.3242	535 Albany St. Boston, MA 02118	contemporary gowns; call for local availability
Helen Morley*	212.594.6404	New York, NY	call for local availability
Herschelle Couturier	415.982.0112	San Francisco, CA	custom evening wear, and gowns; by appointment
Inatome International*	212.966.7777	New York, NY	call for local availability
Jane Wilson-Marquis	212.477.4408	New York, NY	contemporary custom gowns; by appointment
Jeanne's Fantasia	615.352.1726	Nashville, TN	Victorian gowns and headpieces; call for local availability
LAKU	415.695.1462	1069 Valencia San Francisco, CA 94110	
Lily Dong Custom Bridal	408.225.8850	San Francisco, CA	by appointment
Manalé*	212.760.0121	New York, NY	call for local availability
Maria Jung Couturier	305.461.2090	300 Aragon Ave., Ste. 120 Coral Gables, FL 33134	custom gowns and accesssories for attendants; by appointment
Mark Caligiuri	612.339.5772	624 Harmon Pl., Ste. 222 Minneapolis, MN 55403	custom couture gowns; by appointment
Mary Adams	212.473.0237	New York, NY	custom contemporary gowns; by appointment
Milo	214.522.1118	4337 Lovers Lane Dallas, TX 75225	custom dresses; by appointment
Obiko	415.775.2882	794 Sutter St. San Francisco, CA 94109	
Options	800.275.9684	Woodside, NY	tuxedos for women; call for local availability
Pat Kerr	901.525.5223	Memphis, TN	heirloom lace bridal gowns; by appointment; call for local availability

Priscilla of Boston	617.267.9070	137 Newbury St. Boston, MA 02116	gowns and headpieces; call for local availability
Reem Acra/ Reem Bridals*	212.686.8198	New York, NY	custom couture gowns and accessories; by appointment
Richard Glasgow*	212.683.1379	New York, NY	couture bridal gowns; call for local availability
Star Gowns of Distinction	214.278.7560	565 W. Oats Rd. Ste. 136 Garland TX 75043	custom gowns
Thomasina	412.563.7788	615 Washington Rd. Mt. Lebanon, PA 15228	custom gowns, by appointment
Ulla-Maija	212.570.6085	New York, NY	couture gowns; call for local availability
Vera Wang*	212.628.3400 212.575.6400	991 Madison Ave. New York, NY 10023	contemporary gowns, custom couture; by appointment
Wearkstatt*	212.941.6960	New York, NY	contemporary and custom; by appointment or call for local availability
Zazu & Violets'	510.845.1409	1790 Shattuck Ave. Berkeley, CA 94709	

BRIDAL REGISTRY

NAME	PHONE	ADDRESS	COMMENTS
ABC Carpet & Home*	212.473.3000	888 Broadway New York, NY 10003	home accessories, furniture, linens, tableware
The Accent Shop	317.844.5112	1520 E. 86th St. Indianapolis, IN 46240	
Altum Garden Nursery	317.875.7746	11335 N. Michigan Rd. Zionsville, IN 46077	

R C E S

Bardith Ltd.	212.737.3775	901 Madison Ave. New York, NY 10021	antique English pottery and porcelain
Barneys New York*	310.276.4400	9570 Wilshire Blvd. Beverly Hills, CA 90212	
	212.826.8900	660 Madison Ave. New York, NY 10021	
Bauman Rare Books	212.759.8300	301 Park Ave. New York, NY 10022	
Bed Bath & Beyond	201.379.1520	Springfield, NJ	call for local availability
Bloomingdale's	212.705.2800 800.888.2.WED	1000 Third Ave. New York, NY 10022	nationwide registry service
The Bridal Registry Shop	212.431.0077	New York, NY	full-service registration
Brodean*	800.295.4040	3440 Sacramento St. San Francisco, CA 94118	china, linen, flatware, crystal; by appointment
	800.522.7975	377 Broome St. New York, NY 10013	
Calvin Klein Home	212.292.9000	654 Madison Ave. New York, NY 10021	
China Silver & Crystal Shop	206.441.8906 800.759.5817	2809 2nd Ave. Seattle, WA 98121	
Collections	317.283.5251	113 E. 49th St. Indianapolis, IN 46205	
Crate & Barrel	847.272.2888	Northbrook, IL	housewares, tableware; call for local availability catalog; national registry
David Orgell	310.273.6660	320 N. Rodeo Dr. Beverly Hills, CA 90210	
Durr, Ltd.	612.925.9146	4386 France Ave. Edina, MN 55410	home furnishings, table- ware, linens
Domain	206.450.9900	300-120 Ave. NE 6-115 Bellevue, WA 98005	housewares
Earthly Possessions	617.696.2440	10 Bassett St. Milton, MA 02186	tableware
	617.741.5253	7 Main St. Hingham, MA 02043	

Eastern Accent	617.266.9707	237 Newbury St. Boston, MA 02116	home accessories, tableware
Felissimo	800.565.6785	10 W. 56th St. New York, NY 10019	home accessories, flat- ware, tableware
Fishs Eddy	212.420.9020 212.873.8819	889 Broadway New York, NY 10003 2176 Broadway New York, NY 10024	tablesettings, restaurant ware
Fortunoff	516.832.9000	1300 Old Country Rd. Westbury, NY 11590	full-service registry
Gill & Lagodich, Ltd.	212.619.0631	New York, NY	frames
Geary's	310.273.4741	351 N. Beverly Dr. Beverly Hills, CA 90210	
Georg Jensen	800.546.5253 312.642.9160 714.662.2644	683 Madison Ave. New York, NY 10021 959 Michigan Ave. Chicago, IL 60611 South Coast Plaza 3333 South Briston Costa Mesa, CA 92626	sterlingware
Guess Home Collection	800.GUESS.46	New York, NY	call for local availability
Gump's*	415.982.1616	San Francisco, CA	china, crystal, decorative accessories
Hechts	202.628.6661 703-558-1200	1201 G St. NW Washington, D.C. 20005 Arlington, VA	call for local availability
Hollyhock	213.931.3400	214 N. Larchmont Blvd. Los Angeles, CA 90004	
The Home Depot*	800.654.1914		registry; call for local availability
Lenox	800.635.3669	New Jersey	china; call for local availability
L.L. Bean	800.341.4341	Freeport, ME	sporting, camping goods
Mackenzie-Childs	212.570.6050	824 Madison Ave. New York, NY 10021	decorative majolica accessories, tableware

Mikasa	800.833.4681	Secaucus, NJ	china, crystal, flatware; call for local availability
Neiman Marcus	310.550.5900	9700 Wilshire Blvd. Beverly Hills, CA 90212	call for location
NCM Studio, Inc.	716.877.2215	Buffalo, NY	custom china a specialty
Paragon Sporting Goods	212.255.8036	867 Broadway New York, NY 10003	
Pavillon Christofle	310.858.8058	9515 Brighton Way Beverly Hills, CA 90210	
Polo/Ralph Lauren	214.522.5270	58 Highland Park Village Dallas, TX 75205	
Pottery Barn	800.922.5507		housewares, tableware, call for locations
Replacements Limited	800.REPLACE 910.697.3000	1089 Knox Rd. McLeansville, NC 27301 Greensboro, NC	hard-to-find china
Room Service*	214.369.7666	4354 Lovers Lane Dallas, TX 75225	decorative accessories, vintage furnishings
Room with a View	310.453.7009	1600 Montana Ave. Santa Monica, CA 90403	
Secrets	206.523.2464	1023 NE 62nd St. Seattle, WA 98109	linens
Silver Vault*	214.357.7115	5655 West Lovers Lane Dallas, TX 75209	flatware, platters, services
Something Wonderful	317.848.6992	9700 Lakeshore Drive East Indianapolis, IN 46280	
Stanley Korshak*	214.871.3600	500 Crescent Ct., Ste. 100 Dallas, TX 75201	decorative accessories
Steuben	800.424.4240		fine crystal; call for locations
Stupell Ltd. Fine Gifts*	212.260.3100	28 E. 22nd St. New York, NY 10010	china, crystal, flatware
Takashimaya*	212.350.0593	693 Fifth Ave. New York, NY 10022	tableware, decorative accessories

R   E   S   O

Tiffany & Co.*	212.755.8000	New York, NY	china, crystal, sterling, decorative accessories; call for locations
Tower Records	800.474.7890		national registry, music collections
Troy	212.941.4777	138 Greene St. New York, NY 10012	artisan-crafted home furnishings
Ursus Books and Prints	212.772.8787	981 Madison Ave. New York, NY 10021	out-of-print art books
Waterford Wedgwood	800.677.7860		china, crystal; call for locations
William-Wayne & Co.*	212.288.9243	850 Lexington Ave. New York, NY 10021	decorative accessories, tableware
Wolfman-Gold & Good Company*	212.431.1888	117 Mercer St. New York, NY 10012	service and tableware, decorative accessories
Zona*	212.925.6750	97 Greene St. New York, NY 10012	artisan-crafted decorative accessories
	516.324.4100	2 Newtown La. East Hampton, NY 11937	
	970.925.3763	218 South Mill St. Aspen, CO 81611	

BRIDAL SALONS

NAME	PHONE	ADDRESS	COMMENTS
Auer's	303.321.0404	210 Saint Paul St. Denver, CO 80206	full-service salon
B. Hughes Bridal and Formal	615.292.9409	4231 Harding Rd. Nashville, TN 37205	
Barneys New York*	310.276.4400	9570 Wilshire Blvd. Beverly Hills, CA 90212	Vera Wang collection, accessories
Bergdorf Goodman	212.753.7300	754 Fifth Ave. New York, NY 10019	full-service salon

Beverly Brooks for the Bride	913.381.1060	4002 W. 83rd St. Prairie Village, KS 66208	
Bridal & Formal	513.821.6622	300 W. Benson St. Reading, OH 45215	
Bridal Boutique of Carmel	317.844.1780	13720 N. Meridian St. Carmel, IN 46032	
The Bridal Salon at Stanley Korshak	214.871.3611	500 Crescent Ct., Ste. 142 Dallas, TX 75201	full-service salon, wedding consultant
Bridals by Franca	602.943.7973	11725 N. 19th Ave. Phoenix, AZ 85021	
The Bride	714.760.1800	230 Newport Center Dr. Newport Beach, CA 92660	
BRIDES by Peggy Barnes	713.622.2298	2031 Post Oak Blvd. Houston, TX 77056	
The Bride's House	314.621.1833	1010 Locus St. St. Louis, MO 63101	
Casablanca Bridal and Formal	808.943.6688	1649 Kalakaua Ave. Ste. 202 Honolulu, HI 96826	
Catan's Southern Plantation	216.238.6664	12878 Pearl Rd. Strongville, OH 44136	
Chic Parisien	305.448.5756	118 Miracle Mile Coral Gables, FL 33134	
d'Anélli Bridals	303.980.1400	7847 West Jewall Ave. Lakewood, CO 80232	
Davenport's	904.398.7553	1418 San Marco Blvd. Jacksonville, FL 32207	full-service salon; by appointment
Daytons Bridal Salon	612.375.2162	700 Nicollet Mall Minneapolis, MN 55402	
Divine Design	503.635.5090	Lake Oswego, OR	
Exclusive for the Bride	810.647.4999	708 North Woodward Ave. Birmingham, MI 48009	

EXCLUSIVES for the Bride	312.664.8870	311 W. Superior St. Chicago, IL 60610	
Giorgio Armani Boutique	212.988.9191 310.271.5555 415.434.2500	New York, NY Beverly Hills, CA San Francisco, CA	couture collection
Helen Benton	501.338.8119	Helena, AR	custom gowns; by appointment; call for local availability
The House of Broel	504.522.2220	2220 St. Charles Ave. New Orleans, LA 70115	
House of Design	617.476.8933	Boston Design, Ste. 634 One Design Center Place Boston, MA 02210	computer-aided custom design
I Do, I Do . . . by Kiley & Jo	713.522.0456	2005G West Grey Houston, TX 77019	
Immortal Beloved	518.584.0962	486 Broadway Saratoga Springs, NY 12866	
J.J. Kelly Bridal Salon	405.752.0029	12325 N. May St. Oklahoma City, OK 73120	
Joan Gilbert	415.752.1808	San Francisco, CA	custom accessories; by appointment
Kleinfeld*	718.833.1100	8202 5th Ave. Brooklyn, NY 11209	full-service salon
Jeannette Russell Bridal Couture	412.343.2444	1500 Washington Rd. The Galleria Pittsburgh, PA 15228	by appointment
Jessica McClintock	310.273.9690	9517 Wilshire Blvd. Beverly Hills, CA 90210	
Kalima	212.691.9520	135 W. 12 St. New York, NY 10012	custom contemporary; by appointment
Laura's Couture Collection	816.444.1444	317 E. 55th St. Kansas City, MO 64113	
Lisa Hammerquist	518.434.9151	Albany, NY	contemporary custom gowns

Margot Alexis Bridal	602.951.4009	7000 E. Shea Blvd. Scottsdale, AZ 85251	
Marina Morrison*	415.781.7920	212 Sutter St. San Francisco, CA 94108	
Marshall Field's	312.781.3545	Chicago, IL	
Mary Ann Maxwell for the Bride	713.529.3939	3331 D'Amico St. Houston, TX 77019	
Mon Ami	714.546.5700	355 S. Bristol St. Costa Mesa, CA 92626	
Morgane Le Fay	212.879.9700 212.925.0144 310.393.4447	746 Madison Ave. New York, NY 10021 151 Spring St. New York, NY 10012 1528 Montana Ave. Santa Monica, CA 90403	contemporary collection
Neiman Marcus	314.567.9811 214.741.6911	100 Plaza Frontenac St. Louis, MO 63131 1618 Main St. Dallas, TX 75201	
One of a Kind Bride	212.645.7123	89 Fifth Ave., 9th Fl. New York, NY 10011	custom salon
Original Bride Couture	212.997.4697	225 W. 39th St. New York, NY 10018	custom gowns, accessories; by appointment
Patsy's a Bridal Boutique	214.528.1227	4244 Oak Lane Dallas, TX 75219	
Priscilla, The Bride's Shop	617.267.9070 303.355.9491	137 Newbury St. Boston, MA 02116 201 Steele Denver, CO 80206	Priscilla of Boston gowns, accessories, shoes
Renee Strauss	310.657.1700	8692 Wilshire Blvd. Beverley Hills, CA 90211	
Risuleo	310.276.8809	624 N. Doheny Dr. Los Angeles, CA 90069	
Sandra Johnson Couture*	310.247.8206	138 S. Robertson Blvd. Los Angeles, CA 90046	custom couture

Stephane Lessant	201.792.0268	Hoboken, NJ	custom couture; by appointment
Suky Rosan	610.649.3686	49-53 Anderson Ave. Ardmore, PA 19003	
Tatiana of Boston	617.262.4914	13 Newbury St. Boston, MA 02116	
The Ultimate Bride	312.337.6300	106 East Oak St. Chicago, IL 60611	
The Ultimate Bride	314.961.9997	St. Louis, MO	
Vera Wang Bridal House	212.628.3400	991 Madison Ave. New York, NY 10021	
Victoria's Bridal Inc.	206.283.4225	535 W. McGraw Seattle, WA 98119	custom gowns
The Wedding Dress at Saks Fifth Avenue	212.940.4288 404.261.7234	New York, NY Atlanta, GA	full-service salon
White Rose	818.795.8886	34 South Raymond Pasadena, CA 91005	
Yolanda Enterprises	617.899.6470	355 Waverly Oaks Rd. Waltham, MA 02154	
Yumi Katsura*	212.772.3760	907 Madison Ave. New York, NY 10021	gowns, accessories
Zita's Bridal Design	414.276.6827	1122 North Aster Milwaukee, WI 53202	

CALLIGRAPHY

NAME	PHONE	ADDRESS	COMMENTS
Alan Simon	317.257.6968	5338 N. Pennsylvania St. Indianapolis, IN 46220	by hand or computer
An Englishman in L.A.*	213.656.8611	Los Angeles, CA	illuminated wedding certificates, handmade parchment invitations

Anna Pinto	201.656.7402		contemporary hand lettering, design
Barbara Callow Calligraphy	415.928.3303	1686 Union St. San Francisco, CA 94123	
Carole Maurer	610.642.9726	Wynnewood, PA	matching typefaces
Caroline Paget Leake	212.691.2712	New York, NY	copperplate specialist, Victorian and Art Noveau style borders, ornaments
Cheryl Jacobsen	319.351.6603	1131 E. Burlington St. Iowa City, IA 52240	calligraphy and design
Claire Mendelson	212.595.1775 416.784.1426	New York, NY Toronto, Canada	contemporary ketubah art, illustrations
Eleanor Winters	718.855.7964	Brooklyn, NY	copperplate, pen lettering and italics
Evelyn Schramm	214.969.2823	Dallas, TX	
Goldy Tobin	206.454.6143	Seattle, WA	
Heather Belle McQuale*	804.286.2940	Scotsville, VA	script styles, illustrated details
Jack Fitterer	518.325.7172	Hillsdale, NY	illuminator, fine letterer, all stationery, certificates, bookbinding
Jay Greenspan	212.496.5399	New York, NY	ketubah artist, illuminator, florentine to contemporary styles, invitations
Jonathan Kremer	610.664.9625	Narberth, PA	medieval and contemporary, ketubah and wedding certificates
Janet Redstone Fine Calligraphy & Design	312.944.6624 800.484.7919 x3310	Chicago, IL	custom monograms, brochure available
K2 Design	214.522.2344	Dallas, TX	
Kevin Karl	817.926.2888	Fort Worth, TX	

Margaret DiPiazza Inc.*	212.889.3057	New York, NY	handmade paper cones
Margie Reed	206.232.7343	Seattle, WA	
Oggetti	415.346.0631	1846 Union St. San Francisco, CA 94123	
Papineau Calligraphy	510.339.2301	5772 Thornhill Dr. Oakland, CA 94611	
Pendragon Inc.*	508.234.6843	Whitinsville, MA	hand-lettered, hand-painted stationery
Richard Jordan	212.265.2556	New York, NY	Carolingian script, custom designs, decorative painting
Sherry Schlossberg	818.222.2272	23034 Park Dulce Calabasas, CA 91302	
Special Letters	310.316.1533	112 S. Catalina Ave. Redondo Beach, CA 90277	
Stephannie Barba*	212.426.8949	New York, NY	custom design, illustrations
Toni Elling	518.827.6477	Middleburgh, NY	hand-painted vine, leaf motifs

CANDLES

NAME	PHONE	ADDRESS	COMMENTS
American Pie	415.929.8025	3101 Sacramento St. San Francisco, CA 94115	
Antiques & Home Furnishings	817.334.0330	3433 W. 7th Fort Worth, TX 76107	
Barker Co.	206.244.1870 800.543.0601	Seattle, WA	candlemaking supplies
Candelier	415.989.8600	60 Maiden Lane San Francisco, CA 94108	

The Candle Shop	212.989.0148	118 Christopher St. New York, NY 10014	candles and oil lamps, will ship
The Candlestick	415.332.2834 800.972.6777	777 Bridgeway Sausalito, CA 94965	
Creative Candles	800.237.9711	Kansas City, MO	all lengths, all colors
Dadant & Sons	800.637.7468	Hamilton, IL	candlemaking supplies
Fantastico	415.982.0680	559 6th St. San Francisco, CA 94103	
Fillamento	415.931.2224	2185 Fillmore St. San Francisco, CA 94115	
General Wax & Candle Company	818.765.6357	6863 Beck Ave. N. Hollywood, CA 91605	
Hurd Beeswax Candles	707.963.7211 800.977.7211	3020 Saint Helena Hwy. N. Saint Helena, CA 94574	decorative candles
Ilume	213.782.0342	8302 W. 3rd St. Los Angeles, CA 90048	
Inside Out	310.652.9280	521 N. La Cienega Blvd. Los Angeles, CA 90048	
Ken Knight	214.969.5490	2828 Routh St. Ste. 100 Dallas, TX 75201	
Knorr Beeswax Products	619.755.3430 800.807.BEES	14906 Via De La Valle Delmar, CA 92014	
Lamplight Farms	414.781.9590 800.645.5267	4900 North Lilly Rd. Menomonee Falls, WI 53051	
Out of the Dreamtime	360.385.2185 800.643.1658	Port Townsend, WA	votive holders, to the trade only
Perin-Mowen	212.219.3937 214.748.2128	New York, NY Dallas, TX	beeswax candles, to the trade only
Pourette Manufacturing Company	206.789.3188 800.888.9425	1418 NW 53rd St. Seattle, WA 98107	molds and candlemaking supplies

Sample House & Candle Shop	214.871.1501 817.429.7857	2615 Routh St. Dallas, TX 75201 1540 S. University Dr. Fort Worth, TX	
Summer House	415.383.6695	21 Throckmorton Ave. Mill Valley, CA 94941	
Susan Schadt Designs*	800.459.4595	2120 Jimmy Durante Blvd. Del Mar, CA 90210	hand-rolled beeswax candles, candle saucers, holders, accessories, custom work available
Visual Design*	205.556.4164	Tuscaloosa, AL	candle bracelets, decorative accessories

C A T E R E R S

NAME	PHONE	ADDRESS	COMMENTS
A Mano Catering	617.444.2132	301 Reservoir St. Needham, MA 02194	
Affairs to Remember	404.872.7859 404.876.6314	680 Ponce De Leon Ave. Atlanta, GA 30308	
A Joy Wallace Catering Production	305.252.0020	8501 Southwest 129th Terrace Miami, FL 33156	
All in Good Taste	412.321.5516	1520 Monteray St. Pittsburgh, PA 15212	
Along Came Mary	213.931.9082	5365 W. Pico Blvd. Los Angeles, CA 90019	
Ambrosia Catering	801.645.8355	P.O. Box 4005 Park City, UT 84060	
Ann Walker Catering	415.945.0952	5627 B Paradise Dr. Corte Madera, CA 94925	
Another Roadside Attraction	901.525.2624	679 Adams St. Memphis, TN 38105	

Apple Spice Caterers	801.359.8821	620 South West Temple Salt Lake City, UT 84101	
Atrium Catering	612.339.8322	275 Market St., Ste. C25 Minneapolis, MN 55405	full-service custom caterers
Betty Zlatchin Catering	415.641.8599	3386 19th St. San Francisco, CA 94110	
Calihan Gotoff Catering	312.829.4644	942 West Huron Chicago, IL 60622	
Capers Catering	617.648.0900	66A Broadway Arlington, MA 02174	
The Catered Affair	617.982.9333	Accord Park, P.O. Box 26 Hingham, MA 02018	
The Catering Company	816.444.8372	401 E. 54th St. Kansas City, MO 64110	
Catering St. Louis	314.961.7588	829 Hanley Industrial Ct. St. Louis, MO 63144	
Cathy's Rum Cake Catering	602.945.9205	4200 N. Marshall Way Scottsdale, AZ 85251	
Chardonnay's of Jacksonville	904.262.8372	11406-3 San Jose Blvd. Jacksonville, FL 32223	
Chow! Catering	405.752.9991	11212 N. May Ave., Ste. 101 Oklahoma City, OK 73120	
The Common Plea	412.281.5140	308 Ross St. Pittsburgh, PA 15219	
Creative Edge Parties*	212.741.3000	New York, NY	
Creative Gourmets	617.783.5555	32 Antwerp St. Boston, MA 02135	
Crystal Catering	317.925.9506	2625 North Meridian St. Indianapolis, IN 46225	
Dani Foods	214.444.9792	2156 W. Northwest Hwy. Ste. 311 Dallas, TX 75220	

R   E   S   O

David Wehrs Seafood	410.643.5778	St. Michael's, MD	Chesapeake Bay clambakes
Design Cuisine	703.979.9400	2659 S. Shirlington Rd. Arlington, VA 22206	
Duck-Duck Mousse	310.392.4956	2640 Main St. Santa Monica, CA 90405	
Elaine Bell Catering Company*	707.996.5226	Sonoma, CA	Napa wine country
Entertainment Caterers	617.262.2605	7 Lansdowne St. Boston, MA 02215	
Epicurean Catering	303.770.0877	6022 South Holly St. Greenwood Village, CO 80111	
Events by Steven Duvall	803.763.9222	1478 Savannah Hwy. Charleston, SC 29407	
Fascinating Foods	901.276.3555	2160 Central Ave. Memphis, TN 38104	
Feastivities	817.377.3011	5724 Lock Ave. Fort Worth, TX 76107	by appointment
Ferree Florsheim	312.282.6100	5080 North Kimberly, Unit 102 Chicago, IL 60630	
Food Art	504.524.2381	801 Carondelet St. New Orleans, LA 70130	
Food Company	214.939.9270	215 Henry St., Ste. B Dallas, TX 75226	
Food For All Seasons	313.747.9099	1164 Broadway Ann Arbor, MI 48103	
Food in Motion Inc.	212.766.4400	New York, NY	ethnic menus; call for appointment
Gai Klass	310.559.6777	10335 W. Jefferson Blvd. Culver City, CA 90232	
Gracious Catering	414.786.1030	890 Elm Grove Rd. Elm Grove, WI 53226	

Heck's	216.464.8020	Cleveland, OH
Incredible Edibles	816.587.9922	5505 NW Fox Hill Rd. Parkville, MO 64152
J.G. Melons	415.331.0888	100 Ebbtide Rd. Sausalito, CA 94965
Jack Norman Ltd.	414.425.4720	7973 South Hwy. 100 Franklin, WI 53132
Joe McDonall	206.285.7846	570 Roy St. Seattle, WA 98109
Joel's Grand Cuisine	800.335.8994	503 New Hampshire St. Covington, LA 70433
Kates Fine Catering	615.298.5644	619 W. Iris Dr. Nashville, TN 37204
Katherine's Catering	313.930.4270	Domino's Farms Prairie House P.O. Box 985 Ann Arbor, MI 48103
Krane & Rush Catering	414.964.3663	159 E. Silver Spring Dr. Whitefish Bay, WI 53217
L.A. Celebrations!	213.837.8900	1716 S. Robertson Blvd. Los Angeles, CA 90035
La Bocca Fina Fine Catering	510.264.0276	2416 Radley Court, #1 Hayward, CA 94545
La Pêche	502.451.0377	1147 Bardstown Rd. Louisville, KY 40204
Le Petit Gourmet Catering	303.388.5791	4182 E. Virginia Ave. Denver, CO 80222
Lee Epting Catering	770.641.1825 770.641.7772	1010 Kathleen Ct. Roswell, GA 30075
Lewis Steven's Distinctive Catering	602.991.2799	7601 E. Gray Dr. Scottsdale, AZ 85251
Marian's Island-Wide Catering	808.621.6758	79 Mango Place Wahiawa, HI 96786

R   E   S   O

McCall Associates	415.552.8550	888 Brannon St., Ste. 600 San Francisco, CA 94103	
Mood Food Ltd.	212.243.4245	New York, NY	
Moveable Feast	313.663.3278	326 West Liberty Ann Arbor, MI 48103	
Now We're Cooking	415.255.6355	2150 Third St. San Francisco, CA 94107	
O.K. Uniform Company	212.966.1984	New York, NY	cotton aprons, uniforms
Panache Catering	303.369.2009	14100 East Jewell Ave., Ste. 24 Aurora, Colorado 80012	
Partysist Caterers	504.865.1512	8220 Willow St. New Orleans, LA 70118	
Paula LeDuc Catering	510.547.7825	1350 Park Ave. Emeryville, CA 94608	
Pavilion Catering	414.671.2001	4101 W. Greeenfield Ave. Milwaukee, WI 53215	
Poulet	510.845.5932	1685 Shadduck Berkeley, CA 94709	
The Prairie Star Restaurant	505.867.3327	P.O. Box 1509 Bernalillo, NM 87004	
Pronto	810.544.7900	608 South Washington Royal Oak, MI 48067	
Proof of the Pudding	404.892.2359	2033 Monroe Dr. Atlanta, GA 30324	
Ritz Charles	317.846.9158	12156 N. Meridian Carmel, IN 46032	
Robbins Wolfe Catering	212.924.6500	New York, NY	
Rococo	818.909.0990	6734 Valjean Ave. Van Nuys, CA 91406	

The Roostertail Catering Club	313.822.1234	100 Marquette Dr. Detroit, MI 48214
The Ruins	206.285.7846	Seattle, WA
Ruth Meric Catering	713.522.1448	3030 Audley Houston, TX 77098
Sammy's	216.523.5899	Cleveland, OH
Sargeant's Inc.	615.373.9331	Brentwood, TN
Savoy	510.420.6102	3239 Elm St. Oakland, CA 94609
Simply With Style Catering	508.228.6248	63 Summerset Rd. Nantucket, MA 02554
Someone's in the Kitchen	505.986.8077	Route 7, Box 129W Santa Fe, NM 87505
Somerset	310.204.4000	8982 National Blvd. Los Angeles, CA 90034
Sonny Bryan's Smokehouse	214.353.0027	Dallas, TX
South City Kitchen Catering	404.873.7358	1144 Cresent Ave. Atlanta, GA 30309
A Special Event	800.392.2566	536 South Main St. West Bend, WI 53095
Susan Gage Caterer Inc.	301.839.6900	7411 Livingston Rd. Oxon Hill, MD 20745
Susan Holland & Company*	212.807.8892	New York, NY
Susan Mason Inc.	912.233.9737	206 W. Gaston St. Savannah, GA 31401
Taste Catering	415.550.6464	3450 Third St. San Francisco, CA 94124
Taste of Scandinavia	612.482.8876	845 Village Center Dr. North Oaks, MN 55127

Tavola Catering	503.225.9727	625 S.W. 10th Ave. Portland, OR 97205	
Thomas Caterers	317.542.8333	4440 N. Keystone Ave. Indianapolis, IN 46205	
Thomas Preti Caterers	212.764.3188 914.667.2331	Long Island, NY	
Three Tomatoes	303.393.7010	2019 E. Seventeenth Ave. Denver, CO 80206	
Tiger Rose Catering	415.388.3287	15 Madrona Ave. Mill Valley, CA 94941	
Tony's At Home Catering	713.622.6779	4009 Westheimer Houston, TX 77098	
Upper Crust Inc.	502.456.4144	1914 Bardstown Rd. Louisville, KY 40205	
Vivande	415.346.4430	2125 Fillmore St. San Francisco, CA 94115	
Walter Burke Catering Inc.	505.473.9600	P.O. Box 914 Sante Fe, NM 87504	
Wendy Krispin Caterer	214.748.5559	1025 N. Stemmans Ste. 600 Dallas, TX 75207	
Where Dreams Come True	808.943.0196	1814 Poki St. Ste. 302 Honolulu, HI 96822	

CHILDREN'S FASHION

NAME	PHONE	ADDRESS	COMMENTS
Bebé Thompson	212.249.4740	1216 Lexington Ave. New York, NY 10028	
Flowers Down Under	315.685.6285	4521 Jordan Rd. Skaneateles, NY 13153	custom headpieces; by appointment

H.M. Wogglebug	401.751.7787	350 South Main St. Providence, RI 02903	attendants' dresses; by appointment
Jennifer Preddie Designs	212.302.5864	New York, NY	call for local availability
Lisa Shaub	212.675.9701	New York, NY	hand dyed straw millinery; call for local availability
Pegeen	201.442.0799	Ironia, NJ	flower girl, ring bearer fashions; call for local availability
Pinwheels	508.228.1238	7 South Beach St. Nantucket, MA 02554	European children's wear
Sandra Johnson Couture	310.247.8206	138 S. Robertson Blvd. Los Angeles, CA	flower girl dresses; by appointment
Susan Sullivan Design	315.685.8661	Skaneateles, NY	custom work; by appointment
SweePeas	718.680.5766	Brooklyn, NY	custom work; by appointment
Todd Thomas	212.765.7765	New York, NY	custom children's fashion; by appointment
Vivian Nicole	212.760.0121	New York, NY	call for local availability
The Wooden Soldier	800.375.6002	North Conway, NH	catalog

CLEANERS

NAME	PHONE	ADDRESS	COMMENTS
Imperial Gown	800.WED.GOWN		pick-up, delivery, and consultation nationwide
Jeeves of Belgravia	212.570.9130	39 E. 65th St. New York, NY 10021	preservation, restoration

Linens Limited	800.637.6334	240 N. Milwaukee St. Milwaukee, WI 53202	wet cleaning a specialty; minor restoration
Madame Paulette	212.838.6827	1255 2nd Ave. New York, NY 10021	cleaning, restoration, repair work, packed in acid-free box, tissue

CONFECTIONERS

NAME	PHONE	ADDRESS	COMMENTS
Bella Dulce*	212.967.9167	335 W. 38th St. New York, NY 10018	sugar, marzipan keepsakes
Black Hound	212.979.9505 800.344.4417	149 1st Ave. New York, NY 10030	cookies, gifts; mail order available
English Cottage Candies	717.866.4789	631 W. Lincoln Ave. Myerstown, PA 17042	chocolatier, custom shapes
Gloria's Cake and Candy Supplies	310.391.4557	3755 Sawtelle Blvd. Mar Vista, CA 90066	
Godiva Chocolatier	212.984.5900 800.9.GODIVA		on-line service
La Maison du Chocolat	212.744.7117	25 E. 53rd St. New York, NY 10021	chocolates handmade in Paris
Li-Lac Chocolates	212.242.7374	120 Christopher St. New York, NY 10014	handmade chocolates; will ship
Mary's Sweets	214.221.7707	1114 W. Main Lewisville, TX 75067	chocolates, fillings and candymaking supplies
Meadowsweets	800.484.7347 code 4884	Middleburgh, NY	crystallization kits; mail order
Neuhaus Chocolate Shop	214.373.3590	10720 Preston Rd. Ste. 1007 Dallas, TX 75230	imported and handmade chocolates
Richart Design et Chocolates	800.742.4278	7 E. 53rd St. New York, NY 10022	Parisian chocolates, silk screen patterns; mail order

Toraya	212.861.1700	17 E. 71st St. New York, NY 10021	traditional Japanese sweets, tea room; limited shipping

CONSERVATORS & RESTORATION SPECIALISTS

NAME	PHONE	ADDRESS	COMMENTS
Debora Jackson	718.596.9143	82 Schermerhorn St. Brooklyn, NY 11201	custom accessories to match restorations
Gentle Arts	504.895.5628	4500 Dryads St., Ste. B New Orleans, LA 70115	textile and heirloom restoration, antiques only, lace a specialty
Gina Bianco	212.924.1685	New York, NY	textile and costume conservation, gown restorations, custom headpieces; by appointment
Mary Frederickson	806.655.1362	1420 4th Ave., Ste. 22 Canyon, TX 79015	by appointment
Museum Quality Preservation	800.937.2693	9 Laurel Lane Pleasantville, NY 10570	custom conservation, restoration, preservation
Sewtique	860.445.7320	391 Long Hill Rd. Groton, CT 06340	antique fabrics

CONSULTANTS

NAME	PHONE	ADDRESS	COMMENTS
Aloha Enchanted Weddings	808.263.0918	146 Heilili St., Ste. 101 Kailua, HI 96734	
Along Came Mary	213.931.9082	5365 W. Pico Blvd. Los Angeles, CA 90019	

Apples & Oranges Event Planning	707.254.8980	Napa, CA	
Bettina Thompson Stern	202.244.5903	3425 Quebec St. NW Washington, DC 20016	
Bridal Network	415.362.0199	San Francisco, CA	
Celebrations	901.525.5223	Memphis, TN	full-service wedding planners
Colin Cowie Lifestyle	213.462.7183	Los Angeles, CA	by appointment
Connie Kerns	510.339.3370	San Francisco, CA	
Creative Parties	301.654.9292	4933 Auburn Ave. Bethesda, MD 20814	
The Elegant Touch by Ellie	800.575.5509	1193 Kaeleku St. Honolulu, HI 96825	
Event of the Year	212.570.1055	New York, NY	location service
Gai Klass	310.559.6777	10335 W. Jefferson Blvd. Culver City, CA 90232	
Gale Sliger Productions	214.637.5566	1261 Profit Dr. Dallas, TX 75247	
Gary Barvard Event Design	317.687.1920	1205 Park Ave. Indianapolis, IN 46202	party consultant
Gayle Labenow	516.422.0192	Babylon, NY	
Geoff Howell*	212.366.0567	New York, NY	
Jacque Designs	310.859.6424	505 S. Beverly Dr. Beverly Hills, CA 90212	
Kate Edmonds Corporate and Private Events	212.366.4447	New York, NY	
L.A. Celebrations!	213.837.8900	1716 S. Robertson Blvd. Los Angeles, CA 90035	
Lori Draper	406.961.5580	Victor, MT	consultation service

Lynn Schlereth	201.379.5627	Short Hills, NJ	
Marcy Blum Associates*	212.688.3057	251 East 51st St. New York, NY 10022	by appointment
Margo Bouanchaud	504.927.4288	711 Jefferson Hwy., Ste. 2 Baton Rouge, LA 70806	
McCall Associates	415.552.8550	888 Brannan St., Ste. 600 San Francisco, CA 94103	
Michelle Lally	412.731.2028	Pittsburgh, PA	
Monica Hickey	212.666.6721	New York, NY	fashion consultant
Nina Austin*	214.871.3600	Dallas, TX	gown consultant and event planner
Parties, Parties, Parties	415.331.0544	2656 Bridgeway, #202 Sausalito, CA 94965	
Party Concepts	310.820.2255	2218 Canyonback Rd. Los Angeles, CA 90049	
Stanlee Gatti Designs	415.558.8884	1208 Howard St. San Francisco, CA 94103	
Susan Dorenter	201.768.6663	Demarest, NJ	invitation designer and event planner
Tie the Knot	415.968.2564	Mountain View, CA	
Tom Thomas	212.627.9046	New York, NY	event planner and gift specialist
Tricia Windom	912.598.1368	285 Center Dr. Savannah, GA 31406	
Watson & Company*	415.441.5251	San Francisco, CA	
The Wedding Resource	415.626.8147	San Francisco, CA	

DECORATIVE ACCESSORIES

NAME	PHONE	ADDRESS	COMMENTS
All Heart	415.381.8868	32B Miller Ave. Mill Valley, CA 94941	stationery, wrapping paper, frames, crystals
Angéle Parlange Design*	504.895.6511	New Orleans, LA	scripted silk textiles, chairs, table linens, men's accessories
Annie's Treasures	800.872.6888	1388 San Mateo Ave. S. San Francisco, CA 94080	glass votives, fruit baskets
Argentum-The Leopard's Head	415.296.7757	414 Jackson St. San Francisco, CA 94111	antique silver
Art Matters Catalog	800.979.2787	New York, NY	decorative objects by mail
Bennett Bean	908.852.8953	357 Rte. 661 Blairstown, NJ 07825	gilded ceramic bowls; by appointment
Billie Beads	718.372.3954	Brooklyn, NY	millefiore polymer clay objects, ring boxes, hearts
Brian Windsor Art, Antiques, Garden Furnishings*	212.274.0411	272 Lafayette St. New York, NY 10003	antiques, garden furnishings
Brooks Barrel Co.	410.228.0790	Cambridge, MD	natural pine barrels; catalog
The Brown Bag	415.922.0390	2000 Fillmore St. San Francisco, CA 94115	giftwrap, gifts, novelty
Canterbury Woodworks Inc.*	603.796.2258	Boscawen, NH	shaker-style trays, boxes; catalog
Claiborne Gallery*	212.475.3072	452 W. Broadway New York, NY 10012	glassware, furniture; interior design available
Coffin & King*	212.541.9527	New York, NY	gilded decorative objects, custom work; by appointment
Country Originals Inc. & The Design Collection	601.366.4229 800.249.4229	Jackson, MS	home accessories, gifts; catalog

Dan Levy Studio*	212.268.0878	155 E. 29th St., #3N New York, NY 10001	porcelain, earthen-ware; custom design, monogramming available
Daniel Mack Rustic Furnishings	914.986.7293	Warwick, NY	natural form wood furniture; custom design available
David Landis*	212.563.7568	New York, NY	glass candlestick bobeches; call for local availability
De vera	415.558.8865 415.861.8480	334 Gough St. San Francisco, CA 94102 384 Hayes St. San Francisco, CA 94102	home furnishings, Italian blown glass, European antiques
Design via Carioca*	415.642.9321	2123 Bryant St. San Francisco, CA 94110	cast aluminum pots, garden furniture
Ecologia*	908.996.3255	Frenchtown, NJ	sea glass nuggets, frosted bowls, votives, glassware
Elizabeth Meredith	707.763.1532	Petaluma, CA	miniature light strings, parchment cones; call for local availability
Elizabeth Street Gallery	212.644.6969	1176 Second Ave. New York, NY 10021	architectural remnants, garden fixtures, sculpture
Expecting to Fly	415.453.6527	3095 Kerner Blvd. San Rafael, CA 94901	hand-painted dinnerware; custom designs available
Fantastico	415.982.0680	559 Sixth St. San Francisco, CA 94103	dry flowers, gift wrap, wedding invitations
Fillamento	415.931.2224	2185 Fillmore St. San Francisco, CA 94115	home furnishings, accessories
Folly	212.925.5012	13 White St. New York, NY 10013	antique garden accessories, urns, benches
Forget Me Knots	415.921.0838	1738 Union St. San Francisco, CA 94123	bridesmaid wedding favors, accessories
Forrest Jones	415.567.2483	3274 Sacramento St. San Francisco, CA 94115	glassware

The Gardener	510.548.4545	1836 Fourth St. Berkeley, CA 94710	unusual containers, hand-made paper, ceramics
Garden Antiquary	914.737.6054	Cortland Manor, NY	iron, stone sculptures, antique ornaments, fixtures, furnishings; by appointment
Gargoyles	215.629.1700	572 S. Third St. Philadelphia, PA 19147	collectibles and accessories to rent or purchase
Geoff Howell*	212.366.0567	220 W. 19th St. New York, NY 10011	custom decorative objects, illustrations, visuals, events
Gump's	415.982.1616	135 Post St. San Francisco, CA 94108	china, crystal, silver, Asian gifts, stationery
Haas Wood Working, Inc.	415. 421.8273	64 Clementina San Francisco, CA 94105	custom wood-turned curve moldings, Victorian style
Handcraft of South Texas	800.443.1688	Pharr, TX	wire containers; custom design available
Hollyhock	213.931.3400	214 N. Larchmont Blvd. Los Angeles, CA 90004	antique home furnishings, accessories, interior design
Inside Out	310.652.9280	521 N. La Cienega Blvd. Los Angeles, CA 90048	
Kinsman Company	800.733.4146	Point Pleasant, PA	all garden accessories, wire chandelier baskets; catalog
Kiybele Creations	914.273.6659	Armonk, NY	garden accessories; call for local availability
La Maison Moderne*	212.691.9603	144 W. 19 St. New York, NY 10011	decorative objects; registry available
The Loom Company*	212.366.7214	New York, NY	artist representative; by appointment
Marc Musters*	212.713.5781	New York, NY	custom decorative objects, specialists in metal
Michelle Columbine	415.927.8884	415 Corte Madera Town Ctr. Corte Madera, CA 94925	

Monticello Studio	312.527.0559	1533A Merchandise Mart Chicago, IL 60654	reproductions, architectural objects, columns, sconces, boxes
Munder-Skiles	212.717.0150	799 Madison Ave., 3rd Fl. New York, NY 10021	reproduction garden ornaments, furniture; custom work
Naomi's Antiques To Go	415.775.1207	1817 Polk St. San Francisco, CA 94109	American pottery, 1930–1960; registry available
Niedermaier*	212.966.8631 312.266.7077	New York, NY Chicago, IL	gifts; registry available
Pacific Circle Arts	510.540.1233	Berkeley, CA	rattan and grass baskets, Indonesian handicrafts; call for local availability
Pandora's Plasterworks	212.505.7615	New York, NY	plaster cast objects, candlesticks, sconces, ornaments; retail and catalog
Parisé*	212.475.9755	New York, NY	decorative votives, monogrammed linens; call for local availability
Phoenix Imports*	212.608.6670	New York, NY	paper lanterns, sandalwood fans, Oriental imports
Pier 1 Imports	817.878.8000	301 Commerce St. Fort Worth, TX 76102	furniture, kitchen items; call for local availability
Pine St. Papery	415.332.0650	42 Caledonia St. Sausalito, CA 94965	paper goods a specialty
Pullcart	212.727.7089	New York, NY	ceramic studio; by appointment
R. H.	415.346.1460	2506 Sacramento St. San Francisco, CA 94115	garden and home accessories
Rayon Vert *	415.861.3516	3187 16th St. San Francisco, CA 94103	home accessories, linens, furniture, flowers
Rose Tattoo*	305.293.1941	1114 White St. Key West, FL 33040	gold-leafed containers, perfume bottles; custom orders available

R   E   S   O

Room Service*	214.369.7666	4354 Lovers Lane Dallas, TX 75225	home accessories, vintage finds, furniture, design services
Seibert & Rice Fine Italian Terracotta	201.467.8266	Short Hills, NJ	terracotta containers; catalog, will ship
Sue Fisher King	415.922.7276	3067 Sacramento St. San Francisco, CA 94115	ceramics, linens, toiletries; gifts for the house
Sugar and Spice	415.387.1722	3200 Balboa San Francisco, CA 94121	
Summer House	415.383.6695	21 Throckmorton Ave. Mill Valley, CA 94941	candles, jewelry, furniture; gifts for the house
Tail of the Yak*	510.841.9891	2632 Ashby Ave. Berkeley, California 94705	decorative objects, linens, candles, boxes, stationery, vintage jewelry
Treillage	212.535.2288	418 E. 75th St. New York, NY 10021	garden ornaments, weathered furniture, accessories
Turner Martin	415.324.8700	540 Emerson St. Palo Alto, CA 94301	objects for people and their homes
Urban Archaeology	212.431.6969	285 Lafayette St. New York, NY 10012	garden, architectural objects; purchase or rent
Vanderbilt and Co.	707.963.1010	1429 Main St. St. Helena, CA 94574	home accessories, pottery, books, baskets, lamps, French linens, Mediterranean flowers
Where Your Heart Is Designs	503.359.4147	2313 A St. Forest Grove, OR 97116	hand-painted trays, boxes, ribbon work, cards
Wholesale Dried Flowers	415.781.3034	149 Morris St. San Francisco, CA 94107	
Wilkes Home	415.986.4380	375 Sutter St. San Francisco, CA 94108	
Williams-Sonoma	415.362.6904	150 Post St. San Francisco, CA 94108	glassware, flatware, linens; bridal registry available

FABRICS & NOTIONS

NAME	PHONE	ADDRESS	COMMENTS
ABC Carpet & Home*	212.473.3000	888 Broadway New York, NY 10003	slipcovers, tablecloths, decorative accessories
B & J Fabrics, Inc	212.354.8150	New York, NY	chantilly lace, silks a specialty
Bell'occhio	415.864.4048	8 Brady St. San Francisco, CA 94103	
Britex Fabrics	415.392.2910	146 Geary St. San Francisco, CA 94108	vintage buttons
Calico Corners	415.461.0923	340 Bon Air Shopping Ctr. Greenbrae, CA 94901	
Diamond	213.931.8148	611 S. La Brea Ave. Los Angeles, CA 90036	
Fabric Center	508.343.4402	Fitchburg, MA	catalog
Gardner's Ribbons & Lace	817.640.1436	2235 E. Division Arlington, TX 76011	lace, buttons, beads and trims, including vintage
Heaven on La Brea	213.965.8200	Los Angeles, CA	vintage fabrics, trimmings, lace; will ship
Interior Alternatives	302.454.3232	1325 Coochs Bridge Rd. Newark, DE 19713	silk fabrics, sewing materials
International Silks & Woolens	213.653.6453	8347 Beverly Blvd. Los Angeles, CA 90048	
Lacis	510.843.7178	2982 Adeline Berkeley, CA 94703	
M & J Trimming	212.391.9072	1008 Ave. of the Americas New York, NY 10008	notions, custom millinery
Poppy Fabrics	510.655.5151	5151 Broadway Oakland, CA 94611	
Promenade Fabrics	504.522.1488	1520 St. Charles Ave. New Orleans, LA 70130	ribbons, fabrics

Richard Brooks Couture Fabrics	214.739.2772	6131 Luther Lane Dallas, TX 75225	
Roberta Karsch	818.986.2843	13837 Ventura Blvd. Sherman Oaks, CA 91423	
Rose Brand	800.223.1624	New York, NY	theatrical fabrics for draping; call for local availability
Satin Moon Fabrics	415.668.1623	32 Clement San Francisco, CA 94118	
Sheru	212.730.0766	49 W. 38th St. New York, NY 10018	notions, beads a specialty
Silk Surplus	212.753.6511	235 E. 58th St. New York, NY 10022	designer fabrics for slipcovers
Sposabella Lace	212.354.4729	252 W. 40th St. New York, NY 10018	fabrics, custom milllinery, dressmaking
Steinlauf & Stoller	800.637.1637 212.869.0321	234 W. 39th St. New York, NY 10018	threads, sewing notions
Tessuti	212.753.3626	228 W. 39th St. New York, NY 10018	hard-to-find silk tulle
Tinsel Trading Company	212.730.1030	New York, NY	metallics, vintage flowers

FASHION

NAME	PHONE	ADDRESS	COMMENTS
Badgley Mischka	212.921.1585	New York, NY	call for local availability
Chanel	212.688.5055	15 E. 57th St. New York, NY 10022	custom couture
Craig Taylor	800.879.4500	214 Sullivan St. New York, NY 10012	tuxedo shirts for women, ready to wear and custom; by mail

Cynthia Rowley	212.334.1144 312.528.6160	New York, NY Chicago, IL	evening collection, shoes; call for local availability
Debra Morefield	212.226.2647	128 Wooster St. New York, NY 10012	alternative fashion, ready-to-wear and custom
Elizabeth Wayman	212.302.9130	New York, NY	attendants' fashion; call for local availability
525 Made in America	212.921.5688	New York, NY	cotton cashmere, angora, wool sweaters, throws; call for local availability
Galanos	213.272.1445	Los Angeles, CA	call for local availability
George Parkinson	213.933.3348	7372 Beverly Blvd. Los Angeles, CA 90036	contemporary evening wear, alternative bridal
Gucci	800.388.6785 310.278.3451 415.392.2808 214.387.3357	New York, NY Beverly Hills, CA San Francisco, CA Dallas, TX	
Henri Bendel	212.247.1100	712 Fifth Ave. New York, NY 10019	
Issac Mizrahi	800.340.6004	New York, NY	call for local availability
Jacqueline Hope	212.691.4324	New York, NY	call for local availability
Jim Hjelm Occasions	212.764.6960	New York, NY	call for local availability
Kathryn Nixon	212.979.8699	New York, NY	custom dressmaker; by appointment
Les Habitudes	310.273.2883	Los Angeles, CA	contemporary romantic fashions
Liz Claiborne	800.578.7070	New York, NY	attendants' collection; call for local availability
Michael Kors*	212.221.1950	New York, NY	call for local availability
Nicole Miller*	212.288.9779 310.652.1629 415.398.3111 214.630.7300	New York, NY West Hollywood, CA San Francisco, CA Dallas, TX	contemporary attendants' suits, accessories

Norma Kamali	212.957.9797	11 West 56th St. New York, NY 10019	suits, lingerie, accessories
Pamela Dennis	212.354.2100	New York, NY	call for local availability
Philip Shortt & Paul Guzzetta	203.969.7227	200 Henry St. Stamford, CT 06902	custom dress design
Po Couture	212.921.0049	New York, NY	gowns; call for local availability
Richard Tyler	213.624.9299	Los Angeles, CA	custom bridal; by appointment
Robert Danes	212.941.5680	New York, NY	custom bridal; by appointment
Shawn Ray Fons	212.755.5077	New York, NY	custom bridal; by appointment
Suzanne Spellan	718.789.4476	Brooklyn, NY	custom dressmaker; by appointment
Sylvia Heisel	212.719.3916	New York, NY	call for local availability
Timothy Lloyd Pope	212.371.6422	9 W. 57th St. Ste. 4310 New York, NY 10019	fashion consultant; by appointment
Watters & Watters	214.991.6994	Dallas, TX	attendants' gowns; call for local availability

FLORAL DESIGNERS

NAME	PHONE	ADDRESS	COMMENTS
Alexandria May's Topiaries*	212.427.9132	New York, NY	topiaries; by appointment
Alexandra Randall Flowers*	516.862.9291	St. James, NY	herbs, garden flowers a specialty; by appointment
Amaryllis	202.328.8285	Washington, DC	

Andrew Pascoe Flowers	516.922.9561	Oyster Bay, NY	by appointment; will travel
Anthony Ferraz	212.929.2168	New York, NY	wedding and event planner; by appointment
Anthony Garden Boutique Ltd.	212.737.3303	134 E. 70th St. New York, NY 10021	wedding planning
Arrangement	305.576.9922	3841 NE 2nd Ave. Ste. 403 Miami, FL 33137	custom floral design
Ateliér A Work Shop *	214.720.7290	2800 Routh St., Ste. 140 Dallas, TX 75201	custom design
Atlanta Flower Market	770.396.3301	7521 Roswell Rd. Atlanta, GA 30350	
Avant-Gardens	305.554.4300 800.771.7150	9280 SW 40th St. Miami, FL 33165	
Baskets For All Seasons	808.524.0014	147 Huanu St. Honolulu, HI 96813	
Baumgarten Krueger	414.276.2382	225 E. Wisconsin Ave. Milwaukee, WI 53202	
Blong Florists	904.389.7661	4207 St. Johns Ave. Jacksonville, FL 32210	
Bloomers	415.563.3266	2975 Washington Ave. San Francisco, CA 94115	
Blossoms	810.548.7900	2338 Coolidge Berkley, MI 48072	
Blue Meadow Flowers *	212.979.8618	328 E. 11th St. New York, NY 10003	hand-wired bouquets; by appointment
Bomarzo *	415.771.9111	1410 Vallejo St. San Francisco, CA 94109	hand-wired bouquets; by appointment
Botanica	901.274.5767	937 S. Cooper St. Memphis, TN 38103	architectural and naturalistic garden styles
Botanicals on the Park	800.848.7674 314.772.7674	3014 South Grand St. Louis, MO 63118	

R   E   S   O

Bouquets	303.333.5500	1525 Fifteenth St. Denver, CO 80202	
Brady's Floral Design	602.945.8776 800.782.6508	4167 N. Marshall Way Scottsdale, AZ 85251	
Carole Brunet	201.746.4465	Montclair, NJ	foliage, organic materials; by appointment
Castle & Pierpont	212.570.1284	401 E. 76th St. New York, NY 10021	
Charles Radcliff	713.522.9100	1759 Richmond Ave. Houston, TX 77098	
Charleston Florist	803.577.5691	184 King St. Charleston, SC 29407	
Christian Tortu at Takashimaya, NY*	212.350.0100	693 Fifth Ave. New York, NY 10022	unusual combinations, containers
Christopher Bassett*	212.254.0685	New York, NY	organic materials, hand- wired bouquets; by appointment
Christopher Whanger *	214.559.3432	Dallas, TX	country casual style
Claire Marie	415.771.5718	San Francisco, CA	
Claire W. Webber Florals & Events by Design*	800.261.8605 510.261.8606	Oakland, CA	floral and event design; by appointment
Columbine	415.434.3016	1541 Grant St. San Francisco, CA 94133	
The Cottage Garden	404.233.2050	Atlanta, GA	
Country Gardens	216.333.3763	Cleveland, OH	
Covent Gardens	513.232.4422	6209 Corbley Mt. Washington, OH 45230	
Craig Sole Designs	913.649.9929	7928 Conser St. Overland Park, KS 66204	
The Crest of Fine	312.273.2282	417 Fourth St. Wilmette, IL 60091	flowers; by appointment

R C E S

Curtis Godwin	910.484.4547	1404 Raeford Rd. Fayetteville, NC 28305	
Cynthia's Creations	303.699.5938	2727 S. Lewiston St. Aurora, CO 80013	
Cynthia's Floral Designs	800.944.8246 904.398.5824	3915 Hendricks Ave. Jacksonville, FL 32207	
D'Clements	303.399.5543	909 S. Oneida St. Denver, CO 80224	
David Brown Florist	713.521.1191	1208 Fairview Houston, TX 77006	
Delapgar	513.321.2600	3433 Michigan Ave. Cincinnati, OH 45208	
Designs by Jody	847.816.6661	152 Eakre Rd. Lake Bluff, IL 60044	
Devorah Nussenbaum at Verdure *	510.548.7764	Berkeley, CA	herbs a specialty; by appointment
Donald Vanderbrook	216.371.0164	Cleveland, OH	
Elizabeth House	704.342.3919	1431 South Blvd. Charlotte, NC 28203	
Emilia's Flowers	801.943.7301	702 East and 12300 S. Draper Draper, UT 84020	
Enflora	317.634.3434	111 Monument Circle, Ste. 100 Indianapolis, IN 46204	
English Garden	615.352.0094	522 E. Iris Dr. Nashville, TN 37204	
Esprit De Fleur	206.547.7271	Seattle, WA	by appointment
Fioridella	415.775.4065	1920 Polk St. San Francisco, CA 94109	
Florals by Ken & Lisa Gibbons	201.217.0924	Jersey City, NJ	fresh as well as dried bouquets, topiaries, decorative items

R E S O

Floral Supply Syndicate	415.986.5443	670 Brannan St. San Francisco, CA 94107	
Floramor Studio Florist	415.864.0145	569 Seventh St. San Francisco, CA 94103	
Fujikami Florist, Inc.	808.537.9948	1200 Pensacola St. Honolulu, HI 96814	
Flora Nova	503.228.1134	1302 NW Hoyt Portland, OR 97209	
Fiori	612.623.1153	Melrose Flats 17 NE 5th St. Minneapolis, MN 55413	
Florals of Waterford*	201.327.0337	74 E. Allendale Rd. Saddle River, NJ 07458	flowers, fruits, unusual combinations, antique accessories
Florist Grand	808.599.4132	705 S. King St., Ste.100 Honolulu, HI 96813	
The Flower Studio	414.228.9200 414.228.7378	6933 N. Port Washington Rd. Milwaukee, WI 53217	
Flowers on the Square	817.429.2888	311 Main St. Fort Worth, TX 76102	
Foliage Garden	212.989.3089	120 W. 28th St. New York, NY 10001	flowering plants, trees; to buy or rent
Fred Palmer Flowers	505.820.0044	2214 W. Alameda, Box F Santa Fe, NM 87501	
Friendly Flower Gallery	919.596.8747	2208 Halloway Durham, NC 27703	
Garden Center	801.595.6622	678 South 700 East Salt Lake City, UT 84102	
The Garden Gate Creative Design *	800.646.5840 214.220.1272	Dallas, TX	handpainted aisle runners
Glorimundi	212.727.7090	307 Seventh Ave. New York, NY 10001	floral, event design; by appointment
Gary Page Wholesale Flowers	212.741.8928	New York, NY	local and imported flowers, foliage

The Gift Hut	216.777.3688	22086 Lorain Rd. Fairview Park, OH 44126	
Hastings & Hastings	415.381.1272	27 Miller Ave. Mill Valley, CA 94941	
Hepatica	412.241.3900	1119 S. Braddock Ave. Pittsburgh, PA 15218	
Hibiscus	816.891.0808	10010 N. Executive Hills Blvd. Kansas City, MO 64153	
Hilo Airport Flowers	808.935.8275	Hilo, HI	Hawaiian tropical flowers and leis; will ship
Holliday's Flowers, Inc.	901.753.2400	2316 S. Germantown Rd. Germantown, TN 38138	
Incline Florist	800.556.5033 702.831.5043	850 Tanager St. Incline Village, NV 89450	
Indigo V.	415.647.2116	1352 Castro St. San Francisco, CA 94114	by appointment
Jacob Maarse	818.449.0246	655 E. Green St. Pasadena, CA 91101	
Jane Pruitt	912.925.9849	Savannah, GA	
Jennifer Houser	516.725.2667	Sag Harbor, NY	
Joseph Maake Flowers & Decorative Accessories*	516.921.3076	Oyster Bay, NY	fresh and dried flowers
Judith Brandley Florist of Sierra Madre*	818.355.6972	Sierra Madre, CA	by appointment
KLK	415.861.3516	3187 16th St. San Francisco, CA 94103	
Larkspur	612.332.2140	514 N. Third St. Minneapolis, MN 55401	
Larkspur	212.727.0587	39 Eighth Ave. New York, NY 10004	

R   E   S   O

Laurels Custom Florist*	213.655.3466	7964 Melrose Ave. Los Angeles, CA 90046	floral design, event planning
Laurie Stern Floral Art*	510.528.8040	727 Sea View Dr. El Cerrito, CA 94530	Victorian and English country style; by appointment
L. Becker Flowers	212.439.6001	217 East 83rd St. New York, NY 10028	bouquets a specialty
Leslie Palme	718.622.6995	Brooklyn, NY	florals by appointment
Living Creations	801.485.3219	Snowbird, UT	
Loop Flowers	303.750.1717	2773 S. Parker Rd. Aurora, CO 80014	
Magnolias	502.585.4602	1112 S. Brook St. Louisville, KY 40203	
Main Street Floragardens	415.485.2996	P.O. Box 686 San Anselmo, CA	by appointment
Mark Hall of the Renaissance Garden	617.536.6937	Boston, MA	
Marsh Meadows Design	912.925.9849	13214 Whitebluff Rd. Savannah, GA 31419	
Michael Haley Ltd.	904.387.3000	3953 St. Johns Ave. Jacksonville, FL 32205	
Miho Kosuda Ltd.*	212.922.9122	310 E. 44th St. New York, NY 10017	hand-wired bouquets a specialty
Mitch's Flowers	504.899.4843	4843 Magazine St. New Orleans, LA 70115	
Mount Flora	801.649.6910	2519 Creek Park City, UT 84060	
Nanz and Kraft Florist	502.897.6551	141 Breckinridge Ln. Louisville, KY 40207	
Nature's Daughter	908.221.0258	Basking Ridge, NJ	event planning; by appointment

Newberry Brother's Greenhouse & Florist	303.322.0443	201 Garfield St. Denver, CO 80206	
Palmer-Kelly Floral Designs	317.923.9903	5168 N. College Ave. Indianapolis, IN 46205	
Perfect Presentations	504.522.7442	833 Fulton St. New Orleans, LA 70130	
Peter A. Chopin Florist, Inc.	504.891.4455	2800 St. Charles Ave. New Orleans, LA 70115	
Potted Gardens	212.255.4797	23 Bedford St. New York, NY 10013	unusual containers a specialty
Preston Bailey	212.683.0035	New York, NY	
Rayon Vert Extraordinary Flowers*	415.861.3516	3187 16th St. San Francisco, CA 94103	flower designs, decorative accessories
Regalo Flowers	505.983.4900	151 Washington Ave. Santa Fe, NM 87501	
The Renaissance Garden	617.536.6937	Boston, MA	
Robert Bozzini	415.351.2823	San Francisco, CA	by appointment
Ron Wendt Design*	212.290.2428	245 W. 29th St. New York, NY 10001	garden style
Rosewood Florists	803.256.8351	2917 Rosewood Dr. Columbia, SC 29205	
Russell Glenn Floral Design	214.742.3001	2114 Fearrington Dallas, TX 75207	by appointment
Salutations Ink	303.371.2393	5005 Peoria St. Denver, CO 80239	
Silver Birches Custom Design Floristry*	818.796.1431	180 E. California Blvd. Pasadena, CA 91005	
Spring Street Garden	212.966.2015	186½ Spring St. New York, NY 10012	by appointment

Stacey Daniels Flowers*	800.463.7632 914.762.8372	42 Gaunj Dr. Ossining, NY 10562	English garden style; by appointment
Stanlee R. Gatti Designs	415.558.8884	1280 Howard St. San Francisco, CA 94103	full-service event design
Stanley's Garden Works	415.567.6476	San Francisco, CA	by appointment
Suzanne Codi	202.269.4259	111 Quincy Place NE Washington, DC 20002	
Ten Pennies Florist	215.336.3557	1921 S. Broad St. Philadelphia, PA 19148	
TFS*	310.274.8491	616 N. Almont Los Angeles, CA 90069	floral studio, vintage collectibles
Thran's Flowers	702.588.1661	225 Kingsley Grade Stateline, NV 89449	
Tim Condron	412.361.4057	5879 Center Ave. Pittsburgh, PA 15206	
Tommy Luke Florist	503.228.3131	1701 SW Jefferson Portland, OR 97205	
Tommy Thompson	313.665.4222	504 S. Main Ann Arbor, MI 48103	
Trochta's Flowers and Greenhouses	800.232.7307 405.848.3338	6700 N. Broadway Ext. Oklahoma City, OK 73116	
The Tulip Tree	615.352.1466	6025 Highway 100 Nashville, TN 37205	flowers and gifts
Two Design Group*	214.741.3145	Dallas, TX	floral studio, full-service planning
Uptown Flowers	504.899.2923	538 Nashville Ave. New Orleans, LA 70115	
Valorie Hart Designs*	408.720.9506	Sunnyvale, CA	romantic floral designs, full-service planning
Vines	505.820.7770	459 Cerrillos Rd. Sante Fe, NM 87501	

Vollan Blumen Florist	503.236.1713	6663 E. Burnside St. Portland, OR 97215	
VSF*	212.206.7236	New York, NY	full-service planning, sculptural designs
Wayside Garden	812.945.3596	4164 Ross Hollow Rd. New Albany, IN 47150	weddings and large parties a specialty
Wells Flowers	317.872.4267	2160 W. 86th St. Indianapolis, IN 46260	
Whitegate	213.465.1222	562 N. Larchmont Blvd. Los Angeles, CA 90004	
Wildflowers of Louisville	502.584.3412	653 S. Fourth Ave. Louisville, KY 40202	
Winston Florist	617.541.1100	P.O. Box 933 Boston, MA 02117	
Wisteria Design Studio, Ltd.	612.332.0633	275 Market St., Ste. 50 Minneapolis, MN 55405	
The Woods*	310.826.0711	Los Angeles, CA	floral boutique, accessories, gifts; full-service planning
Xylem	412.967.9844	1320 Freeport Rd. Pittsburgh, PA 15238	
Zen Floral Design	214.526.9736	3858 Oak Lawn, Ste. 149 Dallas, TX 75219	
Zezé Flowers*	212.753.7767	New York, NY	

FLORAL SUPPLIES

NAME	PHONE	ADDRESS	COMMENTS
Carolyn Blazier*	404.893.3767	Alpharetta, GA	vintage silk flowers
Central Floral	212.686.7952	40 W. 28th St. New York, NY 10001	tools and supplies

Coast Wholesale Dried Flowers	415.781.3034	149 Morris St. San Francisco, CA 94107	
Coco & Co., Inc.	214.748.1899	2100 Stemmans Freeway Dallas, TX 75207	
Country House	508.475.8463	Andover, MA	catalog
D. Blümchen & Company, Inc.	201.652.5595	162 E. Ridgewood St. Ridgewood, NJ 07450	velvet flowers; catalog
Dorothy Biddle Service	717.226.3239	U.S. Rt. 6 Greeley, PA 18425	catalog
Dulken & Derrick*	212.929.3614	12 W. 21st St. New York, NY 10011	handmade flowers
Everyday Gardener	601.981.0273	2945 Old Canton Rd. Jackson, MS 39216	garden accessories
Fresh Oregon Holly	800.821.0172	St. Helens, OR	fresh cut holly; mail order
G. Wolff Pottery*	203.868.2858	New Preston, CT	hand thrown porcelain, clay; by appointment
Galveston Wreath Company	409.765.8597	Galveston, TX	dried botanicals, berries, flowers, pods
Gardener's Eden	800.822.9600	San Francisco, CA	garden supplies, containers, greenery
Grassroots Garden	212.226.2662	131 Spring St. New York, NY 10012	plants, trees, supplies
Green Valley Growers	707.823.5583	Sebastopol, CA	seasonal flowers, foliage, wreaths
J. Levine Books & Judaica	212.695.6888 800.553.9474	New York, NY	huppahs; catalog
The Marketplace	212.594.8289	245 W. 29th St. New York, NY 10012	rentals
Metalcrafts	703.335.6060	802 Centerville Rd. Manassas, VA 22111	copper containers, metal pails, vases
Moskatel's	213.689.4830	738 S. Wall St. Los Angeles, CA 90014	crafts

Mozayiks	212.219.1160	285 Mott St. New York, NY 10012	mosaic objects, custom huppah poles
New England Garden Ornaments	508.867.4474	North Brookfield, MA	garden structures; catalog
Oak Grove Mills	908.782.9618	Pittstown, NJ	flowering plants
Palecek Basket Co.	800.527.5724	137 World Trade Center 2050 Stemmans Freeway Dallas, TX 75207	to the trade only
Pany	212.645.9526	New York, NY	silk and paper flowers
Paxton Gate	415.255.5955	1204 Stevenson St. San Francisco, CA 94103	garden supplies, landscaping services
Quentin Natural Materials	409.258.5744	Dayton, TX	dried local berries, grasses
Rosedale Nursery	914.769.1300	51 Saw Mill Pkwy. Hawthorne, NY 10532	garden supplies, landscaping services
Smith & Hawken*	800.776.3336		flowering plants, gifts; catalog
Tzin Tzun Tzan*	415.641.0373	1570 Indiana St. San Francisco, CA 94107	decorative folk accessories
Waterford Gardens*	201.327.0721	Saddle River, NJ	water lilies
Wildflowers of Princeton Junction	800.499.4459	Princeton Junction, NJ	dried floral products; catalog

GIFTS

NAME	PHONE	ADDRESS	COMMENTS
American Craft Museum Gift Shop	212.956.6047	New York, NY	artistan crafts, jewelry
Anne-Stuart Hamilton	212.682.6439	New York, NY	custom keepsakes

Baccarat*	212.826.4100	625 Madison Ave. New York, NY 10022	French tableware, crystal pendants
Christie's East	212.570.4830	New York, NY	furnishings, jewelry; auction house
Deborah Schenck	802.295.7916	13 Fox Lane Quechee, VT 05059	framed artwork, decorative objects
Deborah Shapiro*	212.532.2420	New York, NY	custom gifts; by appointment
Dishes Delmar	415.558.8882	P.O. Box 170126 San Francisco, CA 94117	
Felissimo	800.565.6785	10 W. 56th St. New York, NY 10019	flatware and dinnerware
Fillamento	415.931.2224	2185 Fillmore St. San Francisco, CA 94115	
The Gardener	510.548.4545	1836 Fourth St. Berkeley, CA 94710	
Heritage on the Garden	617.426.9500	288 Boylston St. Boston, MA 02116	china, crystal gifts
Ilene Chazanof	212.254.5564	New York, NY	silver accessories; by appointment
Macy's/Union Square	415.397.3333	170 O'Farrell San Francisco, CA 94115	
Mottaheda	212.685.3050	New York, NY	majolica tableware; call for local availability
Museum of Modern Art Gift Shop	800.447.MOMA	New York, NY	artist-designed gifts; catalog
Mxyplyzyk	212.989.4300	New York, NY	specialty gifts, objects
Nat Sherman	800.221.1690	New York, NY	handmade cigars; catalog
Restoration Hardware	415.924.8919	1700 Redwood Hwy. Corte Madera, CA 94925	
Smith and Hawken	415.381.1800	35 Corte Madera Ave. Mill Valley, CA 94941	

Stimuli	212.477.1476	New York, NY	desktop objects, men's accessories
Stoneworks*	800.STONE.61	Tuxedo, NJ	custom engraved stone
Sue Fisher King	415. 922.7276	3075 Sacramento St. San Francisco, CA 94115	
Surprise Packages	800.334.1428 610.277.2300	Bridgeport, PA	gift boxes
Tiffany & Co.	415. 781.7000	350 Post St. San Francisco, CA 94108	
Translations	214.373.8391	4014 Villanova Dallas, TX 75225	dinnerware, glassware and flatware
Tudor Rose Antiques*	212.677.5239	New York, NY	silver accessories, frames, vanity sets
Uncommon Market Inc.	214.871.2775	2701 Fairmount Dallas, TX 75201	antiques, acccessories, lighting
Unlimited Ltd. The Antique Mall	214.490.4085	15201 Midway Dallas, TX 75244	
Vanderbilt and Co.	707. 963.1010	1429 Main St. St. Helena, CA 94574	by appointment
Vertu	214.520.7817	4514 Travis Rd., Ste. 124 Dallas, TX 75205	china and flatware; registry
Williams-Sonoma	415.362.6904	150 Post St. San Francisco, CA 94108	tableware

INFORMATION SOURCES

NAME	PHONE	ADDRESS	COMMENTS
American Rental Association	800.334.2177		national referral service, party rental brochures
Association for Bridal Consultants	203.355.0164	New Milford, CT	membership referral agency; call for local consultant

Cultured Pearl Information Center*	212.688.5580	New York, NY	care, purchase tips; call for brochures
Diamond Information Center	212.210.8169	New York, NY	care, purchase tips; call for brochures
Flower Council of Holland	516.621.3625	Glenwood Landing, NY	information service; call for local availability
The Fragrance Foundation*		145 E. 32nd St. New York, NY 10016	write for brochures
G.I.A. Trade Laboratory	800.421.7250	New York, NY	gemologists; appraisals
International Formalwear Association	312.644.6610 ext. 338	Chicago, IL	local formalwear referrals; call for brochure
National Limousine Association	800.NLA.7007		referral service; call for local service
Neighborhood Cleaners Association	212.967.3002	New York, NY	referral service; call for local cleaning specialist
Second Harvest National Foodbank Network	312.263.2303	Chicago, IL	national list of foodbank distribution
Silver Trust International*	212.689.4737	295 Madison Ave. New York, NY 10017	write for flatware brochures
Society for Calligraphy	213.931.6146	Los Angeles, CA	call for referrals or instruction
Teleflora*	310.826.5253	12233 W. Olympic Blvd. Ste. 118 Los Angeles, CA 90064	call for local availability
Washington Calligraphers Guild	301.897.8637	Merrifield, VA	call for referrals
World Gold Council	212.688.0005	New York, NY	call for brochure

JEWELRY

NAME	PHONE	ADDRESS	COMMENTS
Agatha, Paris	212.758.4301	611 E. 58th St. New York, NY 10022	costume jewelry, faux pearls
Amy Faust	415.642.0620	664 B 29th St. San Francisco, CA 94131	custom silver jewelry
Angela Cummings Boutique*	212.872.8874	954 Fifth Ave. New York, NY 10019	South Sea pearls, wedding bands
Antique Timepieces and Jewelry	415.454.4807	574 San Anselmo Ave. San Anselmo, CA 94960	
Barneys New York*	310.276.4400	9570 Wilshire Blvd. Beverly Hills, CA 90212	
Beads of Paradise	212.620.0642	16 E. 17th St. New York, NY 10010	ethnic beads, gifts
Brenda Schoenfeld*	214.368.4007	8319 Preston Center Plaza Dallas, TX 75225	silversmith, wedding bands
Bulgari	415.399.9141	340 Stockton St. San Francisco, CA 94108	
Camilla Dietz Bergeron*	212.794.9100	New York, NY	estate jewelry; by appointment
Carol Shufro	212.865.9335	New York, NY	wedding bands, earrings, necklaces
Cartier*	212.753.0111 415.397.3180 310.275.4272	New York, NY San Francisco, CA Beverly Hills, CA	jewelry, stationery; registry
Cathy's Antiques & Estate Jewelry	214.871.3737	500 Crescent Court Ste. 140 Dallas, TX 75201	
Christie's East	212.606.0460	New York, NY	auction house: estate jewelry
Collective Antiques	415.621.3800	212 Utah St. San Francisco, CA 94103	

David Clay Jewelers	415.922.4339	1872 Union St. San Francisco, CA 94123	platinum, custom work
Day Lone-Wolf	508.544.8620	77 N. Main St. Orange, MA 01364	Native American designs, custom wedding bands
Dianne's Old and New Estates	415.346.7525	2181 Union St. San Francisco, CA 94123	
Dina Varano	203.526.8866	27 Main St. Chester, CT 06412	custom sterling silver
Dogtown	510.653.1566	Oakland, CA	etched sterling wedding bands; call for local availability
Dumont	310.289.9500	8661 Sunset Blvd. W. Hollywood, CA 90038	vintage, estate jewelry, watches, gifts
Elizabeth Rand*	212.754.1227	New York, NY	gold wedding bands, organic influences
Ezmaralda Gordon*	310.552.1731	Beverly Hills, CA	fine custom jewelry; call for local availability
Fragments	212.334.9588	107 Greene St. New York, NY 10012	costume and fine jewelry, bridal accessories
Gloria Natale*	212.769.4740	New York, NY	handmade wedding bands; by appointment
Haltom's Jewelers	817.336.4051	317 Main St. Ft. Worth, TX 76102	custom work available
Jenny Lessard*	212.966.7010	New York, NY	ancient inspirations; call for local availability
Ken Riney Antiques & Estate Jewelry	214.871.3640	500 Crescent Court, Ste. 154 Dallas, TX 75201	
Kieselstein Cord	212.764.6140	New York, NY	fine jeweley; call for local availability
Lang	415.982.2213	323 Sutter St. San Francisco, CA 94108	antique and estate
Laura Morton Design	310.289.1166	Los Angeles, CA	silver and minerals; bridal collection

Lisa Jenks Limited*	212.777.8708	New York, NY	call for local availability
Lowell Lundeen Jewelry	612.338.8030	430 First Ave. North Minneapolis, MN 55401	custom contemporary jewelry
Lydia's Jewelry	415.398.8288	107 Geary St. San Francisco, CA 94108	
Mansoor Gore	415.327.5667	530 Ramona Palo Alto, CA 94301	custom and antique
Marcia Lorberfeld*	212.354.7507	New York, NY	sterling bands; call for local availability
Mary Vera	214.661.3686	Dallas, TX	antique jewelry dealer
Matthew Trent Inc.	214.871.9170	2530 Cedar Springs Dallas, TX 75201	custom available
Meryl Waitz*	212.675.7224	New York, NY	jewelry, gifts; call for local availability
Mignon Faget, Ltd.*	504.865.1107	New Orleans, LA	sterling wedding bands; call for local availability
Mikimoto*	212.664.1800 800.431.4305	New York, NY San Francisco, CA	cultured pearls
Miriam Haskell	212.764.3332	New York, NY	pearl, crystal, heirloom designs
Mish Jewelry*	212.734.3500	New York, NY	costume and vermeil jewelry
Nancy & Risë*	212.391.1484	New York, NY	sterling cufflinks; call for local availability
Neiman Marcus	415.362.3900	150 Stockton St. San Francisco, CA 94108	
Paris 1925	415.567.1925	1954 Union St. San Francisco, CA 94123	
Patience Morgan Jewelry	914.942.2182	Stony Point, NY	custom jewelry; by appointment
Pave	310.458.3492	1128 Montana Ave. Santa Monica, CA 90403	

Reinstein/Ross	212.226.4513	122 Prince St. New York, NY 10012	ancient motifs; call for local availability
Saity Jewelry	212.308.6570	725 Fifth Ave. New York, NY 10022	Native American jewelry, turquoise, coral, jade
Sidney Mobell	415.986.4747	950 Mason St. San Francisco, CA 94108	
Something Old, Something New	201.224.9224	Edgewater, NJ	wedding bands, posy rings
St. Eligius	415.771.2282	1748 Union St. San Francisco, CA 94123	
Stephen Dweck*	212.764.3030	21 W.38th St. New York, NY 10018	vermeil bands, home accessories
Steven Raspa*	718.746.3871	Malba, NY	salvaged car glass jewelry
Susan Cummins Gallery	415.383.1512	12 Miller Ave. Mill Valley, CA 94941	
Tail of the Yak*	510.841.9891	2632 Ashby Ave. Berkeley, CA 94705	
Tara Peck Designs	908.879.8383	15 Ammerman Way Chester, NJ 07930	silver and gold; custom work
Temple St. Clair Carr*	212.219.8664	New York, NY	gold, platinum bands; call for local availability
Tiffany & Co.*	212.755.8000 310.273.8880 415.781.7000 214.458.2800	New York, NY Beverly Hills, CA San Francisco, CA Dallas, TX	jewelry, stationery; registry
Tribalinks	602.623.8654	267 S. Stone Ave. Tucson, AZ 85701	gold and silver bands
The 23rd St. Custom Jewelry Shoppe	310.828.0833	2319 Wilshire Blvd. Santa Monica, CA 90404	
Union Street Goldsmith	415.776.8048	1909 Union St. San Francisco, CA 94108	
Van Cleef & Arpels*	212.644.9500 310.276.1161	New York, NY Beverly Hills, CA	platinum and diamonds

| Wells-Ware | 212.222.9177 | New York, NY | bracelets, necklaces, custom mementos |

LINENS

NAME	PHONE	ADDRESS	COMMENTS
Alphapuck Designs	212.267.2561	New York, NY	slipcovers, tablecloths; custom work
Angéle Parlange*	504.897.6511	5419 Magazine St. New Orleans, LA 70115	fine linens, decorative accessories; registry
Anichini	802.889.9430	Rt. 110 Turnbridge, VT 05077	fine linens; call for local availability
Ann Gish*	805.498.4447	Newbury Park, CA	fine linens, silks, custom work; call for local availability
Ballroom Elegance	305.477.0477	7830 NW 57th St. Miami, FL 33166	rentals only
Carla Weisburg*	212.620.5276	New York, NY	custom textile design, table linens, pillows
Covered Affairs	516.623.9012	Freeport, NY	custom table linens, rentals; call for local availability
Current	206.622.2433	1201 Western Seattle, WA 98101	linens; registry
Demi Adeniran-Fabrica*	212.587.6340	360 Broadway New York, NY 10013	custom work
Feathers Theatre	412.621.4700	5520 Walnut St. Pittsburgh, PA 15232	linens; registry
Fischer Textiles	619.299.0772	San Diego, CA	table linens; call for local availability
Françoise Nunnalle	212.246.4281	New York, NY	antique linens; by appointment

R   E   S   O

Judi Boisson American Country*	516.283.5466	Southampton, NY	handmade quilts, furnishings
Kate Morrison*	212.740.6024	200 Pinehurst Ave. New York, NY 10033	custom table linens
Kimberly Soles*	718.857.0904	137 7th Ave. Brooklyn, NY 11215	hand-painted linens, men's accessories
The Linen Gallery	214.522.6700	7001 Preston Rd. Dallas, TX 75205	
Linens et al	310.652.7970	165 N. Robertson Blvd. Beverly Hills, CA 90211	
Mark Rossi*	212.924.0522	668 Greenwich St. New York, NY 10014	custom work; catalog
MUIH Inc.*	212.366.4740	220 W. 19th St. New York, NY 10011	custom work
Nancy Angel of Angel Threads*	212.673.4592	New York, NY	slipcovers, huppahs; rentals available
Peacock Alley	214.520.6736	3210 Armstrong Dallas, TX 75205	
Room with a View	310.453.7009	1600 Montana Ave. Santa Monica, CA 90403	
Shaxted	310.273.4320	350 N. Camden Dr. Beverly Hills, CA 90210	
Slips*	415.362.5652	1534 Grant St. San Francisco, CA 94133	custom fabrications, slipcovers
Susan Parrish	212.645.5020	390 Bleecker St. New York, NY 10014	antique quilts, folk crafts
Trouvaille Française*	212.737.6015	New York, NY	antique linens

R C E S

LINGERIE

NAME	PHONE	ADDRESS	COMMENTS
Aricie Lingerie De Marque	415.989.0261	50 Post St. Crocker Galleria San Francisco, CA 94108	
Arlotta*	212.779.0711	New York, NY	foundations; call for local availability
Bettina	415.563.8002	3654 Sacramento St. San Francisco, CA 94118	
Bravo Bras	800.55.BRAVO	7200 France Ave. South, #331 Edina, MN 55435	
Enchantê	312.951.7290	Chicago, IL	lingerie and accessories
Fernando Sanchez	212.989.9166	New York, NY	evening wear; call for local availability
Jezebel	800.537.3235	New York, NY	bustiers; call for local availability
La Perla*	212.570.0050 212.644.4188	New York, NY	silk foundations; call for local availability
Lily	310.724.5757	9044 Burton Way Beverly Hills, CA 90211	
Milltex*	212.779.4366	New York, NY	Poupie Cadolle corsets; call for local availability
Neiman Marcus	310.550.5900	9700 Wilshire Blvd. Beverly Hills, CA 90212	
Pantages	206.528.1922	2655 NE University Village Seattle, WA 98105	
Patricia Gourlay	203.869.0977	45 East Putnam Rd. Greenwich, CT 06830	
Sheers The Bodywear Bar	214.528.7292	4266 Oak Lawn Dallas, TX 75219	
Silk, Satin and Lace	415.435.1237	13 Main St. Tiburon, CA 94920	

RESO

Sue Ekahn/ New York*	212.929.4432	New York, NY	custom couture lingerie; call for local availability
Sydney Bush*	212.563.8023	New York, NY	traditional bridal petticoats; call for local availability
Toujours	415.346.3988	2484 Sacramento St. San Francisco, CA 94118	
Victoria's Secret	800.888.1500	New York, NY	retail stores and catalog
Village Corset Shop	212.463.0365	New York, NY	bustiers, lingerie; custom fittings

LOCATIONS

NAME	PHONE	ADDRESS	COMMENTS
Adamson House	310.457.8185	23200 Pacific Coast Hwy. Malibu, CA 90265	
Alden Yacht Charters	401.683.1782 800.662.2628	Portsmouth, RI	yachts to charter; full service planning
Allen House	810.642.2817	556 W. Maple Rd. Birmingham, MI 48009	historic home and gardens
The America Society	212.249.8950	New York, NY	landmark residence
American Carousel Museum	415.928.0550	633 Beach St. San Francisco, CA 94109	
The American Club at Kohler	414.451.2107	Highland Dr. Kohler, WI 53044	
The Ancient Monastery Spanish	305.945.1462	16711 W. Dixie Hwy. N. Miami Beach, FL 33160	12th-century gothic monastery
Angel Island State Park	415.435.5390	P.O. Box 318 Tiburon, CA 94920	
Arboretum of Los Angeles Country	818.821.3211	301 N. Baldwin Ave. Arcadia, CA 91006	

Archbishop's Mansion	415.563.7872	San Francisco, CA	historic hotel; wedding planning services
Arizona Biltmore	602.954.2540	24th & Missouri Ave. Phoenix, AZ 85016	landmark hotel
Atlanta Botanical Gardens	404.876.5859	P.O. Box 77246 Atlanta, GA 30357	
Auberge du Soleil	707.963.4658	Rutherford, CA	
Avon Old Farms School	860.673.3201	500 Old Farms Rd. Avon, CT 06001	Tudor-style campus, pavillon, stately halls
Balclutha	415.929.0202	San Francisco Maritime National Historic Park Hyde St. Pier San Francisco, CA 94133	historic sailing ship
Bandoilier National Park	505.672.0343	Santa Fe, NM	
Beck Chapel	812.855.7425	University Chancellor's Office Owen Hall, Rm. 100 Indiana University Bloomington, IN 47405	
The Bellevue Hotel	800.221.0833 215.893.1776	1415 Chancellor Ct. Philadelphia, PA 19102	
The Beverly Hills Hotel*	310.276.2251	9641 Sunset Blvd. Beverly Hills, CA 90210	ballrooms and bungalows
The Biltmore Estate	800.408.4405	1 North Pack Square Ashville, SC 28801	historic mansion
The Biltmore Hotel	305.445.1926	1200 Anastasia Ave. Coral Gables, FL 33134	
Bishop's Lodge	505.983.6377	Bishop's Lodge Rd. Sante Fe, NM 87504	mountain chapel and inn
The Blantyre	413.637.3556	Blantyre Rd. Lenox, MA 01240	country estate
Boettcher Mansion on Lookout Mountain	303.526.0855	900 Colorow Rd. Golden, CO 80401	historic mansion

Bonaventura Balloon Co.	800.FLY.NAPA 707.944.2822	133 Wall Rd. Napa, CA 94558	
Boone County Courthouse	317.482.3510	103 Courthouse Square Lebanon, IN 46052	historic courthouse
The Boucvalt House	504.528.9771	1025 St. Louis St. New Orleans, LA 70118	historic French Quarter home
The Breakers	407.655.6611	1 S. County Rd. Palm Beach, FL 33480	ballrooms and suites
Camberly Brown Hotel	502.583.1234	335 West Broadway Louisville, KY 40202	
The Captain Whidbey Inn	360.678.4097	2072 W. Captain Whidbey Inn Rd. Coupeville, WA 98239	coastline inn
Carnegie Museums of Pittsburgh	412.622.3360	4400 Forbes Ave. Pittsburgh, PA 15213	
Castle Hill	508.356.4351	290 Argilla Rd. Ipswich, MA 01938	historic manor
Central Park Conservancy*	212.360.2766	New York, NY	formal gardens, terraces
Century Inn	412.945.6600	Scenery Hill, PA	historic inn and formal gardens
Chalkers	415.512.0450	101 Spear St. 1 Rincon Center San Francisco, CA 94105	
Charles Town Landing	803.852.4200	1500 Old Towne Rd. Charleston, SC 29407	
The Charlotte Inn	508.627.4151	27 South Summer St. Edgartown, MA 02539	
Chateau Marmont	213.656.1010 800.242.8328	8221 Sunset Blvd. Los Angeles, CA 90046	
Cheekwood Botanical Gardens	615.353.2148	1200 Forrest Park Dr. Nashville, TN 37205	
Chicago Cultural Center	312.744.6630	78 E. Washington St. Chicago, IL 60602	

R   C   E   S

Cincinnatian Hotel	513.381.3000	601 Vine St Cincinnati, OH 45202	landmark hotel
City Club	415.362.2480	155 Sansome St. San Francisco, CA 94111	historic club
Claussen's Inn	803.765.0440 800.622.3382	2003 Greene St. Columbia, SC 29205	
The Cleveland Ritz-Carlton	216.623.1300	1515 W. 3rd St. Cleveland, OH 44113	
Cleveland Zoo	216.661.6500	Cleveland, OH	scenic rain forest
Coco Loco	202.289.2626	810 7th St. NW Washington, DC 20001	
Dallas Arboretum & Botanical Garden	214.327.8263	Dallas, TX	
Deer Valley	801.649.1000	Park City, UT	mountain location
Delano Hotel	800.555.5001	1685 Collins Ave. Miami Beach, FL 33139	modern Art Deco hotel; full-service event planning
Demenil Restaurant	314.771.5829	3352 Demenil Place St. Louis, MO 63118	historic mansion and carriage house
Denver Design Center	303.733.2455	595 S. Broadway Denver, CO 80209	
Disney World	407.828.4872	Orlando, FL	full-service planning
The Dunhill Hotel	800.354.4141 704.332.4141	237 N. Tryon St. Charlotte, NC 28202	historic hotel
Dunsmuir House and Gardens	510.562.0328	2960 Peralta Oaks Court Oakland, CA 94604	
East Brother Light Station*	510.233.2385	Richmond, CA	lighthouse station on a private island
Edgewood Terrace Restaurant	702.588.2787	Lake Tahoe, NV	
Elizabeth Park	203.722.6490	Hartford, CT	historic municipal park, walled secret garden

Emporio Armani Express Restaurant	415.677.9010	1 Grant Ave. San Francisco, CA 94108	
Epping Forest Yacht Club	904.739.7200	1830 Epping Forest Dr. Jacksonville, FL 32217	Mediterranean mansion
Eulipions Center	303.295.6814	1770 Sherman St. Denver, CO 80203	Moorish-style ballroom
The Eureka	415.929.0202	Hyde St. Pier San Francisco, CA 94133	permanently docked historic steamboat
EveryMay On-The-Delaware	610.294.9100	Erwinna, PA	country inn and gardens
The Fairmont Hotel	415.772.5293	950 Mason St. San Francisco, CA 94109	
Fairwinds Estate	415.326.7797	Menlo Park, CA	lakefront estate, cruises available
The Fearrington House	919.542.2121	2000 Fearrington Village Center Fearrington Village, NC 27312	historic inn
Five Star Charters	415.332.0306	85 Liberty Ship Way Ste. 112 Sausalito, CA 94965	private charters
The Fogg Museum at Harvard	617.495.0350	32 Quincy St. Cambridge, MA 02138	
The Four Seasons Hotel*	617.338.4400 310.273.2222 206.621.1700 215.963.1500 415.929.2301	Boston, MA Los Angeles, CA Seattle, WA Philadelphia, PA San Francisco, CA	
The Fox Theatre	314.534.1111	527 N. Grand Blvd. St. Louis, MO 63103	
Freemark Abbey	707.963.9694	St. Helena, CA	old-world winery
The Fulton Lane Inn	803.720.2600	202 King St. Charleston, SC 29401	
The Gamble Mansion	617.267.4430 ext. 707	5 Commonwealth Ave. Boston, MA 02116	historic home

R C E S

Gardencourt	502.895.3411	c/o Louisville Seminary 1044 Alta Vista Rd. Louisville, KY 40205	19th-century estate
The Georgian Suite	212.734.1468	3 E. 77th St. New York, NY 10021	
The Georgian Terrace	404.897.1991	659 Peachtree St. Atlanta, GA 30308	ballroom
Gingsberg Collection Showroom	415.621.6060	190 San Bruno Ave. San Francisco, CA 94103	
Green Gables	415.952.1110	Woodside, CA	private estate
Greystone Mansion	310.550.4654	905 Loma Vista Dr. Beverly Hills, CA 90210	
Grant-Humphreys Mansion	303.894.2506	770 Pennsylvania St. Denver, CO 80203	historic home, mountain views
Haas-Lilienthal House*	415.441.5251	San Francisco, CA	historic Victorian home
Halcyon House	202.338.3295	3400 Prospect St. NW Washington, DC 20007	Georgetown mansion
Halekulani	808.923.2311	2199 Kalia Rd. Honolulu, HI 96815	beachfront views
Hall of State	214.421.4500	Dallas, TX	
Hamlin Mansion	415.331.0544	2120 Broadway San Francisco, CA 94115	historic mansion
Harbor View Hotel	508.627.4333	Edgartown, MA	
Hawaiian Chieftain	415.331.3214	San Francisco, CA	18th-century square- rig sail boat
The Heathman	503.241.4100	1001 SW Broadway at Salmon Portland, OR 97205	historic hotel
Heritage House	707.937.5885	5200 N. Hwy. 1 Little River, CA 95456	coastal farmhouse inn

Hidden Valley Castle	203.254.7914	Cornwall, CT	turreted stone chateau, honeymoon cottage
Hornblower Yachts	310.301.6000	13755 Fiji Way Marina del Rey, CA 90292	
Hotel Bel Air	310.472.1211	701 Stone Canyon Rd. Los Angeles, CA 90077	
Hotel Boulderado	303.442.4344	2115 E. 13th St. Boulder, CO 80302	landmark hotel
Hotel del Coronado*	619.435.6611	Coronado, CA	
The Hotel du Pont	302.594.3122	11th & Market St. Wilmington, DE 19801	ballroom and suites
Hotel St. Germain*	214.871.2516	2516 Maple Ave. Dallas, TX 75201	old world inn
Hyatt Regency Scottsdale at Gainey Ranch	602.991.3388	7500 E. Doubletree Ranch Rd. Scottsdale, AZ 85258	
Il Cielo	310.276.9990	9018 Burton Way Beverly Hills, CA 90048	
Indiana Roof Ballroom	317.236.1874	140 W. Washington St. Indianapolis, IN 46204	
Indianapolis Museum of Art	317.923.1331	1200 W. 38th St. Indianapolis, IN 46208	formal garden, river views
Inn of the Anasazi	505.988.3030	113 Washington Ave. Santa Fe, NM 87501	Pueblo-style inn
Inn at Castle Hill	401.849.3800	590 Ocean Dr. Newport, RI 02840	waterfront inn
Inn at Cedar Falls	614.385.7489	21190 St. Rt.374 Logan, OH 43138	log house, converted barn, and gardens
The Inn at Harvard	617.491.2222	1201 Massachusetts Ave. Cambridge, MA 02138	
Inn at Little Washington	540.675.3800	Washington, VA	

Inn at Perry Cabin	410.745.2200	308 Watkins Lane St. Michael's, MD 21663	Chesapeake bayfront inn and gardens
Inn at Weathersfield	802.263.9217	Rt. 106 Weathersfield, VT 05151	Colonial inn
The James Breaky Manor	313.584.5570	125 N. Huron Ypsilanti, MI 48197	historic home, gardens
James Burden Mansion*	212.722.4745	New York, NY	historic home
James Leary Flood Mansion*	415.563.2900	2222 Broadway San Francisco, CA 94115	historic home with bay views
The John Rutledge House	803.723.7999	116 Broad St. Charleston, SC 29401	historic home with a ballroom
The Junior League	713.622.4191	Houston, TX	private location
King's Courtyard Inn	800.723.7000	198 King St. Charleston, SC 29401	walled gardens
Kualoa Ranch	808.237.8515	Kaaawa, HI	tropical gardens
Lake Forest Academy	708.234.3210	1500 W. Kennedy Rd. Lake Forest, IL 60045	historic estate
The Landmark Center	612.292.3225	75 W. 5th St. St. Paul, MN 55102	
Lark Creek Inn	415.924.7766	234 Magnolia Ave. Larkspar, CA 94939	
Le Meridian of Boston	617.451.1900	250 Franklin St. Boston, MA 02110	
The Legion of Honor	415.263.0229	100 34th Ave. San Francisco, CA 94121	elegant museum café and sculpture garden
Lincoln Park Zoo	312.742.2000	2200 N. Cannon Dr. Chicago. IL 60614	historic city park
Locust Grove	502.897.9845	561 Blankenbaker Lane Louisville, KY 40207	18th-century estate and formal gardens
The Lodge at Ponte Vedra Beach	904.273.9500	607 Ponte Vedra Blvd. Ponte Vedra, FL 32082	beach ceremonies and receptions

R E S O

Longview Mansion	816.761.6696	3361 SW Longview Rd. Lee's Summit, MO 64063	historic landmark
Lyford House	415.388.0717	376 Greenwood Beach Rd. Tiburon, CA 94920	
The Lyman Estate	617.893.7232	185 Lyman St. Waltham, MA 02154	historic mansion and gardens
Magnolia Plantation	601.832.8400	16391 Robinson Rd. Gulfport, MS 39503-4817	riverside mansion and gardens
Maison de Ville Hotel	504.528.9206	727 Toulouse St. New Orleans, LA 70130	French Quarter location
Malmaison	314.458.0131	St. Albans, MO	French country inn
Manhattan Penthouse	212.627.8838	80 5th Ave. New York, NY 10011	midtown views
Mansury Mansion	516.878.8862	Center Moriches, NY	historic ballroom
Meadowood Resort	707.963.3646 800.458.8080	900 Meadowood Lane St. Helena, CA 94574	
Memorial Hall	215.685.0122	Fairmount Park Properties West Park Philadelphia, PA 19131	ballroom
Meridian House	202.667.6670	1630 Crescent Place NW Washington, DC 20009	historic mansion, formal gardens
Milwaukee Grain Exchange	414.272.6230	Mackie Building 225 E. Michigan St., Ste. 110 Milwaukee, WI 53202	restored landmark
The Mint Museum	704.337.2000	2730 Randolph Rd. Charlotte, NC 28207	
Miss Pearl's Jam House	415.775.5267	601 Eddy St. San Francisco, CA 94107	
Mission Basilica San Diego del Alcala*	619.281.8449	San Diego, CA	original mission gardens
Mission Inn	909.784.0300	3649 Mission Inn Ave. Riverside, CA 92501	

Missouri Botanical Garden	314.577.5100	4344 Shaw Blvd. St. Louis, MO 63110	
Morton H. Meyerson Symphony Center	214.670.3600	Dallas, TX	
Murat Theatre	317.231.0000	520 N. New Jersey St. Indianapolis, IN 46206	
Myriad Botanical Gardens	405.297.3995	301 W. Reno Ave. Oklahoma City, OK 73102	
Napa Valley Wine Train	707. 253.2111 800. 427.4124	1275 McKinstry St. Napa, CA 94559	
National Building Museum	202.272.2448	401 F St. NW Washington, DC 20001	
The National Cowboy Hall of Fame and Western Heritage Association	405.478.2250	1700 NE 63rd St. Oklahoma City, OK 73111	
The New York Palace Hotel	212.888.7000	455 Madison Ave. New York, NY 10011	ballrooms
Noerenberg Gardens	612.559.6700	2840 N. Shore Dr. Wayzata, MN 55391	lakefront gardens, boathouse
Oak Alley Plantation	504.265.2151	3645 Hwy. 18 Vasherie, LA 70090	historic mansion
Old City Park*	214.421.5141	Dallas, TX	historic village and chapel
Old Federal Reserve Bank Building	415.772.0537	301 Battery St. San Francisco, CA 94111	
Opryland Hotel	615.889.1000	2800 Opryland Dr. Nashville, TN 37205	indoor gardens
Otto Kahn Mansion*	212.722.4747	1 E. 91st St. New York, NY 10028	historic residence
The Pavilion of the Two Sisters	504.488.2896	1 Palm Dr. New Orleans, LA 70124	formal gardens

R   E   S   O

The Peabody Hotel	901.529.4000	149 Union Ave. Memphis, TN 38103	
Petaluma Queen Riverboat	800.750.7501 707.762.2100	255 Weller St. Petaluma, CA 94952	
The Pfister Hotel	414.273.8222	424 E. Wisconsin Ave. Milwaukee, WI 53202	landmark hotel
Philipsburg Manor	914.631.8200	N. Broadway North Tarrytown, NY 10591	working 18th-century farm
Phipps Conservatory	412.622.6915	1 Shendley Park Pittsburgh, PA 15213	formal gardens
Phipps Mansion	303.777.4441	3400 Belcaro Dr. Denver, CO 80209	Georgian mansion
Phipps Tennis Pavilion	303.777.4441	3300 Belcaro Dr. Denver, CO 80209	
The Phoenician	602.941.8200	6000 E. Camelback Rd. Scottsdale, AZ 85251	cactus garden
The Pierre Hotel*	212.838.8000	2 E. 61st St. New York, NY 10021	
Pittsburgh Center for the Arts	412.361.0873	6300 5th Ave. Pittsburgh, PA 15232	
Pittsburgh's Grand Hall at the Priory	412.231.3338	614 Pressley St. Pittsburgh, PA 15212	European-style inn
The Plaza Hotel	212.546.5485	768 5th Ave. New York, NY 10019	ballrooms and terraced suites
The Point	800.255.3530 518.891.5674	HCR #1 Box 65 Saranac Lake, NY 12983	rustic lakefront inn
The Polo Fields Country Club	313.998.3456	5200 Polo Fields Dr. Ann Arbor, MI 48103	
Potomac Boat Club	202.333.9737	3530 Water St. NW Washington, DC 20007	
Powell Gardens	816.697.2600	U.S. Highway 50 Kingsville, MO 64061	botanical gardens and landmark chapel

R C E S

Powell Symphony Hall	314.533.2500 314.286.4148	718 N. Grand Blvd. St. Louis, MO 63103	
The Pratt Mansions*	212.717.1130	New York, NY	historic residence
Prospect Hill	800.277.0844	Trevilians, VA	historic plantation
The Puck Building	212.274.8900	295 Lafayette St. New York, NY 10012	ballrooms
The Radisson Plaza Hotel	810.827.4000	1500 Town Center Southfield, MI 48075	
Rainbow Room	212.632.5045	New York, NY	
Ralph Schnell House	317.925.4600	3050 N. Meridian St. Indianapolis, IN 56208	
El Rancho De Las Golondrinas	505.471.2261	Santa Fe, NM	historic village
The Randall Davey Audubon Center	505.983.4609	P.O. Box 9314 Santa Fe, NM 87504	historic estate
Red Buttle Garden and Arboretum	801.585.5225	18A de Trobriand St. Salt Lake City, UT 84113	
Rembrandt's Restaurant	816.436.8700	2820 NW Barry Rd. Kansas City, MO 64154	rose garden
Renaissance Inn	317.635.9123	1340 N. Alabama St. Indianapolis, IN 46202	historic home and gardens
Rex Hill Vineyard	503.538.0666	North Hwy. 99W Newberg, OR 97132	
Rittenhouse Hotel	800.635.1042 215.546.9000	210 W. Rittenhouse Square Philadelphia, PA 19103	
The Ritz-Carlton	314.863.6300	100 Carondelet Plaza Clayton, MO 63105	
The Ritz-Carlton Philadelphia	800.241.3333 215.563.1600	17th and Chestnut St. at Liberty Pl. Philadelphia, PA 19103	

River Oaks Garden	713.523.2483	2503 Westheimer Rd. Houston, TX 77098	banquet hall and gardens
The Riverplace Hotel	503.228.3233	1510 SW Harbor Way Portland, OR 97201	
Royal Hawaiian Hotel	800.325.3535 808.922.9567	2259 Kalakaua Ave. Honolulu, HI 96815	
Rock and Roll Hall of Fame	216.781.7625	1 Key Plaza Cleveland, OH 44114	
The Ruins	206.285.7846	Roy St. Seattle, WA 98109	interior garden
St. Albans Studio	314.458.5356	St. Albans, MO	stone residence
St. Louis Art Museum	314.721.0072	Forest Park St. Louis, MO 63110	
St. Louis Zoo	314.768.5411	Forest Park St. Louis, MO 63110	lakeside pavilion
St. Michael's Seafood	410.745.3737	3505 Mulberry St. St. Michael's, MD 21663	
St. Paulus Church and Social Hall	415.673.8088	950 Gough St. San Francisco, CA 94102	
Saddle Peak Lodge	818.222.3888	419 Cold Canyon Rd. Calabasas, CA 91302	
Saddlerock Ranch	818.706.0888	31727 Mulholland Hwy. Malibu, CA 90265	working ranch
Saguaro Lake Ranch Resort	602.984.2194	13020 Bush Hwy. Mesa, AZ 85215	
San Ysidro Ranch	805.969.5046	900 San Ysidro Lane Santa Barbara, CA 93108	barn, bungalows, and formal garden
Seelbach Hotel	502.585.3200	500 4th Ave. Louisville, KY 40202	
Seven Gables Inn	314.863.8400	26 N. Meramec Clayton, MO 63105	

R   C   E   S

Sherry Mills Winery	313.668.4817	Ann Arbor, MI	
Shutters on the Beach	310.458.0030	1 Pico Blvd. Santa Monica, CA 90405	
Sir Francis Drake Hotel	415.392.7755	450 Powell St. San Francisco, CA 94102	
Skansonia Ferryboat	206.545.9109	N. Northlake Way Seattle, WA 98103	dry-docked lakeside ferry
Smash Box Studio	310.558.7660	Culver City, CA	photography studios
Snowbird Ski and Summer Resort	801.742.2222	Snowbird, UT	
The Stanhope Hotel*	212.288.5800	995 5th Ave. New York, NY 10028	
Stemson Green Mansion	206.624.0474	1204 Minor Seattle, WA 98101	
Sterling Vineyards	707.942.3300 707.942.3359	Calistoga, CA	
Stern Grove Trocadero Club House	415.666.7035	19th Ave. and Sloat Blvd. San Francisco, CA 94116	
Stone Manor	310.457.6285	Malibu, CA	ocean-view estate, formal gardens
Stow Princess Acres Country Club	508.568.8690	58 Randall Rd. Stow, MA 01775	
Strathmore Art Center	301.530.5889	10701 Rockville Pike N. Bethesda, MD 20852	former estate
Studio 450	212.290.1400	450 W. 31st St. New York, NY 10001	loft with outdoor terraces
Sundance Resort	801.225.4107	R.R. 3, Box A-1 Sundance, UT 84604	
Swedenborgian Church*	415.346.6466	San Francisco, CA	Mission-style chapel, walled garden

Tanque Verde Ranch	602.296.6275	Tucson, AZ	
Tega Cay Country Club	803.548.3500	Old Molokai Dr. P.O. Drawer 39 Tega Cay, SC 29715	
Temple Emanu-El	415.751.2535	2 Lake St. San Francisco, CA 94115	open-air courtyard
Tesuque Verde	505.988.4168	50 E. San Francisco St. Santa Fe, NM 87501	estate and public sculpture garden
Thistle Hill	817.336.1212	1509 Pennsylvania Ave. Fort Worth, TX 76104	historic home
Thomas Bennett House	803.720.1203	Charleston, SC	historic home and gardens
Thomas Fogarty Winery and Vineyards	415.851.1946	14501 Skyline Blvd. Portola Valley, CA 94025	
Union Station	213.625.5865	800 N. Alameda St. Los Angeles, CA 90012	
Union Station Hotel	615.726.1001	1001 Broadway Nashville, TN 37203	
Victoria House Inn	803.720.2944 800.933.5464	208 King St. Charleston, SC 29401	
Villa Montalvo	408.741.3421	15400 Montalvo Rd. Saratoga, CA 95070	
Vizcaya Museum	305.250.9133	3251 S. Miami Ave. Miami, FL 33125	
The Waterford Hotel	800.992.2009 405.848.4782	6300 Waterford Blvd. Oklahoma City, OK 73118	
The Weisman Art Museum	612.625.9494	333 E. River Rd. Minneapolis, MN 55455	
Westerfield House	618.539.5643	8059 Jefferson Rd. Freeburg, IL 62243	rustic home and gardens

The Western Forrestry Conservatory	503.228.1367 ext. 101	4033 SW Canyon Rd. Portland, OR 97221	
Whitehall	502.897.2944	3110 Lexington Rd. Louisville, KY 40206	historic estate
Willow Ridge	303.697.6951	4903 Willow Springs Rd. Morrison, CO 80465	historic mansion
Willow West Country Club	713.437.8217	14502 Fondren Rd. Missouri City, TX 77489	
Windsor Court Hotel	504.523.6000	300 Gravier St. New Orleans, LA 70130	
Woodlawn at Audubon Society	301.652.9188	8940 Jones Mill Rd. Chevy Chase, MD 20815	historic mansion and gardens
Woodruff-Fontaine House	901.525.1469	Memphis, TN	historic mansion
Wrigley Mansion Club	602.955.4079	2501 E. Telewa Trail Phoenix, AZ 85016	

MEN'S FORMALWEAR & ACCESSORIES

NAME	PHONE	ADDRESS	COMMENTS
Alan Flusser CustomShop at Saks Fifth Ave.	212.888.7100	611 Fifth Ave., 6th fl. New York, NY 10022	made-to-measure
Alfred Dunhill	310.274.5351	201 N. Rodeo Dr. Beverly Hills, CA 90210	
Aquascutum of London	415.392.5633	340 Post St. San Francisco, CA 94104	
Ascot Chang	212.759.3333 301.550.1339	New York, NY Beverly Hills, CA	custom dress shirts; by appointment

R   E   S   O

A.T. Harris Formalwear	212.682.6325	11 E. 44th St. New York, NY 10017	
Berk of Burlington Arcade*	212.570.0285	New York, NY	men's accessories; catalog available
Black Tie	415.346.9743	Van Ness at Post San Francisco, CA 94109	
Black and White Formal Wear	415.673.0626	1233 Sutter St. San Francisco, CA 94108	
Brooks Brothers	212.682.8800 214.960.6200 415.397.4500	New York, NY Dallas, TX San Francisco, CA	catalog available
Button Down	415.563.1311	3640 Sacramento St. San Francisco, CA 94118	
Carrott & Gibbs*	303.449.2821	Boulder, CO	silk bow ties, how-to-tie brochure; call for local availability
Cole-Haan*	212.765.9747 800.488.2000	New York, NY	shoe salon; call for local availability
Culwell & Son	214.522.7000	6319 Hillcrest Dallas, TX 75205	sales and rental
David Glazer	212.691.5100	New York, NY	formal accessories; call for local availability
Gene Meyer*	212.980.0110	New York, NY	silk ties; call for local availability
Gianfranco Ferre	310.273.6311 407.659.1071 202.244.6633	Beverly Hills, CA Palm Beach, FL Washington, DC	
Gianni Versace For Men	415.956.7957	50 Post St. San Francisco, CA 94104	
Gitman	800.526.3929	New York, NY	dress shirts; call for local availability
Ike Behar*	212.315.2626	New York, NY	dress shirts; call for local availability
Lord West*	800.275.9684	Woodside, NY	rental; call for local availability

Louis, Boston	800.225.5135	Boston, MA	formalwear, suitings made to order
Paul Smith*	212.627.9770	108 Fifth Ave. New York, NY 10011	
Polo/Ralph Lauren	212.606.2100 310.281.7200 214.522.5270 415.567.7656	New York, NY Beverly Hills, CA Dallas, TX San Francisco, CA	
Presidents Tuxedo	415.989.7642	170 Sutter St. San Francisco, CA 94108	
Saks Fifth Ave. West	310.275.4211	9634 Wilshire Blvd. Beverly Hills, CA 90212	
Selix	415.362.1133	123 Kearny St. San Francisco, CA 94108	
Sulka	212.980.5200 415.989.0600 310.859.9940	New York, NY San Francisco, CA Beverly Hills, CA	accessories; catalog available
Terrence Teng	212.772.1519	New York, NY	silk vests; custom design available
Tuxedo Center	213.874.4200	7360 Sunset Blvd. Hollywood, CA 90046	
The Tuxedo Shop	415.433.5353	Three Embarcadero San Francisco, CA 94111	
Valentino	212.772.6969 310.247.0103	New York, NY Beverly Hills, CA	
Vogel Bootmakers	212.925.2460	19 Howard St. New York, NY 10013	custom shoemakers; by appointment
Wilkes Bashford Company	415.986.4380	375 Sutter St. San Francisco, CA 94108	
Worth & Worth	212.867.6058	331 Madison Ave. New York, NY 10017	collapsible silk top hats, fur felt bowlers

R   E   S   O

MILLINERY & BRIDAL VEILS

NAME	PHONE	ADDRESS	COMMENTS
Amy Downs	212.598.4189	New York, NY	custom design available
Bell'occhio	415.864.4048	8 Brady St. San Francisco, CA 94103	
Bruni Nigh	415.346.3299	2384 Union St. San Francisco, CA 94123	custom design; by appointment
Burke Ladden Gallery	212.786.9550	401 Lafayette St., 5th Fl. New York, NY 10003	vintage fabrications; custom design available
Chapeaux Carine	212.777.8393	125½ E. 17th St. New York, NY 10003	custom design; by appointment
Challoner, NYC*	212.274.1437	New York, NY	headpieces, gloves, handbags; by appointment
Concord Merchandise Corporation	212.840.2720	New York, NY	hat boxes, horsehair veiling, millinery notions
Coup de Chapeaux	415.931.7793	San Francisco, CA	custom design, vintage, millinery restoration
Emma Carlow*	011.44.171.704.0594	London, England	millinery available at Sandra Johnson Couture, Los Angeles
Estee Einstein-One in a Milliner	212.677.2350	184 Second Ave. New York, NY 10003	by appointment
Jessica McClintock	310.273.9690	9517 Wilshire Blvd. Beverly Hills, CA 90210	
Joan Gilbert Bridal Collection	415.752.2456	San Francisco, CA	by appointment
Lafee	213.874.8328	154 S. Larchmont Blvd. Los Angeles, CA 90004	
Lisa Shaub	212.675.9701	615 Hudson St. New York, NY 10014	custom millinery, veils; by appointment

Lola Millinery*	212.366.5708	2 E. 17th St. New York, NY 10003	custom available; by appointment
Manny's Millinery Supply*	212.840.2235	26 W. 38th St. New York, NY 10018	hat boxes, petticoats, notions, veiling; sewing available
Marina Killery Couture Hats Inc*	212.639.9277	214 E. 78th St. New York, NY 10028	custom straw hats; by appointment
Milliners Supply Company	214.742.8284	911 Elm St. Dallas, TX 75202	supplies only
Paris Hats & Veils*	513.948.8888	8910 Reading Rd. Cincinnati, OH 45215	custom crowns and veils
Patricia Underwood	212.268.3774	New York, NY	straws, felts, furs; call for local availability
Staccato	415.381.1746	30 Miller Ave. Mill Valley, CA 94941	
Tia Mazza	212.989.4349	New York, NY	crowns and veils; call for local availability
Zazu & Violets*	510.845.1409	1790 Shattuck Ave. Berkeley, CA 94709	made-to-measure straw hats

MUSIC

NAME	PHONE	ADDRESS	COMMENTS
Baguette Quartet	510.528.3723	San Francisco, CA	
Curtis Music & Entertainment*	908.352.3131	Elizabeth, NJ	string, brass, woodwind ensembles, orchestras and chamber groups
Dick Bright Orchestra	415.826.3425	San Francisco, CA	Craig Sherwood musical director, 3–20 pieces, 1940s–1970s
Eclypse	302.322.1076	Wilmington, DE	jazz ensemble
El Mariachi	215.567.6060	Philadelphia, PA	traditional mariachi

R   E   S   O

Festival Brass	214.328.9330	Dallas, TX	classical musicians all brass instruments
The Full Tilt Band	415.924.0340	San Francisco, CA	
Greg Ball, "White Heat" Orchestra	617.951.7213	Boston, MA	1930's style jazz
Hank Lane Orchestra*	212.767.0600	New York, NY	orchestras, vocals, swing, rock, standards
Janet King	516.671.4519	Long Island, NY	classical harpist; demonstration tape available
Jeff Robbins	214.414.2645	Dallas, TX	jazz trios to contemporary quartets
Ladies Choice String Quartet	310.652.6180	1500 S. Holt Ave. Los Angeles, CA 90035	
La Musica String Ensemble	214.363.6422	5933 Borgundy Rd. Dallas, TX 75230	solo, duo, trio, or quartet
Lester Lanin	212.265.5208	New York, NY	orchestras, vocals swing, rock, standards
Majestic Brass	516.472.5363	Holbrook, NY	classic trumpeters, fanfares
Marcom Savoy and the Hurricanes	415.331.3539	San Francisco, CA	
Paul Lindemeyer Trio	914.693.9055	Ardsley-on-Hudson, NY	classic jazz, vocals; sextext available
Preferred Artists	800.477.8558	Ridgefield, CT	artist representative: swing, motown, R & B
Richard Connick Group	718.545.9638	New York, NY	jazz standards
Sam Kimball Sounds	212.465.9114	New York, NY	full service music broker, house band, reggae, rock, swing, chamber, D.J.
Sterling String Quartet & Sterling Music Ensembles	212.481.7697	New York, NY	classic ensembles, harp, flute, classical guitar, violin

Sterling Trio Flute, Violin and Cello	510.524.2569	San Francisco, CA	
Swing Fever	415.459.2428	San Francisco, CA	
Top Hatters	510.632.5320	855 MacArthur Blvd. San Leandro, CA 94577	
Trinidad International Steelband	415.346.4646	San Francisco, CA	
Willow Productions	617.421.9336	13 Haviland St. Boston, MA 02115	full-service entertainment agency

PARTY RENTALS

NAME	PHONE	ADDRESS	COMMENTS
Abbey Party Rentals	214.350.5373	2525 W. Mockingbird Lane Dallas, TX 75235	also offer tent rentals
Cannonball Party Rentals	214.387.8900	4515 McEwen Dallas, TX 75244	also offer tent rentals
Ducky Bob's Party Rentals Inc.	214.702.8000	14500 Beltwood Pkwy. East Dallas, TX 75244	also offer tent rentals
Fox Tent & Awning Co.	313.665.9126	617 South Ashley St. Ann Arbor, MI 48104	
Frost Lighting	708.729.8200	1880 W. Fullerton St. Northbrook, IL 60614	full-service lighting, special effects
J.G. Willis, Inc.	617.527.0037	Boston, MA	tent rentals
Party Rental Ltd.*	212.517.8750 201.517.8750 301.984.0963	New York, NY Teterboro, NJ Washington, DC	full-service rentals
Partytime Rentals	317.844.5178	1212 S. Range Line Rd. Carmel, IN 46032	

Partytime Tents & Canopies	201.948.2426	Branchvill, NJ	
Peterson Party Center	617.729.4000	Boston, MA	full-service rentals
Resource One	818.343.3451	6925 Canby Ave. Reseda, CA 91335	
Stortz Lighting	212.219.2330	70 Laight St., 1st fl. New York, NY 10021	full-service lighting, special effects
Watts Up!	213.655.5278	8115½ Melrose Ave. Los Angeles, CA 90046	

PHOTOGRAPHY & VIDEOGRAPHY

NAME	PHONE	ADDRESS	COMMENTS
Alex Berliner	213.857.1282	314 N. Brea Ave. Los Angeles, CA 90036	
Babboni's Creative Imaging	414.328.3211	8306 W. Lincoln Ave. West Allis, WI 53219	
Bachrach Photographs	617.536.4730	647 Boylston St. Boston, MA 02116	formal portraits
Bachrach Studio	212.755.6233	New York, NY	formal portraits
Beverly Hall Photography	508.228.2147	Nantucket, MA	also black and white
Bresner Studios	215.546.7277	6729 Castor Ave. Philadelphia, PA 19149	
Cary Hazelgrove Photography	503.228.3783	Nantucket, MA	also black and white
Cheryl Klauss	212.431.3568	New York, NY	

Chris Hartlove	410.426.2829	Washington, DC	photojournalistic style
Christine Rodin	212.242.3260	New York, NY	by appointment
Cilento	414.964.6161	1409 E. Capital Dr. Milwaukee, WI 53217	
Denis Reggie	404.873.8080	75 14th St. NE, Ste. 2120 Atlanta, GA 30309	available in New York and Los Angeles
Evan Kafka	718.349.6987	106 Jackson St. Brooklyn, NY 11211	also black and white
Eyezone Photographics	214.943.6520	Dallas, TX	also black and white
Fred Marcus Photography*	212.873.5588	New York, NY	formal portraits, videography
Grevy Photography	504.522.9825	7433 Maple St. New Orleans, LA 70118	portraits
Hal Slifer	800.234.7755 617.787.7910	Boston, MA	videography
Heirloom Restoration	203.795.0565	New Haven, CT	photographic restoration; appraisal by mail
Hilary N. Bullock Photography	612.338.7516	529 S. 7th St., Ste. 555 Minneapolis, MN 55415	
Jack Caputo	310.273.6181	493 S. Robertson Blvd. Beverly Hills, CA 90211	
James French Photography	214.368.0990	8411 Preston Ave., Ste. 118 Dallas, TX 75225	by appointment
Jamie Bosworth Photography	503.246.5378	8635 SW 9th St. Portland, OR 97219	
Jenny Bissell	216.247.7988	Cleveland, OH	
John Derryberry & Associates	214.357.5457	5757 W. Lovers Lane Ste. 310 Dallas, TX 75209	also black and white; by appointment
John Dolan	212.426.2598	New York, NY	also black and white

John Tilley Photography	214.358.4747	Dallas, TX	also portraits
John Wolfsohn	310.859.9266	9904 Durant Dr. Beverly Hills, CA 90212	
Joyce Wilson	317.786.1769	Indianapolis, IN	also portraits
Julie Skarratt	212.877.2604	New York, NY	also handmade albums
Kaish.Dahl	310.724.7282	9400 Santa Monica Blvd. Beverly Hills, CA 90210	
Keith Trumbo*	212.580.7104	221 W. 78th St. New York, NY 10024	also black and white
Leah Campbell	612.339.9049	510 1st Ave North, Ste. 708 Minneapolis, MN 55403	
Longshots	504.282.3559	1505 Gardena Dr. New Orleans, LA 70122	
Maureen Edwards De Fries	203.740.9343	Brookfield, CT	portraits, custom albums
Mike Posey Photography and Video	504.488.8000	3524 Canal St. New Orleans, LA 70119	also videography
Nelson Hume	212.222.7424	New York, NY	videogaphy and editing services
Phil Kramer Photography	215.928.9189	30 S. Bank St. Philadelphia, PA 19106	
Rob Fraser	212.677.4589	New York, NY	also portraits
Robert Friedel	212.477.3452	New York, NY	also black and white
Robert George	314.771.6622	1933 Edwards Ave. St. Louis, MO 63110	also black and white
Robin Sachs Photography	214.824.0624	Dallas, TX	portraits only, also black and white
Ross Whitaker/ Terry de Roy Gruber Photographers*	212.749.2840	New York, NY	videography also black and white

Sengbush Photography	214.363.3264	6611 Snyder Plaza, Ste. 109 Dallas, TX 75205	
Stephen Photography	502.244.3753	205 South Madison Ave. Louisville, KY 40243	
Susan Bloch	516.549.0203	Huntington, NY	also black and white
Tanya Malott Lawson*	212.677.2540	New York, NY	also black and white
Valerie Shaff	212.475.2819	New York, NY	portraits, sepia and black and white
Wendi Schneider	303.322.2246	Denver, CO	portraits, polaroid transfers, hand painted images
Zalewa Designer Images	800.836.7688 812.951.3259 502.451.0307	9700 State Rd. 64 Georgetown, IN 47122	

PROVISIONS

NAME	PHONE	ADDRESS	COMMENTS
Aristoff Caviar and Fine Foods	310.271.0576 212.581.7118 800.332.7478	West Hollywood, CA New York, NY	caviar, patés, mustards, oils; mail order
Black Hound	212.979.9505 800.344.4417	149 First Ave. New York, NY 10030	fine cookies, gifts; mail order
Browne Trading Company	207.766.2402	260 Commercial St. Portland, ME 04101	caviar; mail order
CMC Company	800.262.2780	Avalon, NJ	ethnic foodstuffs; mail order
Cook Inspired	800.693.3342	Rhinbeck, NY	sweet tarts; mail order; brochure available
Dean & DeLuca	212.431.1691 800.221.7714	560 Broadway New York, NY 10012	mail order; catering available

Dufour Pastry Kitchens	212.929.2800	New York, NY	handmade frozen puff pastry, hors d'oeuvres, empanadas, tart shells
Elia and Jules Esposito's Porchetta	215.271.8418	1627 S. 10th St. Philadelphia, PA 19148	Italian specialties some mail order
Feastivities	817.377.3011	5724 Lock Ave. Fort Worth, TX 76107	gourmet foods and fresh caviar
Honeybaked Ham	800.892.HAMS	Toledo, OH	hams, smoked turkeys, salmon, condiments, pies; mail order, catalog
Malibu Farms	213.278.9750	S. San Pedro, CA	edible pansies; mail order
Marty's	214.526.4070	3316 Oakland Ave. Dallas, TX 75219	fresh caviar
JP Shellfish Company	207.439.6018	Elliot, ME	lobsters, oysters,
Petrossian Boutique	212.245.2217	182 W. 58th St. New York, NY 10019	caviar, provisions; mail order

RIBBONS

NAME	PHONE	ADDRESS	COMMENTS
A Touch of Ivy	609.252.1191	Princeton, NJ	cotton ribbons; call for local availability
Bell'occhio*	415.864.4048	8 Brady St. San Francisco, CA 94103	antique ribbons, silk flowers, wrappings, gifts
Brimar Inc.*	708.272.9585	Northbrook, IL	metallic cording, tassels; call for local availability
C.M. Offray & Son, Inc.*	212.213.4285	New York, NY	call for local availability
Cinderella	212.840.0644	60 W. 38th St. New York, NY 10018	ribbons, trimmings, silk flowers; catalog

Gardener's Ribbons & Lace	817.640.1436	2235 E. Division Arlington, TX 76011	vintage and one-of-a-kind ribbons
Hyman Hendler*	212.840.8393	67 W. 38th St. New York, NY 10018	unique ribbons
Impressions/ Just Accents*	212.481.6127	New York, NY	wired silk organza ribbons; call for local availability
International Silks & Woolens	213.653.6453	8347 Beverly Blvd. Los Angeles, CA 90048	
Karyn Sanders Sweet Material Things*	914.895.2519	Wallkill, NY	ribbonwork, accessories; mail order
Kel-toy	510.645.4885	San Francisco, CA	craft paper ribbons, raffia, papers; catalog; call for local availability
Leslie DeFranesco	718.624.1706	Brooklyn, NY	flat ribbonwork creations; by appointment
Loose Ends	503.390.7457	Salem, OR	braids, ribbons, paper flowers; catalog
Margaret Wolfe	310.322.1397	Los Angeles, CA	hand-dyed ribbons, Victorian ribbonwork
Midori Inc.*	206.282.3595	Seattle, WA	organza, silk ribbons; call for local availability
Moskatel's	213.689.4830	738 S. Wall St. Los Angeles, CA 90014	
Paulette C. Knight	800.642.8900 415.626.6184	San Francisco, CA	wired, silk ribbons; call for local availability
Renaissance Buttons	312.883.9508	826 Armitage Ave. Chicago, IL 60614	Victorian trimmings, buttons
The Ribbonry	419.872.0073	119 Louisiana Ave. Perrysburg, OH 43551	ribbons, kits, books, accessories
Tender Buttons*	212.758.7004 312.337.7033	New York, NY Chicago, IL	

V V Rouleaux	011.44.171.730.3125	London, England	ribbon, trimmings, braids; mail order
Vaban Gille Inc.*	800.VABAN.06 404.523.3465	Atlanta, GA	imported silk, wired ribbons; call for local availability

S H O E S

NAME	PHONE	ADDRESS	COMMENTS
Amy Jo Gladstone	718.899.8010	Long Island City, NY	boudoir slippers, silk shoes; custom work
Bruno Magli	212.752.7900	677 5th Ave. New York, NY 10022	
Capezio Dance Theatre Shop	212.245.2130	1650 Broadway New York, NY 10019	ballet slippers; catalog
Christin Loboutin*	212.737.3333	30 E. 67th St. New York, NY 10021	call for local availability
Diego Della Valle	800.4.JP.TODS	New York, NY	
Dolly Duz	407.368.7288	2200 Glades Plaza Boca Raton, FL 33431	
Dyeables	800.431.2000	Patterson, NY	dyable shoes, handbags; catalog; call for local availability
Giordano's	212.688.7195	1150 2nd Ave. New York, NY 10021	size 4-6 only; catalog
Helene Arpels	212.755.1623	470 Park Ave. New York, NY 10021	shoes, evening slippers, accessories
Kenneth Cole*	800.KEN.COLE 212.675.2550	New York, NY	catalog available
Kitty's Antiques and Collectibles	214.416.5160	Dallas, TX	old lace-ups

Manolo Blahnik	212.582.3007	15 W. 55th St. New York, NY 10019	call for local availability
Neiman Marcus	310.550.5900	9700 Wilshire Blvd. Beverly Hills, CA 90212	
Patrick Cox	212.759.3910	702 Madison Ave. New York, NY 10021	call for local availability
Peter Fox Shoes*	212.431.7426 213.393.9669	New York, NY Santa Monica, CA	catalog available
Robert Clergerie	212.207.8600 310.276.8907	New York, NY Los Angeles, CA	call for local availability
Sigerson and Morrison	212.219.3893	242 Mott St. New York, NY 10012	
Stuart Weitzman	212.750.2555	625 Madison Ave. New York, NY 10022	hard to find sizes
Susan Bennis Warren Edwards	212.755.4197	12 W. 57th St. New York, NY 10019	call for local availability
Vanessa Noel*	212.333.7882	12 W. 57th St., Ste. 901 New York, NY 10019	call for local availability
Walter Steiger	212.688.5050	New York, NY	call for local availability

STATIONERY

NAME	PHONE	ADDRESS	COMMENTS
Arak Kanofsky Studios*	201.792.3458	111 First St. Jersey City, NJ 07302	custom invitations, favors, printmaking studio
The Beverley Collection	904.387.2625	4217 Chippewa Dr. Jacksonville, FL 32210	engraved invitations
Blue Marmalade*	612.927.8774	Minneapolis, MN	computer-generated calligraphy, whimsical invitations

BOHO Designs	415.441.1617	San Francisco, CA	custom invitations
Campbell Stationers & Engravers	214.692.8380	8318 Preston Center Dallas, TX 75225	
Cartier*	212.753.0111 415.397.3180 310.275.4272	New York, NY San Francisco, CA Beverly Hills, CA	engraved stationery, jewelry; bridal registry
Claudia Laub Studio*	213.931.1710 800.221.3728	Los Angeles, CA	letterpress, custom design; catalog
Crane & Co. Papermakers	617.247.2822	Prudential Center 800 Boylston St. Boston, MA 02199	calligraphy available
Crane & Company*	800.IS.CRANE	Dalton, MA	call for local availability; publishes *Crane's Blue Book* (invitation etiquette)
Creative Intelligence	213.936.9009	Los Angeles, CA	custom invitations, table accessories, packaging
Custom Card Bar	714.854.3690	4255 Campus Dr. Irvine, CA 97215	gifts, presentations
Ellen Weldon*	212.925.4483	273 Church St. New York, NY 10013	engraving, printing, calligraphy
Embrey Papers	310.440.2620	11965 San Vincente Blvd. Los Angeles, CA 90049	
Empire Stamp & Seal	212.679.5370	New York, NY	blind embosses, custom rubber stamps
I.H.M. Systems*	516.589.5600	710 Johnson Ave. Bohemia, NY 11716	full service printer, engraving, embossing
J & M Martinez Graphique de France	800.444.1464	9 State St. Woburn, MA 01801	letterpress stationery, journals; call for local availability
Jam Paper	212.255.4593	611 Ave. of the Americas New York, NY 10011	card, paper stock, envelopes
Judith Winslow	609.683.1584	116 Patton Ave. Princeton, NJ 08540	stationery, paper, product design

Just Robin	310.273.9736	9171 Wilshire Blvd. Beverly Hills, CA 90210	
Kate's Paperie*	212.941.9816	561 Broadway New York, NY 10012	custom invitations, ribbons, albums, gifts
Maria Thomas*	508.234.6843	27 Prospect St. Whitinsville, MA 01581	custom invitations, calligraphy, programs, scrolls, place cards
Menash Signatures	212.595.6161 800.PEN.SHOP	New York, NY	fine writing instruments, accessories, catalog
Mrs. John L. Strong*	212.838.3848	699 Madison Ave. New York, NY 10021	custom engraving
100th Monkey Productions*	818.398.3132	Pasadena, CA	preprinted stationery, polaroid transfer images
Paper Access*	212.924.7318	23 W. 18th St. New York, NY 10011	papers, embossing supplies; catalog
The Paper Garden	210.494.9602	San Antonio, TX	stationery, rubber stamps
Paper Place	512.451.6531	4001 N. Lamar Austin, TX 78756	stationery, fine papers
Paper Routes	214.828.9494	404 Exposition Dallas, TX 75226	handmade papers
Printemps	203.226.6869	18 Avery Pl. Westport, CT 06880	custom stationers
The Printery*	516.922.3250	43 W. Main St. Oyster Bay, NY 11771	hand-letterpress stationery, custom invitations, ephemera
Prometheus*	714.240.1052	Capistrano Beach, CA	glass pens, Italian inks, albums, papers; call for local availability
Prose and Letters*	408.293.1852	San Jose, CA	custom stationery, calligraphy; by appointment
PS The Letter	817.731.2032	5122 Camp Bowie Blvd. Ft. Worth, TX 76107	
Purgatory Pie Press*	212.274.8228	19 Hudson St. #403 New York, NY 10013	hand letterpress, custom stationery; by appointment

Ruffles & Flourishes	509.627.5906	Richland, WA	blind embossing, molded paper stationery; call for local availability
Scriptura	504.897.1555	5423 Magazine St. New Orleans, LA 70115	
Silberman-Brown Stationers	206.292.9404	1322 5th Ave. Seattle, WA 98101	invitations
SoHo Service*	212.925.7575	69 Greene St. New York, NY 10012	custom stationery, printing, graphic design, letterpress
Soolip Paperie & Press	310.360.0545	8646 Melrose Ave. West Hollywood, CA 90069	
Studio Z Mendocino*	707.964.2522	711 N. Main St. Fort Bragg, CA 95437	letterpress stationery; call for local availability
Through the Grapevine	612.906.0932	1040 Lake Susan Dr. Chanhassen, MN 55317	invitation design
Twelve Dozen Graphics*	914.945.0921	Ossining, NY	custom invitations, graphic design
William Ernest Brown Stationers	214.891.0008	Dallas, TX	
Write Selection	214.750.0531	314 Preston Royal Center Dallas, TX 75230	
Zorn Design Studio	213.344.9995	1800 Diamond Ave. S. Pasadena, CA 91030	

TRANSPORTATION

NAME	PHONE	ADDRESS	COMMENTS
Antique Autos	310.323.9028	8306 Wilshire Blvd. Beverly Hills, CA 90212	
Bonaventure Hot Air Balloons	707.944.2822 800.FLY.NAPA	Napa, CA	brochure

The Border Bus	214.855.0296	1801 N. Lamar Dallas, TX 75202	decorated charter bus
Carey International Limousine Service	800.336.4646	Washington, DC	booking office for 400 national locations: chauffeured limousines, buses, vans
Cartwright Ranch & Stables	817.249.2490	Fort Worth, TX	horse-drawn carriages
Chateau	212.246-0520	New York, NY	horse-drawn carriages; brochure
Classic Car Suppliers	310.657.7823	1905 Sunset Plaza Dr. W. Hollywood, CA 90069	
Colonial Parking Incorporated	302.651.3600	Wilmington, DE	valet service, uniformed attendants
Doubletree Farms	214.631.4096	Dallas, TX	horse-drawn carriages, wagons
Five Star Limousines of Texas Inc.	214.234.5466	13541 Floyd Circle Dallas, TX 75243	limousiness and Rolls Royces
Integrated Transportation Services	800.487.4255	Los Angeles, CA	chauffeured limousines; brochure
Lifestyle Transportations, Inc.	617.381.0600	2 Betty St. Everett, MA 02149	
McKinney Avenue Trolley	214.855.0006	3155 Oak Grove Dallas, TX 75204	trolley cars for charter through historic and arts districts of Dallas
Meyer Valet Parking	800.VALET.PK	New York, NY	uniformed attendants
Mogel's Classic Auto*	909.622.1617 818.967.4852	Ontario, CA Burbank, CA	chauffered antiques, vintage sports cars, limousines; call for local availability
Napa Valley Model A Rentals	707.944.1106	Yountville, CA	antique cars; brochure

New York Pedi-cabs	212.604.4279	New York, NY	chauffeur-pedaled pedi-cabs; call for local availability
Sailaway	212.825.1976	New York, NY	1938 teak and mahogany yawl; rentals; brochure
Shamrocks Carriages	414.272.6873	Milwaukee, WI	
Superior Location Van Service Ltd.	201.579.7374 800.888.3488	Newton, NJ Miami, FL	location van rentals, location finder
Yellow Rose Carriages	317.634.3400	1327 Northlake Rd. Indianapolis, IN 46202	horse-drawn vehicles

VINTAGE FASHIONS

NAME	PHONE	ADDRESS	COMMENTS
Amazon Dry Goods	319.322.6800	2218 E. 11th St. Davenport, IA 52803	Victorian fashions, accessories, patterns, books, shoes; catalog
Ann Lawrence	505.982.1755	369 Montezuma, #210 Santa Fe, NM 87501	by appointment
Cornelia Powell*	404.365.8511	Atlanta, GA	vintage textiles and accessories; call for local availability
Departures from the Past*	415.885.3377	San Francisco, CA	fashions, petticoats, costumes, accessories
Gene London	212.533.4105 212.929.3349	New York, NY	fashions, accessories, gowns
Georgian Vintage Gowns	404.365.8511	271 E. Paces Ferry Rd. Atlanta, GA 30305	
Golyester Antiques*	213.655.3393	136 S. La Brea Los Angeles, CA 90046	one-of-a-kind fabrics, fashions, notions, jewelry

The Perfect Wedding

J. Peterman Company	800.231.7341	Lexington, KY	catalog available
Jana Starr Antiques*	212.861.8256	236 E. 80th St. New York, NY 10021	Edwardian period fashions, accessories, laces, linens, refitting
Jean Hoffman Antiques*	212.535.6930	207 E. 66th St. New York, NY 10021	antique gowns, lace, accessories; restoration
Last Tango in Paradise	305.532.4228	Miami, FL	fashion, accessories, menswear
Legacy	212.966.4827	109 Thompson St. New York, NY 10012	fashion, accessories, headpieces and veils
Lily	310.724.5757	9044 Burton Way Beverly Hills, CA 90211	
Mary Ellen & Company	219.656.3000 800.669.1860	100 N. Main St. North Liberty, IN 46554	Victorian reproductions, petticoats, parasols, accessories; catalog
Past Patterns	317.962.3333	217 S. 5th St. Richmond, IN 47375	historic patterns for men and women, accessories, undergarments
1909 Company	800.339.1909 212.343.1658	New York, NY	fashion, accessories, period and reproductions; catalog
Out of the Past	718.748.1490	9012 3rd Ave. Brooklyn, NY 11209	fashions and accessories
Paris 1900	310.396.0405	2703 Main St. Santa Monica, CA 90405	
Time After Time	213.653.8463	7425 Melrose Ave. Los Angeles, CA 90046	
Trouvaille Française	212.737.6015	New York, NY	linens, laces, Victorian fashions, petticoats; by appointment

R   E   S   O

WEDDING CAKES

NAME	PHONE	ADDRESS	COMMENTS
Ana Paz Cakes	305.471.5850	1460 NW 107th Ave., Unit D Miami, FL 33172	custom designer
Ann Amernick	301.718.0434	Chevy Chase, MD	
Ashley Bakery	803.763.4125	Charleston, SC	
Bettina Thompson Stern	202.244.5903	3425 Quebec St. NW Washington, DC 20016	
Betty van Norstrand	914.471.3386	6 Leonard Rd. Poughkeepsie, NY 12601	hand-painted miniature sugar work a specialty
Cake and Cookies by Maria	610.767.7109	240 Willow Rd. Rural Rt. 1 Walnutport, PA 18080-9657	custom cakes
The Cakery	303.797.7418	5151 S. Federal Blvd. Littleton, CO 80203	fondant a specialty
The Cakeworks*	213.934.6515	Los Angeles, CA	tromp l'oeil portraits; by appointment
Cheryl Kleinman Cakes*	718.237.2271	448 Atlantic Ave. Brooklyn, NY 11215	Wedgwood cakes
Classic Cakes	317.844.6901	Indianapolis, IN	
Colette's Cakes	212.366.6530	327 W. 11th St. New York, NY 10014	sugar work, sculptural creations; by appointment
Cravings	314.961.3534	8149 Big Bend Welster Groves, MO 63119	buttercream a specialty
Debra Yates	816.587.1095	5418 NW Venetian Dr. Kansas City, MO 64151	marzipan a specialty
Donald Wressel*	310.273.2222	Los Angeles, CA	The Four Seasons pastry chef; spun sugar a specialty
Frosted Art by Arturo Diaz*	214.760.8707	1546 Edison St. Dallas, TX 75207	pastillage flowers, grooms' cakes

Gail Watson Custom Cakes*	212.967.9167	335 W. 38th St. New York, NY 10018	pastillage, buttercream; by appointment
Hansen Cakes	213.936.4332	1072 S. Fairfax Ave. Los Angeles, CA 90019	
Jan Kish-La Petite Fleur*	614.848.5855	633 Oxford St. Worthington, OH 43085	cakes, marzipan fruits, favors; brochures
Jane Stacey	505.473.1243	2092 Calle Contento Santa Fe, NM 87505	custom designs
Jessica Bartl at the New French Bakery	612.341.9083	124 N. 4th St. Minneapolis, MN 55401	also tortes
John and Mike's Amazing Cakes*	206.869.2992	14934 NE 31st Circle Redmond, WA 98052	architectural and theme cakes
Karen English Cakes	505.466.7617	23 Camino Valle Santa Fe, NM 87505	marzipan, charlotte
Katrina Rozelle Pastries and Desserts*	510.655.3209 510.837.6337	Oakland, CA Alamo, CA	fondant a specialty; by appointment
Le Gateau Cakery	214.528.6102	3128 Harvard Dallas, TX 75205	
Le Royale Icing by Margaret Lastick	708.386.4175	35 Chicago Ave. Oak Park, IL 60302	custom cakes
Les Friandises	212.988.1616	972 Lexington Ave. New York, NY 10021	patisserie, custom cakes
Margaret Braun*	212.929.1582	New York, NY	sugar objects, trompe l'oeil jeweling a specialty; by appointment
Masterpiece Cakes	817.322.4043	1700 9th St. Wichita Falls, TX 76301	custom cakes; pastillage marzipan a specialty; will ship
Michel Richard	310.275.5707	310 S. Robertson Blvd. Los Angeles, CA 90048	
Patticakes	818.794.1128	1900 N. Allen Ave. Altadena, CA 91001	

Paul Jerabek Special Affairs Catering*	214.351.3607	5010 Elsby Ave. Dallas, TX 75209	custom cakes, buttercream
A Piece of Cake	803.881.2034	Charleston, SC	
Rosie's Creations, Inc.	212.362.6069	New York, NY	custom cakes, miniature pastillage details, cake toppers
Rosemary Watson	800.203.0629 201.538.3542	Morristown, NJ	custom cakes, lace mold detailing; mail order
Rosemary's Cakes, Inc.*	201.833.2417	299 Rutland Ave. Teaneck, NJ 07666	custom cakes, buttercream
Sima's	414.257.0998	817 N. 60th St. Milwaukee, WI 53213	
A Spirited Cake	214.522.2212	3014 Montecello Dallas, TX 75205	
SUD Fine Pastry	215.592.0499	801 E. Passyunk Ave. Philadelphia, PA 19147	custom cakes, pastries, molded flowers
Susan Kennedy Chopson	615.865.2437	644 Delaware Ave. Madison, TN 37115	
Sweet Dreams	901.725.1265	1441 Jackson St. Memphis, TN 38107	custom cakes
A Taste of Europe by Gisela	817.654.9494	4817 Brentwood Stair Fort Worth, TX 76103	
This And That	803.744.6791	Charleston, SC	
Topia Ltd.	503.230.1986	25-6 NW 23rd Pl. #269 Portland, OR 97210	custom cakes; by appointment
Victoria's Fancy Wedding Cakes	320.352.2636	417 North Oak St. Sauk Centre, MN 56378	royal icing a specialty

WINES & SPIRITS

NAME	PHONE	ADDRESS	COMMENTS
Ale-in-the-Mail	800.573.6325	Plainview, NY	microbrews by mail, gift packages
Champion	206.284.8306	108 Denny Way Seattle, WA 98109	local wines by mail
Chicotsky's Liquor Store	817.332.3566	3429 W. 7th Fort Worth, TX 76107	
D. Sokolin Co.	800.WINE.WIR	Southampton, NY	fine wines, Champagne; catalog
International Wine Center	212.268.7517	231 W. 29th St., Ste. 210 New York, NY 10001	tastings, classes, brochure
Kobrand Wine*	800.628.2921	New York, NY	Champagne selecting; distributors of Taittinger, Domaine Carneros
Kreston Liquors	302.652.3792	904 Concord Ave. Wilmington, DE 19802	wine, Champagne, spirits, beer, ice, event consultation
Marty's	214.526.7796	3316 Oak Lane Dallas, TX 75219	
Morrell & Co.	212.688.9370	535 Madison Ave. New York, NY 10022	fine wines, Champagne; catalog
Partners in Wine	313.761.2333	111 E. Mosley Ann Arbor, MI 48104	
Sherry-Lehmann	212.838.7500	679 Madison Ave. New York, NY 10022	fine wines, Champagne; catalog
Tony's Wine Warehouse and Bistro	214.520.9463	2904 Oak Lawn Dallas, TX	

CALENDAR

PERFECT

A WEDDING CALENDAR

Good organization and a realistic schedule are the keys to planning any wedding. The guidelines that follow are suggestions based on my experience helping brides across the country. But you can produce miracles with far less time—some of the most memorable weddings I have attended have been put together in months and even in a few weeks. The less time you have, the simpler your plan should be.

WEDDING

Twelve months before the wedding

.... Choose your engagement ring.

.... Create a wedding planner diary: Purchase a sturdy sketchbook with handsome paper, small enough to fit in your purse. Add pockets, using heavyweight paper, to hold swatches, ribbons, snapshots, proposals, maps and more.

.... Make an alphabetical index on index cards for names and addresses and information on vendors.

.... Consider the style and budget of your wedding ~ this will become more complete as details are decided.

.... Choose the members of your wedding party.

.... Make a wedding party address list with phone numbers and give a copy to each member and to all the parents.

.... Begin investigating wedding and reception sites.

Eleven months ahead

.... Start looking for a wedding gown.

.... Hire a consultant.

.... Review photography portfolios.

.... Review videographers' sample videos.

.... Request audio tapes of musicians and schedule opportunities to view performances.

.... Meet with caterers, then request a time to see your favorites at work.

.... Look at florists.

.... Begin planning your honeymoon: Consult with a travel agent, visit travel bookstores, and research recent travel features in magazines and newspapers at your local public library or on the internet.

PERFECT

Nine months ahead

.... Visit your officiant to determine the structure of the ceremony and the wedding requirements.

.... Compile an invitation list with addresses; get request lists from your fiancé and all the parents. On index cards make an alphabetical index of the guests' names and color code checkmarks on the cards to acknowledge RSVPs and thank you-notes posted.

.... Actively shop for your bridal gown; finalize selections.

.... Register for gifts.

.... Finalize the menu and book the caterer.

.... Review the contracts and hire a photographer and a videographer.

.... Approve the repertoire and book the musicians.

.... Schedule appointments with your favorite florists.

.... Consult with a stationer, a graphic artist, or a calligrapher for the invitations.

Six months ahead

.... Order your bridal gown.

.... Shop for and order the bridesmaids' gowns.

.... Design and order the invitations, announcements, and thank-you notes.

.... Order a ketubah or illuminated wedding certificate.

.... Have a good haircut and a beauty consultation.

.... Begin the search for transportation options such as a limousine, antique car, or hot-air balloon.

.... Walk through your locations for the wedding and reception with your florists to discuss the options.

.... Order a prototype bouquet and request a proposal from your favorite florists.

.... Plan the rehearsal dinner with your fiancé and your future in-laws.

Five months ahead

.... Book the florist.

.... Review your beauty and fitness regime.

.... Reserve a block of hotel rooms for out-of-town members of the wedding party and guests.

Four months ahead

.... Review all details with the wedding consultant.

.... With your parents, schedule a final tasting or viewing with the caterer, the florist, and the consultant.

.... Finalize the guest list.

.... Order the wedding rings.

.... Confirm the delivery date for the wedding gown and bridesmaids dresses, and schedule the fittings.

.... Investigate the local wedding license requirements.

.... Order your custom-made accessories.

.... Inquire about newspaper announcement requirements and deadlines.

.... Plan the bridesmaids' luncheon.

.... Update your insurance.

Three months ahead

.... Meet with the florist to discuss your order.

.... Finalize the menu and all the details with the caterer.

.... Schedule a portrait session with the photographer to receive prints for newspaper announcements.

.... Make an appointment with the hair and makeup consultants for the portrait and the wedding date.

.... Purchase your wedding-day lingerie and shoes before the fittings.

.... Address the invitations.

.... Select the men's formal wear.

Eight weeks before

.... At the first bridal gown fitting, select a headpiece.

.... Schedule the blood tests, if necessary.

.... Mail the invitations.

.... Shop for gifts for the wedding party.

.... Sit for your bridal portrait.

.... Make sure the bridesmaids schedule their fittings.

.... Schedule a champagne and wine tasting.

.... Prepare a preliminary seating plan.

Six weeks before

.... Submit announcements to the newspapers.

.... Shop for the groom's gift.

.... Select thank-you gifts for the parents.

.... Write and post thank-you notes for every gift as it arrives and
definitely within two weeks of receipt.

.... Send out invitations to the bridesmaids' party.

.... Attend a second fitting and finalize the accessories.

Four weeks before

.... Obtain a marriage license.

.... Confirm the honeymoon reservations.

.... Pick up the wedding rings and inspect the engravings.

.... Shop for additional honeymoon clothing, lingerie, and rehearsal
dinner outfit.

Meet with the officiant to finalize the ceremony details and the
rehearsal schedule.

.... Review wedding plans with your parents.

.... Submit a final request list to the musicians, the photographer,
and the videographer.

Three weeks before

.... Schedule a dress rehearsal with the hair stylist and bring the headpiece with you.

.... Schedule the final beauty appointments.

.... Prepare a wedding day itinerary with the consultant.

.... Review details with the caterer; prepare the final guest count.

.... Confirm again with the florist.

Two weeks before

.... Arrange for transportation connections for out-of-town wedding party members.

.... Review, then print, the wedding day directions with phone numbers, and give it to all the drivers.

.... Address the wedding announcements to be mailed on the wedding day.

.... Double check the final details with all members of the wedding party.

.... Have a final fitting, and take your dress or have it delivered to your home the day before your wedding.

.... Consolidate your accessories and toiletries, and obtain any missing items.

.... Prepare an emergency kit.

.... Pack the bridesmaids' kits.

.... Reconfirm details and payments with all the vendors.

.... Submit a final guest count to the caterer.

.... Finalize the seating plan.

.... Submit names for place cards to the calligrapher.

One week before

.... Purchase travelers' checks for the honeymoon.

.... Review items to be packed for the honeymoon and purchase any missing items.

.... Prepare the wedding toasts.

.... Host a bridesmaids' party: distribute the wedding day accessories and hand out the gifts.

.... The groom attends his bachelor party.

.... Reconfirm manicure and beauty appointments.

.... Review the schedule with the wedding consultant and your parents.

.... Inspect your gown and the veil.

Two days before

.... Pack your honeymoon clothes.

.... Have a manicure.

.... Write notes to your parents for them to receive day after the wedding.

The day before

.... Tape a wedding day schedule to your mirror.

.... Be sure the wedding gown, all accessories, and the emergency kit are in your dressing area.

.... Review last-minute changes with the consultant.

.... Distribute directions, schedule, and a phone list to all; keep extra copies handy.

.... Make sure significant guests have wedding-day transportation.

.... Give announcements to your honor attendant to be mailed on the wedding day.

.... Rehearse the ceremony twice.

.... Attend a rehearsal dinner.

.... Get some sleep.

NOTES

PERFECT